"This excellent book covers in extensive detail the many vicissitudes of modern psychoanalytic work with same-sex couples. It is comprehensive and ground-breaking in its range of topics, and much needed to break the silence and ignorance that too often prevail in this area. All the experienced contributors maintain the necessary tension between understanding the internal and the external sources of conflict in same-sex relationships. It will be an invaluable resource for years to come, to all couple therapists whatever their identities."

– Joanna Ryan,
The Site for Contemporary Psychoanalysis; co-author of
Wild Desires and Mistaken Identities: Lesbianism and Psychoanalysis

"If a successful outcome of psychoanalysis or psychotherapy is an ability to relate to the otherness of the other, then in the tradition of Ralph Roughton who encouraged us to engage in Rethinking Homosexuality, Damian McCann has produced an edited volume of challenging papers by accomplished clinicians to foster such rethinking about sexual otherness in couples. The book thus appeals to psychoanalysts to adopt new ways of thinking about sexuality when treating couples, which is based in contemporary research-based understandings and not in otherwise-biased thinking and clinical practices that have historically done much harm, both to patients and candidates."

– Dr Timothy Keogh,
President, Australian Psychoanalytical Society

"In 2021 seventy-two jurisdictions across the world still criminalise homosexuality; in eleven of these the death penalty can be imposed. This outstanding edition reminds us that we cannot afford to be complacent and that it is essential that psychoanalysis engages with these external realities as well as applying its well-honed approach to investigating the internal world of the patient. The contributors challenge us to be mindful of the heteronormative biases and prejudices that continue to affect psychoanalytic thinking and practice even when we like to think that we are open and liberal. They powerfully illustrate through their work with couples that psychoanalysis has much to offer to our understanding of sexuality and gender as long as it can stand up to the self-questioning and scrutiny that contribute to the evolution of any discipline. This book is highly recommended. It is also essential reading."

– Prof. Alessandra Lemma,
Psychoanalysis University College London
and Anna Freud National Centre For Children and Families

Same-Sex Couples and Other Identities

This book provides a contemporary exploration of psychoanalytic theory and its application to therapy with lesbian, gay, bisexual, trans and queer relationships, challenging heteronormative practice and introducing new perspectives on working with gender and sexual diversity.

In this wide-ranging collection, international contributors draw on key aspects of couple psychoanalytic theory and practice, whilst also expanding hetero and mono-normative frames of reference to explore the nature of relating in open, closed and poly relationships. Developments in regard to gender and sexuality within the contexts of family and culture and an examination of same-sex parenting are also included, as are psychosexual considerations and the process of aging. A major focus of the book is the importance of the therapist's own gender and sexuality in the clinical encounter and how to manage adjustments in approach to counter the dominance of heteronormative thinking in practice.

The first book of its kind to incorporate an in-depth examination of same sex, queer, bi-sex, trans and queer relationships in regard to psychoanalytic thinking and practice, *Same-Sex Couples and Other Identities* is a vital resource for psychoanalytically informed psychotherapists, counsellors and practitioners working with a diverse range of clients.

Damian McCann, D.Sys.Psych, is a couple psychoanalytic psychotherapist working at Tavistock Relationships, London, and adjunct faculty member of the International Psychotherapy Institute (IPI), Washington, DC. He is a full member of the British Psychoanalytic Council and has a particular interest in working with gender and sexual diversity in psychoanalytic practice.

The Library of Couple and Family Psychoanalysis
Series Editors: Susanna Abse, Christopher Clulow, Brett Kahr, and David Scharff

The library consolidates and extends the work of Tavistock Relationships and offers the best of psychoanalytically informed writing on adult partnerships and couple psychotherapy.
   Other titles in the series:

Clinical Dialogues on Psychoanalysis with Families and Couples
Edited by David E. Scharff and Monica Vorchheimer

Couple Stories: Application of Psychoanalytic Ideas in Thinking About Couple Interaction
Edited by Aleksandra Novakovic and Marguerite Reid

Psychoanalytic Approaches to Loss: Mourning, Melancholia and Couples
Edited by Timothy Keogh and Cynthia Gregory-Roberts

A Couple State of Mind: The Psychoanalysis of Couples and The Tavistock Relationships Model
Mary Morgan

Engaging Couples: New Directions in Therapeutic Work with Families
Edited by Andrew Balfour, Christopher Clulow, and Kate Thompson

Interpretation in Couple and Family Psychoanalysis: Cross-Cultural Perspectives
Edited by Timothy Keogh and Elizabeth Palacios

Marriage and Family in Modern China: A Psychoanalytic Exploration
David E. Scharff

Same-Sex Couples and Other Identities: Psychoanalytic Perspectives
Edited by Damian McCann

Same-Sex Couples and Other Identities

Psychoanalytic Perspectives

Edited by
Damian McCann

LONDON AND NEW YORK

Cover image: Getty

First published 2022
by Routledge
2 Park Square, Milton Park, Abingdon, Oxon OX14 4RN

and by Routledge
605 Third Avenue, New York, NY 10158

Routledge is an imprint of the Taylor & Francis Group, an informa business

© 2022 selection and editorial matter, Damian McCann; individual chapters, the contributors

The right of Damian McCann to be identified as the author of the editorial material, and of the authors for their individual chapters, has been asserted in accordance with sections 77 and 78 of the Copyright, Designs and Patents Act 1988.

All rights reserved. No part of this book may be reprinted or reproduced or utilised in any form or by any electronic, mechanical, or other means, now known or hereafter invented, including photocopying and recording, or in any information storage or retrieval system, without permission in writing from the publishers.

Trademark notice: Product or corporate names may be trademarks or registered trademarks, and are used only for identification and explanation without intent to infringe.

British Library Cataloguing-in-Publication Data
A catalogue record for this book is available from the British Library

Library of Congress Cataloging-in-Publication Data
A catalog record has been requested for this book

ISBN: 978-1-032-18678-8 (hbk)
ISBN: 978-0-367-36446-5 (pbk)
ISBN: 978-1-003-25570-3 (ebk)

DOI: 10.4324/9781003255703

Typeset in Times New Roman
By KnowledgeWorks Global Ltd.

Contents

Acknowledgements	ix
List of contributors	x
Series editor introduction	xiv

Introduction   1
DAMIAN McCANN

1 **Sexuality and gender in development: Facets of bedrock and beyond**   8
PAUL E. LYNCH

2 **Revitalizing the Oedipal model for LGBTQ couples and families**   24
SHELLEY NATHANS

3 **Family matters: The impact of family and sociocultural context on LGBTQ identities and psychodynamics**   43
ANDI PILECKI ELIZA-CHRISTIE

4 **Cultural and intercultural considerations in working with same-sex couples**   60
PATRICIA PORCHAT

5 **Exploring unconscious anxieties for couple psychoanalytic psycho-therapists working with same-sex couples: The same or different?**   74
KATE THOMPSON

viii Contents

6 **Bisexual people and their partners in relational psychoanalytic couple therapy: Aesthetic conflict, multiple selves and the uncontainable** 89

ESTHER RAPOPORT AND IRIT KLEINER PAZ

7 **Queer relationships: unmapped intimacies** 105

IGGY ROBINSON AND ALICE KENTRIDGE

8 **The fear of difference and desire to differentiate: Working with two transitioning couples** 122

LINSEY BLAIR AND DOROTA MUCHA

9 **They *'went in two by two'*: The challenge for couple psychotherapists of working with those in open and polyamorous relationships** 135

DAMIAN McCANN

10 **Psychosexual considerations in working LGBTQ+ couples and individuals** 151

MARIAN O'CONNOR

11 **The process of ageing for same-sex couples** 166

DAVID RICHARDS

12 **Responding to the challenge that same-sex parents pose for psychoanalytic couple and family psychotherapists: Confronting implicit bias!** 179

DAMIAN McCANN AND COLLEEN SANDOR

13 **The LGBTQ couple choice of therapist he/she/they, straight or gay: Creativity vs defense** 192

COLLEEN SANDOR

14 **Understanding and responding to intimate partner violence and abuse in same-sex couple relationships** 205

DAMIAN McCANN

Index 220

Acknowledgements

When Susana Abse and Brett Kahr approached me with the idea of editing this book for The Library of Couple and Family Psychoanalysis, I had no hesitation whatsoever in accepting. In many respects, this invitation provided me with the opportunity of bringing together years of experience in thinking, writing and teaching about gender and sexuality within the fields of psychoanalytic and systemic practice, and it also afforded me the possibility of reaching out to experts, colleagues and friends from around the world to showcase their thinking and practice with same-sex couples and also with gender and sexual diversities more generally. I am therefore eternally grateful to all those who have contributed to the endeavour in bringing this book to print, for their generosity of time and the sharing of their knowledge and clinical wisdom from which I have no doubt many practitioners within the field will benefit enormously.

I am also grateful to Mary Morgan, Stanley Ruszczynski, Christopher Clulow, Shelley Nathans and Kate Thompson, all of whom generously offered to read and provide suggestions on my own chapters. I particularly want to thank Colleen Sandor, friend, mentor and co-author, for her constant presence and encouragement and her steadying hand. It is hard to imagine the amount of work that goes into editing a book like this, but it is so rewarding to know that it will join other recent publications that foreground developments in thinking and practice in our work with LGBTQ individuals, couples and families.

I wish to thank my colleagues at Tavistock Relationships for their contribution over many years to a deepening of my thinking, and am also eternally grateful to David Scharff, Jill Savage Scharff and Janine Wainlass for welcoming me into their wonderful institute (The International Psychotherapy Institute (IPI), Washington, DC) and for allowing me to share my thinking and practice with same-sex couples in the US, Russia and China.

Finally, I wish to thank Susanna Abse and Brett Kahr for their kind invitation and to Routledge for its support in the publication of this book.

Contributors

Linsey Blair, is a psychodynamic and psychosexual couple therapist. She is a graduate of Tavistock Relationships where she also worked as a clinical lecturer and faculty staff. Since relocating to Ireland in 2018, she now works in private practice in Galway and continues to teach, supervise and write.

Alice Kentridge, is a psychodynamic psychotherapist working in the NHS and in private practice. She was part of the founding of the Queer Analytic Circle, a group connecting with and developing new thinking with queer analytic practitioners. She is involved with the Queer Social Dreaming Matrix and has written on art, the body and sexuality.

Itit kleiner-Paz, Ph.D, is a clinical psychologist, working in Tel-Aviv as an individual and couples' therapist. She is also a supervisor and teacher of psychoanalytic and relational couples' therapy. Her Ph.D. was concerned with the application of language philosophy to the understanding of couples' communication, and she is the author of "The Coupled Unconscious" a textbook for psychoanalytic couples' therapy (in press).

Paul E. Lynch, MD, is on the faculty of the Boston Psychoanalytic Society and Institute and the China American Psychoanalytic Alliance. He has a private practice in Boston, MA, and is co-editor, with Alessandra Lemma, of *Sexualities; Contemporary Psychoanalytic Perspectives* (Routledge, 2015).

Damian McCann, D.Sys.Psych, is a couple psychoanalytic psychotherapist working as head of learning and development at Tavistock Relationships, London, and is an adjunct faculty member of the International Psychotherapy Institute (IPI), Washington, DC. He is also a consultant systemic psychotherapist and has many years' experience of working with children, adolescents and their families and of supervising a range of professionals both individually and in groups. He has a particular interest in working with gender and sexual diversity in psychoanalytic practice and has published and taught widely on this topic. His doctoral research was concerned with understanding the meaning and impact of violence in the couple relationships of gay men, and he is involved in developing approaches to working with couples in which there is violence and abuse.

Dorota Mucha, is individual and couple psychotherapist and psychosexual and relationship therapist at Tavistock Relationships. Public speaker, lecturer, clinical supervisor and founder of Us In Therapy, a psychosexual clinic at the Sexual Health Clinic NHS Trust, where she is lead therapist. She has featured in Vice, Soho Theatre, Trafalgar Studios, Soho House and Attitude Magazine.

Shelley Nathans Ph.D., is on the facilities of the California Pacific Medical Centre, the Psychoanalytic Couple Psychotherapy Group, the Psychoanalytic Institute of Northern California. She is the director and producer of the film, *Robert Wallerstein: 65 years at the Centre of Psychoanalysis.* She is on the international advisory board of the journal, *Couple and Family Psychoanalysis,* and is Chair of the Board for the Psychoanalytic Couple Psychotherapy Group. She is co-editor (with Milton Schaefer) of *Couples on the Couch: Psychoanalytic Couple Psychotherapy and the Tavistock Model* (Routledge, 2017). She is in private practice in both San Francisco and Oakland, California.

Marian O'Connor, is a psychoanalytic couple psychotherapist and a psychosexual therapist. She is head of psychosexual training at Tavistock Relationships. Her most recent publications are *Polyamory; a Romantic Solution to Wanderlust?* in Love, Sex and Psychotherapy in a Post-Romantic Era, Routledge, 2021 and *Let's talk about sex* in Engaging Couples: New Directions in Therapeutic Work with Families, Routledge, 2019. She has a private practice in London.

Andi Pilecki Eliza-Christie, is a licensed professional counsellor and psychoanalyst practicing in Pittsburgh, Pennsylvania, where she works primarily with LGBTQ adolescents and adults. She is a graduate of The International Institute of Psychoanalytic Training (IIPT), within The International Psychotherapy Institute (IPI). Her writing includes chapters in Jill Scharff's *Psychoanalysis Online II and III,* addressing the Internet as a transitional space for trans and TGNC patients, and psychoanalytic considerations of Internet use as both adaptive and defensive among LGBTQ and socially isolated populations.

Patricia Porchat, Ph.D., is a psychoanalyst and associate professor in psychoanalytic psychotherapy of adolescents and adults at the Psychology Department – Bauru School of Sciences, at UNESP - São Paulo State University. Member of the NEEPPSICA Lab - Nucleus of Psychoanalytical Studies, Extension and Research at UNESP. Also, a member of the NUDHES Research Group in Health, Sexuality and Human Rights of the LGBT Population, linked to the Department of Collective Health of Santa Casa de São Paulo School of Medical Sciences. Ph.D. in Clinical Psychology at the University of São Paulo. Author of books and articles on psychoanalysis and queer studies and on psychoanalysis and transgender issues, published in Brazil, Argentine and France. In 2019, she was a visiting professor at the Paris Diderot University at CRPMS (Centre de Récherches, Psychanalyse, Médecine et Societé) with a research grant from The São Paulo Research Foundation, FAPESP.

Esther Rapport, PsyD, is a clinical psychologist and psychoanalytic candidate practicing individual psychotherapy and couples therapy in Tel Aviv. She teaches relational psychoanalytic psychotherapy, with an emphasis on gender, social issues and LGBTQ, in Israel and beyond. She is the author of 'From Psychoanalytic Bisexuality to Bisexual Psychoanalysis: Desiring the Real (Routledge, 2019), and finalist of the Bisexual Book Award.

David Richards, is a psychodynamic psychotherapist and supervisor in private practice, working with individuals and in organisational settings. He has worked extensively in the public and private sectors, in fields of HIV and managing a community counselling service for older adults. He was senior tutor on the MSc in Psychodynamic Counselling and Psychotherapy at Birkbeck College London and lectures regularly in the areas of sexuality and identity. He is a long-standing member of the BPC Advisory Group on Sexual and Gender Diversity and contributed a chapter on 'Sexuality and Supervision' in *Sexuality and Gender Now: Moving Beyond Heteronormativity.*

Iggy Robinson, is a London-based psychodynamic therapist working in private practice and the third sector, primarily with trans, non-binary and queer individuals. They help to run the Queer Social Dreaming Matrix, and were involved in establishing the Queer Analytic Circle.

Colleen M. Sandor, is a psychologist and psychoanalyst in Salt Lake City Utah where she is in private practice. She co-founded a Master's in Mental Health Counselling program at Westminster College where she has taught for the last 18 years. Colleen is a faculty member of the International Psychotherapy Institute (IPI) and a teaching analyst for the International Institute for Psychoanalytic Training (IIPT). She is the former co-director of the Salt Lake City chapter of IPI and is currently the co-director of IIPT. Colleen's research and practice focuses on individuals and couples and on work within the LGBTQ community.

Kate Thompson, is a couple psychoanalytic psychotherapist and faculty staff member at Tavistock Relationships, where she leads on the Couple Therapy for Depression Training for NHS practitioners and is also clinical lead for Tavistock Relationships Parenting Services. She has developed Behavioural Couple Therapy for Alcohol Misuse and is involved in the application of MBT for separated parents in conflict. She is the editor of the forthcoming publication of Couple and Family Psychoanalysis focused on separation and divorce.

Series editor introduction

Same-Sex Couples and other Identities: Psychoanalytic Perspectives
Susanna Abse

This book is the 13th title in the Library of Couple and Family Psychoanalysis. An international series, begun in 2009, which is dedicated to publishing the best of contemporary theory and practice in the field of psychoanalysis with couples and families.

The psychoanalytic world has a complex history in its understanding and treatment of sexual diversity. On the one hand, Freud championed the idea that all humans were bisexual at core, a radical idea at the time. On the other hand, we know that there have been darker periods, where psychoanalysts institutionally consolidated an idea of homosexuality as perversion and discriminated against gay and lesbian candidates applying to train. This discrimination which was most overt in America was also covertly at play in the UK. Further, until this century, it would be reasonable to suggest, that even where there has been a generally non-pathologising atmosphere within our field, heterosexuality has been considered a marker of psychological health.

Since 2014, the British Psychoanalytic Council has published a bibliography of key texts in sexuality and gender which aims to develop and support a more progressive approach to the teaching of sexuality in our institutions. An update of these texts was completed in 2020 and a review of them shows that the great majority of these texts date from the beginning of this century and indeed, most date from its second decade. Is this testament to the freeing of a great creativity in our understanding of sexuality? I believe it is. However, in the bibliography there is extraordinarily little which addresses clinical work and theorising about same-sex couples, a grave lack which this collection of papers aims to fill.

Psychoanalytic theorising on sexual diversity has been largely derived from work with individuals, and whilst this has given us invaluable insights into the nature of human sexuality, there has been a gap in understanding the different needs of same-sex couples and how homosexuality is expressed within the couple relationship.

Thirty-five years ago, I began my career as a counsellor at the London Marriage Guidance Council and I began my experience of working with same-sex couples at the same time. Many gay couples made their way to

London Marriage Guidance Council seeking help, yet there was little discussion about their particular needs, or how our heterosexist attitudes might shadow our capacity to work with them. And, it seemed, there was no literature to deepen thinking either. Soon after, I began a psychoanalytic training in work with couples at The Tavistock Institute for Marital Studies (now Tavistock Relationships) and was introduced to Noreen O'Connor and Joanna Ryan's classic and ground-breaking book, *Wild Desires and Mistaken Identities*. I think I was lucky; I doubt there were many psychoanalytic trainings that were, at that time, using this as a core text. My training offered a progressive space to discuss sexuality, and together with my fellow trainees and teachers, we had many lively discussions about human sexuality and whether "disturbances" in Oedipal development could really explain its diversity. It is intensely shocking, given that Tavistock Relationships was relatively forward thinking in the psychoanalytic, that it has taken nearly thirty years for a book such as this to emerge.

Perhaps it has taken this long, because sadly it takes this long for ideas to change and prejudices to begin to abate. The psychoanalytic world can be painfully slow to embrace anything new or challenging and our attitude to sexual diversity shows this most graphically. Additionally, though I know there have been senior couple psychoanalytic psychotherapists who were in lesbian or homosexual relationships themselves, they were not overt about this and would not have embraced writing, lecturing or theorising in this area. They were, if not in the closet, certainly not "out and proud". It has taken this long for gay and lesbian couple psychotherapists to take up their voice, and I for one, am grateful to them.

O'Connor, N., and Ryan J., 1993. *Wild Desires and Mistaken Identities: Lesbianism and Psychoanalysis*. Virago, Reprinted Karnac (2003): London.

Introduction

Damian McCann

This book is coming to print at a time when important developments are taking place within the field of psychoanalysis, as it attempts to redress the shameful neglect and pathologizing of gender and sexual minority individuals, couples and family relationships conducted over many years. There is, however, still much work to be done in order to help therapists reflect on and attend to the dominance of heterosexism both in their minds and within their practice. Freud's own struggle, for instance, to integrate his ideas — that we are all inherently bisexual — against the powerful forces of monosexuality and heteronormativity has resulted historically in psychoanalysts holding views, as outlined by Giffney (2017, p. 28), in which homosexuality was seen as a "developmental arrest" (Segal, 1990); bisexuality as an "immature regression to fantasy" (Rapoport, 2009) and transsexuality as a "marker of a psychotic structure" (Millot, 1990). Unsurprisingly, therefore, psychoanalytic thinking and practice in regard to gender and sexuality has found itself under increasing scrutiny. In 1991, the American Psychoanalytic Association was forced to issue a statement opposing and deploring public and private discrimination against male and female homosexual oriented individuals, and in 1999, it went further in opposing reparative therapy. Similarly, in 2011, the British Psychoanalytic Council made its own statement opposing "discrimination on the basis of sexual orientation" and refusing to accept a homosexual orientation as evidence of "disturbance of the mind or in development". Yet, attention has been drawn to the fact "that while we live, increasingly, within political and social cultures whose official language oppose discrimination and celebrates difference, the effects of prejudice continue to be felt in subtle and more explicit ways by those whose sexuality and gender do not fit within heterosexual norms" (Waddell *et al.,* 2020, p. xii).

The field, therefore, is actively engaged in a crucial and painful process of 'working through' its own internal conflicts in regard to its failure to fully and respectfully engage with gender and sexuality. The increasing number of publications in recent years provides evidence of the fact that much thought and attention is now being focused on the development of theory

DOI: 10.4324/9781003255703-101

and practice specifically in regard to psychoanalysis with lesbian, gay, bisexual, trans and queer (LGBTQ) individuals, couples and families, including: *Uncoupling Convention: Psychoanalytic Approaches to Same-Sex Couples and Families (D'Ercole & Drescher, 2004); Sexualities: Contemporary Psychoanalytic Perspective (Lemma & Lynch, 2015); Clinical Encounters in Sexuality; Psychoanalytic Practice and Queer Theory (Giffney & Watson, 2017); From Psychoanalytic Bisexuality to Bisexual Psychoanalysis: Desiring in the Real (Rapoport, 2019); Sexuality and Gender Now: Moving Beyond Heteronormativity (Hertzmann & Newbigin, 2020),* and this book now adds its own further contribution to this endeavour. Taken together, these publications point to the direction in which the field must go if it is to recover its reputation for cutting edge thinking and practice with this particular population. After all, psychoanalysis has a long history of raising some profound and difficult questions for us all to think about and it must not fight shy of continuing to do so, although it can only do this if it puts its own house in order. Indeed, LGBTQ individuals, couples and families need us to do this thinking, so that when they seek our help, we do not continue to fail them. To avoid this, we must resist the pull towards heteronormative thinking, as well as the temptation to pathologize difference, both of which crucially undermine our therapeutic endeavours to work meaningfully, respectfully, sensitively and effectively with this particular clinical population.

In writing this introduction, I am reminded of the subtle and not so subtle ways in which homophobia and heterosexism operate to oppress and to disturb. Many years ago, when I began working at a Child & Adolescent Consultation Service (now referred to as CAMHS), I had no difficulty in 'coming out' as a gay man. However, the silence that pervaded that disclosure, together with the discomfort that hung in the air — as members of staff engaged with me but in a somewhat disengaged manner, eventually led me to doubt myself and to painfully withdraw. It was as if I was in a darkened room unable to turn on the light to see exactly what was going on and, more importantly, to understand why it was going on. However, after some months of sitting in the dark whilst contemplating leaving my post, the bubble finally burst. On the day in question, another member of staff was heading out, and in an effort to be friendly, I asked if she was going to lunch. The individual in question, who for months had avoided any direct eye contact answered, whilst addressing my knees, that she "was off to the hospital to see a woman who has just had a homosexual, I mean a hysterectomy". In that moment, we were both confronted with the truth of what had been going on in the collective unconscious of the organization, namely, that my sexuality had in some profound way disturbed the natural order, a disturbance that was clearly projected and lodged in me.

Following the parapraxis, the gloves were finally off and I was then confronted with the idea that although cross-gendered co-therapy sessions were a regular feature of practice at the clinic, some of the female members of staff did not feel comfortable working with me in this way. I was told that my sexuality would somehow skew the transference and countertransference dynamics, since inevitably I would only be interested in the men. I find it surprising at the time that I was so understanding and accepting of this madness, but that is what happens when homophobia and heterosexism reign, namely, that it silences and disempowers those who are its victims. And, if we think of the public outrage towards Peter Tatchell's gay rights campaign for equality mounted over the past fifty years, we again witness just how disturbing it is for heterosexual privilege to be challenged. A similar fight is now taking place in regard to trans and those who identify as queer, in that they too challenge and trouble the foundation of taken for granted assumptions concerning gender. Darren Langridge (2008) in his 'queer critique of lesbian and gay models of identity' asks 'Are you angry or are you heterosexual', a reference to the challenge for LGBTQ individuals in fitting in or fighting back. Although this book demonstrates that I have indeed found my voice, it is interesting that I still feel the pressure to tone-down the ranting quality of some of my writing to fit in with the more conventional style of analytic writing, otherwise I risk being seen as just angry and attacking. But in truth, I am angry for the harm that has been done in the name of psychotherapy over so many years to those who identify as lesbian, gay, bisexual, trans and queer, and who have had their sense of otherness reinforced by a discipline that has for so long basked in the security of its heterosexual privilege.

In terms of the book itself, I am grateful for having enlisted such a panoply of international experts within the field, all of whom have generously shared their ground-breaking ideas. I believe that the ideas contained in this book will contribute enormously to the further development and refinement of theory and practice in our work with same-sex couples, and those who are bisexual, trans, and who identify as queer.

Paul Lynch MD in his chapter on Sexuality and Gender in Development: Facets of Bedrock and Beyond, suggests, that in regard to psychoanalysis, we have never had a comprehensive explanation of the developmental path from infantile sexuality to latency, the Oedipus complex and adult sexuality. He therefore helps to navigate a path through the complex relationship between the development of gender and sexuality for individuals and their relationships with others, whilst also examining facets that continue to influence contemporary psychoanalysis and those that have moved beyond.

Shelley Nathans PhD revitalizes the Oedipal theory, divorcing it from its historical heterosexist bias and highlighting its relevance for working with LGBTQ couple and family relationships. She emphasises the triadic structure of the Oedipal situation, which she feels is more salient than the specific gender identification or sexual orientation of the individuals.

Andi Pilecki Eliza-Christie concentrates on the impact of family and sociocultural factors on LGBTQ identities. She utilises Link Theory and intersectionality to examine diversity among queer people, whilst also questioning the focus in psychoanalytic practice on intra-psychic and inter-psychic at the expense of the impact of wider contextual forces that shape the inner and relational lives of LGBTQ individuals, couples and families.

Patricia Porchat PhD focuses on cultural and intercultural considerations in working with same-sex couples in Brazil. She shows convincingly how the dominance of sexism and patriarchy, that fundamentally shapes heterosexual couple relationships in Brazil, is also an influential factor in structuring and shaping the dynamics of same-sex couple relationships.

Kate Thompson explores unconscious anxieties for couple psychoanalytic psychotherapists working with same-sex couples. As a heterosexual and cis-gendered woman, she is interested in understanding the challenges posed for straight therapists working with the intimate world of same-sex couple relationships. She considers the nature of the transference and countertransference dynamics in the work and emphasises the importance of supervision in understanding and working with difference.

Esther Rapoport & Irit Kleiner Paz in their chapter on bisexuality acknowledge that it is a complex sexual identity and that through its unpredictability and failure to hold with the binary notion of opposites, it is perceived as a threat to patriarchal social order. They also believe that bisexuality poses a threat to relationships, insofar as it disobeys heteronormative logic and signifies openness to change. They call for an exploration of the conscious and unconscious meanings of bisexuality as a practice, fantasy, self-identity or ideation and through the use of case scenarios offer a glimpse into their work with bisexual couples.

Iggy Robinson & Alice Kentridge offer a rich exposition of their thinking on queer relationships. Written by queer psychotherapists and in a style that honours queer thinking, the chapter immediately pulls us into uncharted territory. They say that they bring a focus on relationships that "search" beyond the borders of conventional relationship models, because they see this variety of relationships and queer negotiations in their work, because they live them in their partnerships, and because they are so easily erased by the clear-cut categories that exist in the world around them. Essentially, they capture the essence of queer relationships in their wide-ranging critique.

Linsey Blair and Dorota Mucha examine the nature of the therapeutic experience of the transitioning couple. At the heart of their exploration is the question of whether couples can transition together when one of the partners decides to their gender dysphoria. Through case scenarios, they consider each of the couple's shared unconscious phantasies linked to the fear and management of difference and the struggle for differentiation in the face of the transition. They say that it is their hope that in writing this chapter, that developments in thinking and practice relating to couples were

Introduction 5

one or both partners decide to transition will continue to be thought about within the profession.

Damian McCann reflects on and explores the nature of relating in open and polyamorous relationships, especially given that the primary focus on dyadic functioning in mainstream couple psychoanalytic thinking and practice has inevitably limited its interest in and understanding of the relevance of its theory to those in open and polyamorous relationships. Through the use of case examples, he applies thinking related to the 'couple state of mind', 'creative couple functioning', 'attachment', 'desire and sex', to these particular relational configurations. He touches on the technical challenges in working with those in non-exclusive relationships and emphasises the importance self-reflectivity for therapist's working with difference.

Marian O'Connor provides a rich examination of the psychosexual considerations in working with LGBTQ+ couples and individuals. She draws on research conducted in 2010, which confirms that a majority of therapists feel ill-equipped to work with LGB clients. With that in mind, her clinical examples offer an affirmative, integrated approach, using a psychoanalytically informed stance to explore relationship issues and unconscious blocks to a free expression of sexuality, psychoeducation to inform and to counteract sexual myths and behavioural exercises to work directly with the body.

David Richards speaks of the process of ageing for same-sex couples. I am so pleased that David agreed to write this chapter, as it reminds us of the awful situation many gay men and women had to endure prior to the Sexual Offences Act legislation in 1967 which finally implemented the recommendations of the Wolfenden report of 1957. David says, "Both men and women have spoken to me, in the context of the forbidden and illegal act of forming same sex relationships of the 'frisson' and appeal of transgressing these prohibitions". He also examines the tension between those whose lives were blighted by these unimaginable prohibitions and the greater freedoms afforded the young of today. Ageing is rarely an easy process for us all, but for many LGBTQ individuals and couples, there are particular challenges and complexities which David thankfully shares with us in his chapter.

Damian McCann & Colleen Sandor examine the challenges that same-sex parents pose for psychoanalytic couple and family psychotherapists. They approach this important topic through the lens of implicit bias and remind therapists of the need to be aware in working with the LGBTQ population of their own unconscious bias as well as that of the internal state of the client. They examine the routes to parenthood and the particular challenges same-sex parents experience in the outside world. They examine the implicit bias that permeated same-sex parenting research and outline the body of knowledge emanating from these studies. Finally, they explore, through a number of case scenarios, the ways in which implicit bias impacts same-sex parenting and the ways in which these parents may feel freer to construct parenting differently and not necessarily within prescribed gendered roles.

Colleen Sandor explores the LGBTQ couple's choice of therapist and the possible meanings attached to this. For instance, she considers, whether in seeking out a gay or lesbian therapist or a therapist of the same assumed gender, the choice is made for defensive purposes or in an effort to enhance creativity, or both. By exploring a couple's transference to the therapist and the therapist's countertransference in relation to the couple, it becomes possible to see and understand the unconscious choices at play for individuals and couples choosing to work with an LGBTQ therapist rather than one who is straight or vice versa. In addition, she reminds us that these couples come with unique relational and intrapsychic challenges that therapists whatever their affiliations must understand and respect.

Damian McCann believes that same-sex domestic violence and abuse remains a shockingly neglected area of practice, especially given that the incidence of intimate partner abuse in these couples is comparable to or even higher than that seen in heterosexual couple relationships. He therefore attempts to understand the nature of the abuse in same-sex couple relationships as well as exploring the causes of such abusive dynamics. Through the use of two contrasting case scenarios, he reflects on the nature and meaning of the violence and abuse within these couple relationships. In an attempt to understand the abusive dynamics, he draws on ideas relating to the sadomasochistic couple fit, together with attachment theory and ideas relating to stage discrepancy. He calls for a greater interest and investment in same-sex partner abuse to ensure that such couples are not pushed to the margins of society, especially as this only serves to perpetuate their silence and neglect.

References

D'Ercole, A., & Drescher, J. (Eds.) (2004). *Uncoupling Convention: Psychoanalytic Approaches to Same-sex Couples and Families*. New York: Routledge.

Giffney, N. (2017). Clinical encounters in sexuality: Psychoanalytic practice and queer theory. In N. Giffney & E. Watson (Eds.) *Clinical Encounters in Sexuality*, 19–43. Earth, Milky Way: Punctum Books.

Giffney, A.N., & Watson, E. (Eds.) (2017). *Clinical Encounters in Sexuality*, 19–43. Earth, Milky Way: Punctum Books.

Hertzmann, B.L., & Newbigin, J. (Eds.) (2020). *Sexuality and Gender Now: Moving Beyond Heteronormativity*, xi–xiii. Abington, Oxon: Routledge.

Langridge, D. (2008). Are you angry or are you heterosexual? A queer critique of lesbian and gay model of development. In L. Moon (Ed.) *Feeling Queer or Queer Feelings?: Radical Approaches to Counselling Sex, Sexualities and Genders*, 23–35. Routledge/Taylor & Francis Group.

Lemma, A., & Lynch, P.E. (Eds.) (2015). *Sexualities: Contemporary Psychoanalytic Perspectives*. East Sussex: Routledge.

Millot, C. (1990). *Horsexe: Essay on Transsexuality*, trans. Kenneth Hylton. New York: Autonomedia.

Rapoport, E. (2009). "Bisexuality in psychoanalytic theory: Interpreting the resistance". *Journal of Bisexuality 9 (3–4)*, 279–95.

Rapoport, E. (2019). *From Psychoanaltyic Bisexuality to Bisexual Psychoanalysis*. Abingdon, Oxon: Routledge.

Segal, H. (1990). "Hanna Segal interviewed by Jacqueline Rose." In *Hanna Segal, Yesterday, Today and Tomorrow*, 237–57. London and New York: Routledge 2007.

Waddell, M., Catty, J., & Stratton, K. (2020). Series Editors' Preface. In L. Hertzmann & J. Newbigin (Eds.) *Sexuality and Gender Now: Moving Beyond Heteronormativity*, xi–xiii. Abington, Oxon: Routledge.

Chapter 1

Sexuality and gender in development

Facets of bedrock and beyond

Paul E. Lynch

Much has changed in the realm of sexuality and gender since Freud's time, and yet many of Freud's original body-focused terms persist in our common parlance — anal obsession, oral fixation, etc. As psychoanalytic theory evolved from biology and drive theory to the increasingly more abstract concepts of object relations, ego- and self-psychology, and interpersonal and relational psychoanalysis, the language of the body, of infantile sexuality, and of drive theory continued in psychoanalytic discourse, mostly unintegrated with the newer theories. The role of the body and biology in concepts of both gender and sexuality has competed with the role of the mind and social influences. I will review some of the fluctuations in what has been and what may now be considered bedrock, looking at facets which continue to influence contemporary psychoanalysis and facets from which we have moved beyond.

While some believe there was a simpler time when psychoanalytic theories about psychosexual development and gender were straightforward and clear, that is a fallacy. Psychoanalysts always believed that developmental considerations were central to clinical work, yet theories of sexuality, the very heart of psychoanalysis, have been fragmented from the start. We've never had a comprehensive explanation of the developmental path from infantile sexuality to latency, the Oedipus complex, and adult sexuality. Freud knew this, and he didn't. He fluctuated in his *Three Essays on the Theory of Sexuality* (Freud, 1905) between establishing such theoretical pathways and disrupting them, often diverging diametrically from his text in his footnotes (Dimen & Goldner, 2011). Consider, for example, the basic connection between the sexual instinct and the sexual object. Freud said, "We are thus warned to loosen the bond that exists in our thought between instinct and object. It seems probable that the sexual instinct is in the first instance independent of its object; nor is its origin likely to be due to its object's attractions" (p. 148). In loosening this bond between instinct and object, Freud disrupted the existing theories of sexuality. However, Freud apparently did not entirely appreciate the full force and effect of this concept of a sexual instinct fully independent of the sexual object, and as

DOI: 10.4324/9781003255703-1

Davidson (1987) puts it, "Freud's mental habits never quite caught up with his conceptual articulations" (p. 63).

Thus, rather than marking out a clear path from infantile erogenous zone sexuality to adult whole object relations, Freud widened and blurred the developmental path by breaking the link between aim (drive) and object — even if at other times it appears that he still thought of them as inter-dependent. Freud emphasized that we are born with a constitution which varies from one to another in its biological or physiological components, and that our constitution interacts with our various accidental experiences arising in the family and environment (p. 239). Since neither constitution nor experience alone can predict a sexual outcome, we are hard pressed to outline any individual's path, even in retrospect, due to the number of variables involved in the interaction of constitution and experience.

Lacking reliable knowledge of what guides any one individual on the path from infantile sexuality to childhood, latency, and adult sexuality, psychoanalysts nonetheless endorse Freud's idea that adult sexuality only makes sense as an iteration of earlier experience. As he puts it, "The innumerable peculiarities of the erotic life of human beings as well as the compulsive character of the process of falling in love itself are quite unintelligible except by reference back to childhood as being residual effects of childhood" (p. 229). Ironically, it does seem obvious when we think about adult sexuality to trust that it is built on the residual effects of childhood experience, even though those building blocks are mostly obscure.

Sexuality in infancy, and the pre-Oedipal body and mind

It was bodily experiences and erotogenic zones that took center stage in Freud's study of Infantile Sexuality, in the second of his *Three Essays*, and it was the body's demands on the mind for psychic work that established the wishes and desires that became the initial interests of mental energy, or libido (Aisenstein & Moss, 2015). Chodorow (2012, p. 34) notes Freud's surprising absence of psychological theorizing about the mind in his work on infantile sexuality, as compared with his interest in the body and behavior. Even with the addition of Libido theory, we are left with many intriguing ideas and observations, but nothing that holds them together coherently and guides the path to an individual's adult sexuality.

The early contributions of others in the psychoanalytic movement began to shift the focus away from Freud's roots of psychosexuality in physiology and the organs of the body. For example, Fairbairn's shift from "pleasure seeking" to "object seeking" diminished the bodily sexuality of such seeking. Melanie Klein's shift from pleasure and unpleasure to the good or bad breast also moved the primary emphasis of psychosexual development from the body and the drive to the object, and to the realm of fantasy. After further developments in ego- and self-psychology, French analyst Andre Green (1995) felt things had gone too far and asked, "Has Sexuality Anything To Do With Psychoanalysis?" Green lamented that genital sexuality and the Oedipus complex were not getting due attention as *the* central figures in all mental life.

One of the shifts that drew psychoanalytic attention away from sexuality and Oedipus has been referred to as "the widening scope" of indications for analysis (Stone, 1954). With the treatment of narcissistic and border-line character pathologies, attention shifted to the dyadic relations of pre-Oedipal development. In the pre-Oedipal period, we see a shift from bodily discomfort and desperation to a recognition that an Other can disappoint. If you are a small baby, the all-or-nothing violent swings of pre-Oedipal emotion are part and parcel of coping with life while learning that some-times Mommy is available (good object), and sometimes she is no place to be found, or present but disappointing (bad object).

Roots of sexuality in body, mind, and relationship

A mother most often tends to a child's physical and sensual needs without conscious awareness of sexuality, and at times we psychoanalysts do much the same with our patients, despite the sexual foundations of psychoanaly-sis. Mary Target (2015) built on work that she and Peter Fonagy have done over many years (e.g. Fonagy & Target, 1996, 2007) in the realm of attach-ment between mother and child, and laid out a developmental model of sex-uality that holds together body and mind in a relational context. Target, like Green, recognized that reducing adult personality to a version of early object relations risked desexualizing it. However, she showed that infant observa-tion need not be ignorant of sexuality, or of the mother's role in the infant or child's developing psychosexuality. Essential to Target and Fonagy's model of development is the way that affective self-understanding develops out of primary object relationships in the processes of mother's *mentalization* of the infant's affective state, and her *affective mirroring* of it. As the infant's mind develops in the context of the caregivers' mentalization, it is influenced by unconscious messages or "enigmatic signifiers" (Laplanche, 1995 & 1997) conveyed (unconsciously) as the earliest communication of the caregivers' unconscious feelings about sexuality.

Target proposes a common failure of mirroring in relation to infantile sexual excitement, even from mothers who are otherwise adept at reflect-ing and mirroring other emotional states. The infant experiencing sexual tension in the presence of a sensitive and responsive parent would gener-ally not be offered a congruent, metabolized representation of his or her sexual excitement or pleasure, even though other feelings may be reflected in a mostly attuned way. Without mirroring, sexual excitement is poorly reflected and one would expect it not to be well recognized or integrated in the growing child's sense of his social self. Rather than a developmental problem, Target postulates that the unresolved, unmentalized, and obscure state of childhood sexual feelings may provide the impetus in adolescence and beyond to search for a partner outside the family with whom to express, share, and potentially contain sexual excitement.

In the infant and caregiver milieu, which Laplanche (2002) calls the "Fundamental Anthropological Situation," most sexual communications are not conscious for the adults themselves — let alone for the infant who lacks ability to understand the sexual dimensions that are unconsciously present during the acts of ordinary care. Because we are sense-making beings, Scarfone (2019) notes that we will always try to translate the obscure sexual elements, but "for lack of any possible "code" regarding the Sexual, the child's interaction with the adult in this domain is necessarily clouded with enigmas" (p. 1252). What we hear from adult patients then "comes cloaked under layers of translations, retranslations, displacements, sublimations, [and] fixated in character traits and symptoms" (p. 1253).

We see that the primary experience of sexuality is established outside of consciousness — often surprising us, feeling found, feeling new, and exciting — with enigmas of the past repeatedly translated in the light of current experience. Our innate sexuality is shaped by our experience — but mostly outside our awareness, and therefore it can repeatedly be experienced as both authentic and alien, and as taking us beyond our own bounds (Stein, 2008). However, enigmatic signifiers of gender and sexuality are also affected by restrictive forces and cultural codes, "the normative unconscious at the root of repressions" as Evzonas (2020, p. 652) has elaborated. He proposes a model of enigmatic messages to be translated, which takes into account an intersectional approach (encompassing gender, ethnicity, social classifications, religion, etc.) by considering power relations and cultural patterns of oppression (p. 636).

Sexuality in the "Oedipal" mind

Once "Oedipal" development is in motion, the child recognizes that she is actually part of a triangle, rather than the sole focus of attention, and she wants to return to her dyadic place of importance by possessing one parent and getting rid of the other. In the concrete version of this theory, the child wants to copulate with the parent, although in reality the child probably does not have conscious knowledge of the facts of copulation. So, we have a situation now that involves desires that are not primarily physical, which now prominently involve fantasy — a fantasy that a small child could take the place of an adult as lover or mate of another adult, and could be victorious in competition for the coveted position as the desired or chosen one.

Holtzman and Kulish (2000, 2003) have well established the inappropriateness of the Oedipal myth for female development, yet the Oedipal label remains firmly fixed to our thinking about this period of development for all sexes and genders. In contemporary psychoanalysis, Oedipal development is not necessarily about being male, or heterosexual. However, essential elements, including desire, jealousy, fantasy, triangular competition, and the acceptance of triangular relations, remain essential to our thinking about maturational development and the beginnings of more object-focused and less narcissistic relations. The dynamics of maturation, growth, and change that we associate with the term "Oedipal" remain indispensable in clinical work, even though original bedrock assumptions about binary gender and compulsory heterosexual object choice have not stood the test of time.

Today, there is more acceptance of variety in Oedipal configurations of gender and sexual object choice, and contemporary psychoanalysts are also more ready to see that environmental factors play a part in an individual's Oedipal drama. These factors are clinically relevant. Among others, Isay (1987) and Rose (2007) have written about the painful sequelae of empathic failure when families fail to recognize or engage with a homosexual child's affections for a same-sex parent. When the family can tolerate and play along with the drama of romance, competition, and aggression, as they typically do when daddy's little girl wants to marry daddy, then they assist the child to work out the disparities between wishful fantasies and reality. However, maturation and growth may be impeded if the family is not empathically attuned to the child's struggles, or if they respond punitively to signals of sexuality or aggression (as they might when they detect signs that their little boy has a special interest in daddy).

At puberty, under the influence of biology and hormones, an adolescent's desire may appear to be very much of and for the body, yet movement also continues in the mind in the direction of desire for a whole person, or "whole object relations." Particularly because the movement here is in the mind, the variety of individual desires may be endless (Chodorow, 2012).

The tradition of "normal" and universal lines of development for gender and sexuality has fallen from favor. Harris (2009), whose book title refers to gender as "soft assembly," turns away from prescriptive linear developmental lines and toward chaos theory for an understanding that no particular outcome can be predicted in any one case, due to the number of interacting variables, including identifications, bodily experiences, proscriptions, and prescriptions from parents, family, and society. Developmental theory now allows for more uncertainty, more variables, and acceptance that we cannot predict outcomes from known facts. Fiorini (2017) has also found it useful to look outside of psychoanalysis for theories of complexity to get beyond our binary, dichotomous limitations, and she offers a paradigm of hyper-complexity and thinking at intersections and limits between categories.

From enigmatic signifiers to explicit dangers

As the child develops over the years and begins to learn in new ways, she detects both unconsciously and consciously her caregivers' feelings, judgments, and reactions to her subjectivities and emotional states of mind. Education gradually shifts from enigmatic and unconscious messages to more explicit ones — for example, the celebration of expressions of early sexuality that conform to expected (heterosexual) norms and the admonition of desires and behaviors deemed outside the norm. As censures from society compound those within the family, the young person who holds what Sullivan (2003) called "de-legitimized" desires, understands that it is dangerous to express oneself freely.

The danger in the environment is something that Freud warned us about, yet with regard to anti-homosexual bias in his cultural milieu, he often ignored what he knew about it. Freud (1923) told us that the ego serves three masters, and is "consequently menaced by three dangers: from the external world, from the libido of the id, and from the severity of the super-ego. Three kinds of anxiety correspond to these three dangers, since anxiety is the expression of a retreat from danger" (p. 56). Gulati and Pauley's (2020) reconsideration of Freud's (1910) *Leonardo Da Vinci and a Memory of His Childhood* demonstrates beautifully how Freud failed in writing this "pathography" to consider the dangers to Leonardo from his environment, including dangers well-known to Freud, and failed to consider the adaptive skills of Leonardo's psyche to cope with those dangers. Although Freud wrote in other places (1935) that homosexuality cannot be classified as an illness, Gulati and Pauley show that with regard to Leonardo, he failed to fully comprehend the concept of a healthy homosexual.

The anxieties expressed in response to the danger of social admonition for unsanctioned desires and identities make it more likely that the child will learn to conceal, feel abnormal, and feel shame. The sequestration of desires becomes more fraught and more conscious with the onset of puberty and adolescent sexual development. In another example of knowing and not knowing, Freud (1912) showed that excessive opposition to an adolescent's sexual object choices could lead to sequestration of sexual pleasure and potency from loving intimacy. He described this phenomenon in detail with regard to heterosexual men, but failed to see how well suited his schema was for understanding the problems of love, sex, and shame that some gay men struggle with (Lynch, 2002).

If the family or the environment strongly opposes the youth's choice of new objects, it decreases the value of the objects for the person concerned and impedes the enjoyment of sensuality in affectionate, intimate relationships. For gay men who have trouble integrating intimacy with sex, I have emphasized the need for exploration of the shame and anxiety that results from the failure of the family or the social environment to sanction a homosexual boy's erotic desires (Lynch, 2015). Excessive anxiety and shame over the danger of unacceptable desires leads to sequestration of sexual desires from intimate relations, and relegates the sexual to fantastic expression with unfamiliar or denigrated others (in anonymity, with strangers, etc.).

Early unconscious and conscious proscriptions against particular desires, failures of recognition, Oedipal rejection, overt familial interdictions in adolescence, and pervasive societal admonitions, all accrue to create anxiety and shame for outlawed and de-legitimated desires, which interferes with the ability to enjoy sexual pleasures with a valued and loved partner. When no tolerance for particular desires exists, those desires are best kept from those one loves. Freud described the devastating effect of these environmental dangers on the individual:

> *Where they love they do not desire and where they desire they cannot love. They seek objects which they do not need to love, in order to keep their sensuality away from the objects they love [1912, p. 183].*

While some clinicians still avoid the origins of such phenomena, or even dismiss sex without attachment as "perversion," I have found that appreciation and attention to the shame that underlies the disconnection is more useful to help patients work through it.

Gender: Anatomy is destiny?

As with sexuality, psychoanalytic conceptions of gender began with a focus on the body and were troubled in later iterations by various emphases on social and environmental forces. Freud first used his famous phrase, "Anatomy is destiny," in 1912 to acknowledge the close proximity and overlap of sexual organs with excremental organs, to emphasize the animalistic nature of sex. In 1924, he used it again in reference to the morphological smallness of the little girl's clitoris, as compared to the larger penis of a playfellow of the opposite sex. He said this causes her to perceive that a wrong was done to her, and is "a ground for inferiority" (p. 178). The errors of Freud's ways with regard to understanding women have been well exposed and examined for decades. Yet, the base of Freud's point, that biology or anatomy affects psychic development and self-perception, was a cornerstone of early psychoanalytic theorizing about gender and gender identity development, and it remains compelling for many today. Consider the prime importance of anatomy, for example, to the transgender person who declares the need to modify his/her anatomy in order to align it with gender identity and alleviate mental suffering.

Second-generation psychoanalysts, including Karen Horney and Clara Thompson, argued that culture played a larger role than anatomy in determining who felt inferior rather than privileged, by determining which traits were regarded as valued and masculine, such as agency, strength and independence. They exposed gender as a cultural creation whereby social meanings were assigned to biological differences. In a cultural context of power and social constraints, they also exposed some traits that were assumed to be feminine, such as seductiveness, as compensatory defenses in the male dominated economy of power and influence.

Despite the compelling arguments for social influence as a primary determinant of gendered personality, connections between biology and gender identity held their ground. Indeed, many of the developmental theorists who sought to understand female development from the perspective of the girl, actually returned to anatomy. Concepts like *core gender identity* (Money, 1973) and *primary femininity* (Stoller, 1968) were introduced. Several prominent papers were published by female analysts about female genital anxiety, which focused significantly on the qualities of the girl's vagina. Bernstein (1990) wrote that a girl's fear of access to the genitals, fear of diffusivity, and fear of penetration, "complicates the formation of ego boundaries and a firm sense of self" (p. 163). For Mayer (1995), conflicts about primary femininity were rooted not in the phallic castration complex or penis envy, but rather in fantasies of danger to the female genital. Schiller (2012) proposed a labial framework to represent female psychosexuality in terms of the wetness of lips rather than phallic stiffness.

Social construction and regulation of gender

'I am certainly not being thorough, but I hope that I am conveying the way in which the material body has played and continues to play a role in what is thought about gender. This is the case despite persuasive postmodern arguments that the body is just a surface on which is inscribed a series of culturally determined meanings. Biological differences are originally observed and interpreted, and social constructions are initially inscribed, in the very same environment — first and foremost in the context of the family. The family is the primary engine for differentiating, educating, and enforcing along biological and binary gendered lines. Our experience of gender and our psychoanalytic attempts at understanding those experiences all take place within a culture, or an ether, of family structures and definitions which rely heavily on the traditional gender binary. Today we try to recognize our context and acknowledge its influence, but when it comes to culture and family structures, it is hard to find an outside from which to look in.

Butler (1990) argues that there is no essence of gender to be expressed, and gender is nothing without its performative acts. There is no original masculine or feminine to be expressed or imitated. Rather than expressing something innate or inborn, gender is nothing more than a series of social significations inscribed on and performed by a body. In this schema, gender characteristics and gender acts are "the way in which a body shows or produces its cultural signification," because "there is no preexisting identity by which an act or attribute might be measured; there would be no true or false, real or distorted acts of gender, and the postulation of a true gender identity would be revealed as a regulatory function" (p. 141).

16 Paul E. Lynch

Butler's ideas are helpful in thinking both about the individual's use of binary gender traits for settling on a coherent identity, and about the tensions in our current culture which denigrate outliers for the benefit of simplified, coherent norms. Butler shows that the differentiation of the gender binary is a process whereby the culture regulates and controls the boundaries, thereby creating Others and expelling or excreting people or traits which threaten to destabilize coherence. We end up with dirty or polluting people at the margins, who must be defined as "not us," not normal, and expelled from the inner world of our "normal" subjectivity. In this regard, Butler shows the social construction of gender to be a limiting and regulatory process. Here we see some of the cover for violence; uncivil attempts to rid an individual or a society of its unwanted elements. It is this constraining process that Corbett (2001) argues against in his paper, "More Life: Centrality and Marginality in Human Development". Corbett acknowledges our need for some coherence, "a culture's need to read pattern," but proposes also "a culture's need for individuals who reach beyond patterns" (p. 329).

For the individual, these constricted processes of identification show themselves in a form that Butler (1995) refers to as "melancholy gender". In the process of incorporating identifications within the male or female binary, non-conforming identifications are repudiated.

However, gendered identifications and desires that are not allowed into consciousness cannot be consciously repudiated or mourned. For example, under the forces of compulsory heterosexuality, one cannot admit knowledge of an early desire for a same-sex parent. Such desire is not consciously lost and mourned in the course of development in our culture, but as Butler puts it, it is "foreclosed," as if it never existed. It requires vigilance to keep the knowledge or affective memory of its actual existence at bay, and thus repetitive repudiation ironically reifies that which is repudiated. Therefore, masculinity or femininity is haunted by that which it has repudiated outside of awareness — a melancholic identification is maintained with that which has been foreclosed. This process is easiest to see in clinical work when the repudiation is especially strong — in characters of extreme gender stereotypes, rigidly and desperately reaffirming their gendered identifications by aggressive repudiation of characteristics of the perceived "opposite sex."

Gender in foreground and background

Construction of gender in a field of many variables becomes a very personal project (Chodorow, 2002), and one in which we are all burdened by infantile ideals of masculinity and femininity that are ingrained in our social order. What Kaplan (1991) calls "The Perverse Strategy" is a defensive maneuver that involves a deception of self to protect against anxiety and painful knowledge about shame-filled identities and desires — particularly about our failures at gender purity. In her book about female perversions, she shows how socially normalized gender stereotypes are both the crucibles of the classic perversions and also central to all human behavior. Kaplan shows that the manifest experience of gender stereotypes is used to foreground in consciousness a coherent and shameless gendered identity, as a deception to protect against anxiety about latent, shamed, and disavowed aspects of oneself (often perceived as belonging to the opposite sex). In a male perversion, Kaplan states that "the perverse or fetishistic strategy admits into consciousness (foreground) a defensive, phallic, narcissistic exaggeration of masculinity" (p. 12), as a way of obscuring feminine strivings that hover in the background. In the female perversions, the impersonations or performances (foreground figurations) are based on female-gender stereotypes — submissiveness, dependency, cleanliness, intellectual mistiness. One familiar example of the perverse strategy was described by Joan Riviere (1929) in *Womanliness as Masquerade* — where she wrote, "women who wish for masculinity may put on a mask of womanliness to avert anxiety and the retribution feared from men" (p. 303). Idealized femininity is performed then, in order to deceive both performer and observer about the true motivations underlying the behavior, and to keep at bay anxieties over impure gender identities; to remain coherent gender-wise, and keep oneself in the realm of the normal.

Kaplan (2000) states, "the fetishistic strategy is ubiquitous. It infiltrates every living situation whether that situation entails writing books or analyst-patient relationships or gender identity. In all these situations, a vivid manifest presence should be suspected of obscuring a latent absence. Or, put another way, a vivid foreground should be suspected of obscuring a background that is potentially threatening" (p. 354). As in Butler's melancholic gender, what cannot be conscious cannot be valued or mourned, and aspects of gender identities and same-sex attractions that are "foreclosed" by gender idealizations and heterosexist strictures are repeatedly renunciated in the performance of perverse strategies. With different styles, both Butler and Kaplan show that civil structures aim to maintain sexual and gender coherence and conformity. Their work shows how non-conforming identities and behaviors are boxed into categories and extruded from "normal," in order to protect the bourgeois family, its gender idealizations, and the social order it represents. Yet, along the way, we all fail to meet idealized conventions of gender and sexuality, and repeated renunciations of non-conforming aspects of ourselves via perverse strategies attempt to protect us from the truth of non-conformity.

In managing anxiety, the foregrounding of a vivid presence works well because it is also enlivening. We would not want to be reminded at every moment that our new suit, colorful dress, athletic achievements, or sexual adventures are distractions from our primitive fear of annihilation, ridicule, or exclusion. Yet, they are all enacted within the foreground/background strategy, employing gender stereotypes to animate our lives with emotions that feel good.

Yanof (2000) has shown that gender is imbued with layered meanings that can be employed creatively in changeable compromise formations. In contrast to Freud's static gender of anatomic destiny, her work affirms the functional benefits and uses of dynamically changeable gender identity. It also asserts that gender is constantly being reorganized under the influences of biology, object relations, and social construction, and that gender animates conflicts outside the domain of gender and in turn is impacted by non-gendered conflicts as well.

Gender: Anatomy as destination?

For a few decades at least, psychoanalysis was moving steadily toward the recognition that much of our gender bifurcating was fetishistic and defensive, and that all people were capable of multiple identifications without diffusion or fragmentation of self. Treating caricatures of gender stereotypes as defensive compromises, we came to value fluidity and the ability to both empathize and identify across the binaries of sex and gender. We came to think that openness and psychic penetrability are good for men (Elise, 2001), just as strength and agency are good for women.

Many of us were thus challenged by certain trans subjectivities that seemed to be resisting the sharing of characteristics across genders. While liberated women and metrosexual men were enjoying new freedom to blur and blend gender norms, some transsexuals seemed to argue for the necessity of the binary, for the segregation of gender characteristics, and even for the essentialist, biological distinctions that others worked so hard to undo. Here was an irony: gender transitioning was scorned as an unacceptably radical transgression by conservative gender watchdogs, yet it was perceived as a conservative turn toward biologic essentialism by progressive advocates of fluidity and flexibility. In some cases, trans folks appeared to value gender stereotyping, and hoped to embody and perform a gender idealization.

Of course, there are as many trans subjectivities as there are trans people, and they shouldn't be lumped together — I simply want to acknowledge this body-based challenge to our hard-won progressive idealizations of fluidity and flexibility. Unfortunately, the hard emphasis on the physical body's gender characteristics and on the performance of traditional gender role behavior would be too easily labeled as defensive if we now idealize fluidity. Instead, we must renew our commitment to listen to individual and unanticipated unique subjectivities.

Many psychoanalytic theoreticians have attempted in recent decades to bring some of the previously marginalized sexual and gender minorities into the mainstream fold (Moss, 2015). González (2019) wrote, "Psychoanalysis today posits an exceedingly complex relationship between gender, sexuality, the body, and the social, one that tends towards agnosticism on its resolution and highlights the enigmatic" (p. 65). However, recent publications have shown that not all psychoanalysts are comfortable with the enigmatic, and some still show a predisposition for diagnosing pathological etiologies and regulating behavior.

The editors of *The International Journal of Psychoanalysis*, under the heading of "Psychoanalytic Controversies," recently asked whether we can think psychoanalytically about transgenderism (Blass, 2020). Bell's (2020) answer to the question is to raise alarm about our current social order, in which he asserts children are infected through "social contagion" with sudden and urgent needs to get hormone blockers or genital surgeries, and to accuse our current culture of preventing thoughtfulness about such actions. In contrast, Saketopoulou (2020) sees no need for analysts to add affective charge to these matters and suggests that we lower the temperature of our discussions, and instead focus on what we learn from patients. Evzonas and Laufer (2019) name psychoanalytic theory and treatment, along with family and social forces, as potentially contributing elements of violence to the complex dynamics of gender subjectivity. In this setting of anxiety about the actions of transitioning, and with the tendency of clinicians to diagnose and regulate away our discomforts, the ability of the clinician to recognize and examine countertransference is absolutely central to good therapeutic work.

Countertransference

The benefits of psychoanalytic technique, which exposes and explores an individual's conflicts with curiosity and assists in living more freely in any given sex, gender, or sexual orientation, are far more transformational than any accomplishment of received theory. However, for the technique to work, each analyst and patient has to address the prejudices that we are steeped in in our families and cultures, and for the clinician that includes paying attention to any prejudices that are stirred up by particular patients. As Dimen (2001) warned us, "the ambiguous power of diagnosis" involves the power to name and the power to blame.

Much more than an open mind and good intentions are required to become aware of our prejudices and tendencies to distance ourselves from and objectify patients who make us uncomfortable. Evzonas & Laufer (2019) provide a cautionary tale of a therapist who espoused a progressive approach, but in retrospect realized that his personal history and received psychoanalytic theories contributed to particular countertransference feelings, which in turn gave rise to unwitting objectifications of his first trans patient. In reconsidering the case of Cal, a trans patient who fled treatment, they came to believe that the therapist's persistent interest in the clever and compelling logic of his own theories about the origins of Cal's trans identity diverted him from closer attention to Cal's concerns and subjectivities, and thereby contributed to Cal's flight from the treatment (and from being labeled as pathological for his trans experience). Yet they also ask,

"In the context of political correctness and activism that has transformed the stigma of transgenderism into empowerment and agency, does the analytical clinician have the right to question trans identities without being accused of normativity?" (p. 412). They quote Lemma (2018), who argues that "the challenge is to tread the fine line between a dialogue based on an equidistant curiosity about meaning and function that is core to an analytic approach, and a posture of implicit skepticism" (p. 1089).

Herein lies the delicate intricacy of therapeutic technique, and the paramount importance of examining countertransference. The therapist must be sufficiently clear about his own prejudices so that his inquiries may come from genuine curiosity and generosity, so that what Lemma calls "skepticism" remains firmly in the service of exploration and not condemnation (not "inquiries" in the service of imperious naming and blaming interpretations), and may possibly be received as such by patients who have already been traumatized by society's judgements of their desires and identities. Evzonas and Laufer bravely acknowledge in their retrospective evaluation of Cal's flight from treatment that aspects of countertransference had led the therapist "to search aggressively and hastily for the etiology" of Cal's gender identity (p. 409), and that the therapist would have had to transform his own attitudes in order to have been more helpful to his patient.

Along with interrogating our individual prejudices, we must also be vigilant about examining our professional, traditional biases. We are all, individually and collectively, at risk of behaving like Freud in knowing and not knowing — in claiming theories that fail to affect our clinical behavior. We have to wonder, for example, why we hang on to terminology that is not precise. Why do we stick with "Oedipus complex" rather than "Triangulation" or some other word or words with fewer idiosyncratic and variable connotations? Are we unwittingly holding on to some of the heterosexist history of "the Oedipal," even though we acknowledge that maturation into triangular relations is important for all genders and sexual orientations? When we use non-specific traditional terminology, we may perpetuate biases that we have theoretically eschewed. Here is an opportunity for us to learn from Freud's shortcomings — to avoid knowing and not knowing, and instead to have the courage of our convictions to scrutinize our application of theory as actively as we evolve the theories themselves.

References

Aisenstein, A. & Moss, D. (2015). Desire and Its Discontents. In *Sexualities: Contemporary Psychoanalytic Perspectives*, Lemma, A. and Lynch, P.E. (Eds.) (pp. 63–80). New York & London: Routledge.

Bell, D. (2020). First do no harm, *The International Journal of Psychoanalysis*, 101(5):1031–1038.

Bernstein, D. (1990). Female genital anxieties, conflicts and typical mastery modes. *International Journal of Psychoanalysis*, 71:151–165.

Blass, R.B. (2020). Introduction to "Can we think psychoanalytically about transgenderism?", *International Journal of Psychoanalysis*, 101(5):1014–1018.

Butler, J. (1990). *Gender Trouble; Feminism and the Subversion of Identity*. New York & London: Routledge.

Butler, J. (1995). Melancholy gender — Refused identification, *Psychoanalytic Dialogues*, 5(2):165–180.

Dimen, M. (2001). Perversion is us? *Eight notes, Psychoanalytic Dialogues*, 11(6):825–860.

Dimen, M. & Goldner, V. (2011). *Gender and Sexuality*. In *Textbook of Psychoanalysis*, Gabbard, G.O., Litowitz, B.E., and Williams, P. (Eds.) (pp. 133–152). Washington DC: American Psychiatric Publishing.

Chodorow, N. (2002). Gender as a Personal and Cultural Construction. In *Gender and Psychoanalytic Space: Between Clinic and Culture*, Dimen, M. and Goldner, V. (Eds.) (pp. 238–261). New York: Other Press.

Chodorow, N. (2012). *Individualizing Sexuality; Theory and Practice*. New York & London: Routledge.

Corbett, K. (2001). More life: Centrality and marginality in human development, *Psychoanalytic Dialogues*, 11(3):313–335.

Davidson, A.I. (1987). How To Do the History of Psychoanalysis: A Reading of Freud's *Three Essays on the Theory of Sexuality*. In *The Trial(s) of Psychoanalysis*, Meltzer, F. (Ed.) (pp. 39–64). Chicago: The University of Chicago Press.

Elise, D. (2001). Unlawful entry: Male fears of psychic penetration, *Psychoanalytic Dialogues*, 11(4):499–531.

Evzonas, N. (2020). Gender and "race" enigmatic signifiers: How the social colonizes the unconscious, *Psychoanalytic Inquiry*, 40(8):636–656.

Evzonas, N., & Laufer, L. (2019). The therapist's transition, *The Psychoanalytic Review*, 106(5): 385–416.

Fiorini, L.G. (2017). *Sexual Difference in Debate: Bodies, Desires, and Fictions*. New York & London: Routledge.

Fonagy, P., & Target, M. (1996). Playing with reality: I. Theory of mind and the normal development of psychic reality, *International Journal of Psychoanalysis*, 77:217–233.

Fonagy, P., & Target, M. (2007). The rooting of the mind in the body: New links between attachment theory and psychoanalytic thought. *Journal of the American Psychoanalytic Association*, 55(2):411–456.

Freud, S. (1905). *Three Essays on the Theory of Sexuality*. Standard Edition, 7:123–246.

Freud, S. (1910). *Leonardo da Vinci and a Memory of his Childhood*. Standard Edition, 11:57–138.

Freud, S. (1912). *On the Universal Tendency to Debasement in the Sphere of Love (Contributions to the Psychology of Love: II)*. Standard Edition, 11:177–190.

Freud, S. (1923). *The Ego and the Id, Chapter V, The Dependent Relationships of the Ego*. Standard Edition, 19:48–59.

Freud, S. (1924). *The Dissolution of the Oedipus Complex*. Standard Edition, 19:171–180.

Freud, S. (1935). Letter to an American mother." Published as Historical Notes - A Letter from Freud, *American Journal of Psychiatry*, 107(1951):786–787.

Green, A. (1995). Has sexuality anything to do with psychoanalysis?, *International Journal of Psychoanalysis*, 76:871–883.

González, F.J. (2019). Writing gender with sexuality: reflections on the diaries of Lou Sullivan, *Journal of the American Psychoanalytic Association*, 67(1):59–82.

Gulati, R. & Pauley D. (2020). Reconsidering Leonardo Da Vinci and a memory of his childhood, *Journal of the American Psychoanalytic Association*, 68(3):359–406.

Harris, A. (2009). *Gender as Soft Assembly*. New York & London: Routledge.

Holtzman, D. & Kulish, N. (2000). The feminization of the female Oedipal complex, part I: A reconsideration of the significance of separation issues, *Journal of the American Psychoanalytic Association*, 48(4):1413–1437.

Holtzman, D. & Kulish, N. (2003). The femininization of the female Oedipal complex, part II: Aggression reconsidered, *Journal of the American Psychoanalytic Association*, 51(4):1127–1151.

Isay, R. (1987). Fathers and their homosexually inclined sons in childhood, *Psychoanalytic Study of the Child*, 42:275–294.

Kaplan, L. (1991). *Female Perversions*. Northvale, NJ: Aronson.

Kaplan, L. (2000). Further thoughts on female perversions, *Studies in Gender and Sexuality*, 1(4):349–370.

Laplanche, J. (1995). Seduction, persecution, revelation, *International Journal of Psychoanalysis*, 76:663–682.

Laplanche, J. (1997). The theory of seduction and the problem of the other, *International Journal of Psychoanalysis*, 78:653–666.

Laplanche, J. (2002). *Freud and the sexual*. Fletcher, J., House, J., & Ray, N. (Trans., 2011). New York: UIT-The Unconscious in Translation.

Lemma, A. (2018). Trans-itory identities: Some psychoanalytic reflections on transgender identities, *International Journal of Psychoanalysis*, 99(5):1089–1106.

Lynch, P.E. (2002). Yearning For Love and Cruising for Sex: Returning to Freud to Understand Some Gay Men. In *Annual of Psychoanalysis, Vol 30*, Winer, J.A. & Anderson, J.W. (Eds.) (pp. 175–189). Hillsdale, NJ: The Analytic Press.

Lynch, P.E. (2015). Intimacy, Desire, and Shame in Gay Male Sexuality. In *Sexualities: Contemporary Psychoanalytic Perspectives*, Lemma, A. & Lynch, P.E. (Eds.) (pp. 138–155). New York & London: Routledge.

Mayer, E.L. (1995). The phallic castration complex and primary femininity: Paired developmental lines toward female gender identity, *Journal of the American Psychoanalytic Association*, 43:17–38.

Money, J. (1973). Gender role, gender identity, core gender identity: Usage and definition of terms, *Journal of the American Academy of Psychoanalysis*, 1(4):397–402.

Moss, D. (2015). Sexual Aberrations. In *Sexualities: Contemporary Psychoanalytic Perspectives*, Lemma, A. & Lynch, P.E. (Eds.) (pp. 177–188). New York & London: Routledge.

Rose, S.H. (2007). *Oedipal Rejection; Echoes in the Relationships of Gay Men*. Amherst, NY: Cambria Press.

Riviere, J. (1929). Womanliness as a masquerade, *International Journal of Psychoanalysis*, 10:303–313.

Saketopoulou, A. (2020). Thinking psychoanalytically, thinking better: Reflections on transgender, *International Journal of Psychoanalysis*, 101(5):1019–1030.

Scarfone, D. (2019). The sexual and psychical reality, *International Journal of Psychoanalysis*, 100(6):1248–1255.

Schiller, B.M. (2012). Representing female desire within a labial framework of sexuality, *Journal of the American Psychoanalytic Association*, 60(6):1161–1197.

Stein, R. (2008). The otherness of sexuality: Excess, *Journal of the American Psychoanalytic Association*, 56(1):43–71.

Stoller, R.J. (1968). The sense of femaleness, *Psychoanalytic Quarterly*, 37:42–55.

Stone, L. (1954). The widening scope of indications for psychoanalysis. *Journal of the American Psychoanalytic Association*, 2(4):567–594.

Sullivan, N. (2003). *A Critical Introduction to Queer Theory*. New York: New York University Press.

Target, M. (2015). A developmental model of sexual excitement, desire and alienation. In *Sexualities: Contemporary Psychoanalytic Perspectives*, Lemma, A. & Lynch, P.E. (Eds.) (pp. 43–62). New York & London: Routledge.

Yanof, J. (2000). Barbie and the tree of life: The multiple functions of gender in development. *Journal of the American Psychoanalytic Association*, 48(4):1439–1465.

Chapter 2

Revitalizing the Oedipal model for LGBTQ couples and families[i]

Shelley Nathans

Many years ago, my 4-year-old daughter and I were playing with her doll-house together. She was pretending the dollhouse was a hotel and I was the assistant, assigned to hand her objects for placement in various rooms. We had a collection of small dolls, and she was grouping them into families, each family residing in different rooms in the hotel. The families she was making consisted of four dolls: one father, one mother, and two children. All was going well until she made another family, and I stupidly said, "Wait dear, I think you made a mistake. This family doesn't have a Daddy." She looked at me incredulously and said, "Mommy, what's the matter with you? Can't you see they're lesbians!"

She was right of course; I could not see. Although at that time, I consciously believed I comfortably accepted the variety and multiplicity of family life, my unconscious bias had blinded me, leading me to organize our play according to familiar heterosexual structures. But it isn't only pretend play that suffers from this confining myopia. Clinical theory shapes what we see, how we see it, what we do not see, and most importantly, what we do and don't do in clinical practice. In the original myth of Oedipus Rex, Sophocles reveals how blindness to reality may ardently seduce us into following comforting illusions and result in excruciating tragedy — a defense for which we pay a hefty price. It leaves us handicapped by restricting our capacity to apprehend and accept reality and renders us less able to navigate our way in the world. These same biases in our theoretical formulations restrict our vision, blind us, and impede us from obtaining a fuller appreciation of the complexities of contemporary couple relationships and family life.

In this chapter, I revitalize Oedipal theory, divorcing it from its historical heterosexist bias, and highlighting its relevance for working with a variety of couple and family relationships, including lesbian, gay, bisexual, transgender, queer (LGBTQ) and single parent households. Rather than focusing on how Oedipal dynamics affect the psychosexual development of children, I will orient the discussion to adult relationships in non-heteronormative couples and families. I will emphasize the triadic structure of the Oedipal situation — a structure that is, in my view, more salient than the specific

DOI: 10.4324/9781003255703-2

gender identifications or sexual orientations of the individuals. I want to highlight the importance of keeping Oedipal dynamics in mind when treating couples and families, with a particular emphasis on highlighting triadic relationships in diverse couples and families.

The necessity of a contemporary Oedipal model for modern couples and families

Clearly, there is a lag between psychoanalytic theory and the reality of present-day family relations, where many families are not composed of two parents, one of whom identifies as male, the other as female. In clinical practice, I work with individuals and couples who live in a multiplicity of family configurations: straight couples, single-parent families, blended families, multi-generational families, families that include surrogates, families that include both adoptive and biological parents, couples who have separated and divorced and continue living in the same household, same-sex couples, lesbian and gay male couples with children, couples who define themselves as queer or gender fluid, transgender couples and couples with transgender children, couples with open relationships, adults whose parents who have come out of the closet in later life, and couples who decide to remain together when one of the partners comes out as gay or transgender after many years of marriage.

Oedipal theory, and its centrality to the development of psychic structure, has been a signature hallmark in psychoanalytic theory. This developmental arena has been viewed as the fertile ground for myriad psychological impediments and symptom formations. Correspondingly, the necessity of traversing this anxiety-ridden psychic terrain has been regarded as essential for the development of mature psychic functioning and for understanding the dynamics of individuals, couples, and families from a psychoanalytic point of view.

Beginning with Freud, and throughout most of psychoanalytic theory, the primary parent has been deemed to be the mother, while the infant, mother, and father constituted both the literal and psychic triad. If we consider Oedipal theory from a contemporary view, we can challenge the fundamentalist assumption that equates psychological health with specific traditional family structures, from the concrete requirement of specific parental bodies (females and males), or with the inflexible demand of binary symbolic functions (maternal and paternal). Conceived in this way, it is incumbent on us to revise what conventional psychoanalytic theorists envisioned and apply Oedipal theory to non-traditional families, families with two parents of the same sex, gender-fluid parental couples, or single-parents. As clinicians, we must challenge the assumption that non-heteronormative couples and families are necessarily different from traditional families with regard to the essential aspects of Oedipal dynamics, and we must integrate this revision into psychoanalytic theory and practice. In this chapter, I contemporize the Oedipal model to demonstrate that, in all types of families — including those not constituted within heteronormative structures — children and adults alike must come to terms with the anxieties and demands of the Oedipal situation. By using Klein's (1928, 1946) term, the Oedipal situation, as opposed to the Oedipus complex, I am referring to a range of contemporary perspectives that pertain to triads, triangulation, and triadic experience that extend well beyond that which Freud, Klein, and others had originally posited (Britton, 1989).

There is no reason to assume same-sex, non-binary parental couples, or single-parent families offer less opportunity for the psychological development associated with the Oedipal situation and the achievement of triangular psychic space. In my view, this potential is bi-directional and applies to both child and adult development. For example, a child being raised by a single parent must come to recognize that they do not have exclusive possession of that parent due to the parent's relationship to other important persons or activities outside of the infant-parent dyad. Similarly, the parent must also come to terms with Oedipal anxieties because these may flow in both directions, between generations. Conceived in this way, Oedipal anxieties, and their associated beneficial developments, are bi-directional, exacting mutual influence on both adults and children (Abse, 2012). Parenting often forces adults to confront the realities of separateness, the limits of their omnipotent control, and the anxieties associated with inclusion and exclusion in relation to their child's life. Well-functioning family life requires both children and adults to develop, tolerate, and manage these types of issues, along with all the other complexities inherent in triadic relating.

The developmental achievements and mature psychological functioning theorized to result from the sufficiently good enough negotiation of Oedipal territory are not, therefore, the exclusive province or privilege of heterosexual two-parent families. Correspondingly, since the children and adults in LGBTQ and single-parent families are not inherently less psychologically healthy than those in heterosexual families (Manning, et al., 2014), it is also true that they are not less free from the same Oedipal troubles that may afflict us all.

Contemporary psychoanalytic theory and Oedipal theory

Over the past few decades, contemporary psychoanalytic theory has tended to drift away from the Oedipus complex as a central organizing principle (Loewald, 1979; Seligman, 2018) for several reasons: in part due to a general de-emphasis of sexuality and erotics (Elise, 2019, Green, 1995); in part due to an increased emphasis on pre-Oedipal phenomenon (Aron, 1995); and in part due to the contemporary critique of gender and sexual developmental theory embedded in classical theory. A convincing case could be made for dispensing with the Oedipal model entirely due to its heterosexist bias and the history of its many injurious and problematic applications. This includes the erroneous and damaging explanation of female psychosexual development (Benjamin, 1988, 1995; Elise, 2019); the pathologizing of lesbian, gay, and queer persons, and the resultant perpetuation of misguided beliefs about homosexuality (Corbett, 2001); the antiquated view restricting gender to rigid binary, rather than fluid identifications (Aron, 1995; Barden, 2011; Butler, 1995; Corbett, 2001, 2008; Harris, 2005); and the prejudicial impact of unconscious racism embedded in Oedipal theory (Bertoldi, 1998, Nast, 2000). These limitations have led to the development of an important and compelling theoretical turn that argues against the deleterious effects of a theory of universally fixed linear developmental structures, and promotes, instead, a model of gender and sexuality based on complexity, variety, fluidity, and multiplicity (Chodorow, 1996; Corbett, 2001, 2008; Harris, 2005).

However, others have challenged the classical model of the Oedipus in terms of its heteronormative foundations while, at the same time, advocating for its value as central to psychosexual development. The common aim of these contemporary psychoanalytic re-workings of the Oedipus complex has been to reassert its significance as a developmental milestone in individual psychosocial development (e.g., Davies, 2003, 2015; Elise, 2019; Lingiardi and Carone, 2019) and to promote increased, non-linear assumptions regarding gender identification and object choice (e.g., Heineman, 2004; Gonzales, 2009).

Aron (1995), working from a relational psychoanalytic framework and incorporating the work of Britton (1989), contemporized Klein's notion of the combined parental figure in the Oedipal situation to emphasize how it may be metaphorically used in ways that do not privilege heterosexuality, allowing for myriad sexual identifications and arrangements that do not fall along rigid binary lines. Moreover, Aron recontextualized the concept of the primal scene, extending it beyond the idea of a terrorizing traumatic landscape to a vehicle for psychic development that allows for the internalization of patterns of relating, or what Aron termed, "systems of perceived relations among others," that form the basis of a cohesive sense of self and mature psychic relating (Aron, 1995).

Davies (2003), also writing from a relational theoretical perspective, has argued for reestablishing the primacy of the Oedipus complex as a major developmental milestone but, at the same time, disentangling it from assumptions about sexual orientation and object choice. She wrote, "I hope to offer a model for understanding this critical phase of development in which multiple pathways lead to an assortment of potential outcomes, focused not on sexual orientation or object choice but, rather, on the particular qualities of intimacy, eroticism, and a deeply resilient mutuality" (Davies, 2003, p. 7).

Accordingly, Davies (2015) and Lingiardi and Carone (2019) have advocated rethinking the Oedipus complex in favor of a model of "Oedipal complexity," positing that a child's development would not necessarily be pre-determined by their parent's gender or sexual orientation. In this view, psychological development depends upon both pre-Oedipal and Oedipal factors, as well as the parent's own psychological development, including the parent's early relational events, and the internalization of their own parental figures.

Some authors have challenged and stretched the orthodox geometry of the Oedipal metaphor in creative and useful ways. Hertzmann (2011) has used the concept of the creative couple, an idea based on the Oedipus complex, to examine internalized homophobia in lesbian and gay couples. Seidel (2019), in a challenge to the traditional fixed binary assumptions about maternal and paternal functions often assumed in parenting, proposed a geometry that symbolizes fluidity resting on top of triangular structure. She offers the idea of an expansion of the Oedipal triangle to a shape resembling an ice cream cone (a triangle topped with a semi-circle). Corbett (2001), in a discussion of non-traditional family romance, has critiqued the "assumed correspondence between heterosexuality, reproduction, family and reality" (Corbett, 2001, p. 618). Corbett described the primal scene in lesbian and gay families, multiple-parent families, and single-parent families as having "multiple circulating narratives." Ehrensaft (2014) focused on the ubiquity of reproductive technology and the possible genetic and non-genetic ways in which babies may be conceived in our time. She advocated replacing triangles with Oedipal circles to expansively include sperm donors, birth surrogates, gestational carriers, same-sex, and trans-gender couples.

Oedipal theory in psychoanalytic couple and family theory

Oedipal theory has served as an essential pillar in the psychoanalytic theory of couples and families, particularly in the literature born out of the British object relations model developed at the Tavistock Clinic since the 1940s (Grier, 2005b; Nathans, 2017; Ruszczynski, 1993). A number of concepts, derived from Oedipal theory, have been used to describe mature forms of relating. These include the concept of "linked separateness" (Balfour, 2005); "triadic space" (Britton, 1989); a "capacity for separation and triadic relating" (Fisher, 1999); the "marital triangle" (Ruszczynski, 2005); "a couple state of mind" (Morgan, 2001); and "creative coupling" (Morgan, 2005).

Similarly, Oedipal theory, and its associated difficulties with triangular relating, have been employed to describe a variety of disturbances in couple and family relationships. Since a complete review of this literature is beyond the scope of this chapter, I offer examples of some of the significant applications of theory in this domain. A number of authors have described problematic narcissistic forms of relating as deriving from Oedipal issues (Fisher, 1999; Morgan, 1995; Rosenthall, 2005; Ruszczynski, 1995, 2005). Sexual difficulties in couple relationships have been linked to Oedipal problems with inclusion and exclusion (Balfour, 2009; Morgan, 2019), primal scene anxieties (Grier, 2005a; Rosenthall, 2005; Sehgal, 2012), and other problems with triadic relating (Colman,

2009). These dynamics have also been used to understand a variety of parenting difficulties (Balfour, 2005; Morgan, 2005), as well as the intractable issues that often beset high conflict separating and divorcing couples (Shmueli, 2012; Vincent, 2001).

Despite the theoretical contributions that valuably link the Oedipal situation to couple and family life, the vast majority of the clinical material in the psychoanalytic couple and family literature has been exclusively restricted to heteronormative coupling and has contained a glaring dearth of references to non-traditional family structures (McCann, 2017). In one sense, this may be a reflection of the general trend in contemporary psychoanalytic theory to remove sex, sexuality, and erotics from a central role in the Oedipal narrative, but I think there is something more at play, something born out of heterosexual privilege and bias. Does this not reflect an historical heterosexist bent, a viewpoint linked with the shameful psychoanalytic history of pathologizing differences in gender identities and sexual preferences, a blindness that erases those who do not conform to what has been deemed normative?

The Kleinian Oedipal model

Unlike Freud, Klein (1928) viewed what she termed the "Oedipal situation" as beginning in early infancy, when the infant turns away from the mother in frustration and moves toward the father, creating the initial triangle constituted by the infant, mother, and father. This frustration, along with the child's awareness of the parental relationship, is fundamental to the structure of the Oedipal triangle in the psyche. Klein argued that coming to terms with the recognition of the parental couple, the sexual link between them, and the reality of being excluded from this relationship are fundamental to the development of psychic functioning and the achievement of what she termed "depressive position" capacities. This includes the capacity to integrate good and bad experiences, rather than relying on defensive splitting. The integration of good and bad experiences, of both love and hate, is essential to the development of a number of mature psychological capacities associated with depressive position functioning, including: the ability to view the world with nuanced, non-categorical complexity; a greater tolerance of ambivalence towards oneself and others; a concern for others; an awareness of one's potential to be destructive; a capacity for guilt; and the capacity to accept and mourn loss.

In this model, these depressive position capacities are associated with mature psychological and sexual functioning and are achieved through the anxiety-laden trek through the Oedipal triangle. However, it is important to remember that in healthy development, the achievement of these capacities necessarily rests on *a secure dyadic foundation* with a primary caretaker: a "secure attachment" (Main, 2000); a "good enough mother" (Winnicott, 1965); or a mother who provides containment for the infant's unmetabolized emotional experience (Bion, 1962). Without a secure dyadic bedrock, the traverse through Oedipal terrain will likely be more anxiety-ridden and treacherous.

In reality, none of us ever fully or completely arrives at the depressive position, and regressions to less mature psychic states are part of everyday life. The anxieties we encounter in the Oedipal domain will inevitably resurface at different times in our lives, especially in intimate relationships.

The Oedipal situation and the capacity to think

Contemporary Kleinian theorists have extended Klein's theory of the Oedipal situation to show how it provides essential bedrock to other aspects of mature psychic functioning, with a particular emphasis on the development of the capacity to think that rests on triangular space (Britton, 1989). If the child is able to accept the reality of the parental couple and tolerate being excluded from this dyad, the child can have the experience of observing a parental couple and being observed by a parental couple — a parental couple that *observes and thinks* about the child. Over time, the child's experience of observing the parental couple thinking about them promotes the internalization of the mental apparatus for observation and thinking.

In Bion's model of the mind, thinking is composed of two elements: a mind and the thoughts or feelings contained in the mind. In early dyadic relating, the primary parent serves the psychic function of receiving the child's unmetabolized emotional states and provides containment through the processes of thinking, as well as offering something containing back to the child (Bion, 1962). The parental couple also performs a containing function from within a triadic structure by demonstrating a model of a relationship between two people who can observe the child, think about this together, and offer something useful back. Through the processes of projective and introjective identification, the child can internalize the parental couple, along with its psychic functions (to observe and to think). This promotes the mature capacity to subsequently observe and think about oneself, to tolerate both excluding others and being excluded, to be a participant in a relationship while being observed, and to be an observer of a relationship from an outsider's point of view.

The Oedipal situation and the capacity to form mature intimate relationship

The development of flexible psychic triangulation is also crucial to the capacity to form mature intimate relationships, as it allows for a form of linked separateness (Balfour, 2005) that rests on a capacity for observation and on a capacity for being observed in relation to others. This creates an ability to share psychic space and to maintain a sense of one's own separateness while, at the same time, being linked in relation to another without an overwhelming fear of engulfment. From the depressive position, within this flexible triangular space, exclusion from the parental couple or its subsequent symbolic representations will not be experienced as catastrophic. The wish to attack and triumph over an internal parental couple will be diminished. Rivalry will be experienced as less destructive, will not be equated with death to the dyad, and will therefore be less anxiety producing. Consequently, there will be a more flexible capacity to integrate a symbolic or actual third because it will not be imbued with such threatening aspects. Rather than engaging in denial, splitting, projection, and the enactment of unresolved Oedipal conflicts, it will be more possible for a person to integrate sexual and emotional intimacy, and more likely for them to introject a creative parental couple as an internal object (Frisch & Frisch-Desmarez, 2010; Morgan, 2005; Morgan & Freedman, 2000; Nathans, 2012, 2016, 2017, 2018).

Navigating the complexities of the Oedipal situation, in a relatively less problematic way, has other important implications for the capacity to form a creative couple relationship, maintain loyalty to it, and refrain from enacting unresolved Oedipal dynamics through infidelity or other types of boundary violations (Nathans, 2012). Since the Oedipal situation requires a gradual relinquishment of the phantasy of exclusive possession of the desired parent, as well as acceptance of the reality of being excluded from the parental couple, this promotes a capacity to tolerate loss and results in an increased capacity for mourning (Nathans, 2012, 2017, 2018).

Finally, mature psychic functioning is associated with what Morgan has described as the internalization of a creative couple:

> "The creative couple" is primarily a psychic development, one in which it is possible to allow different thoughts and feelings to come together in one's mind, and for something to develop out of them. This capacity obviously has a major impact on an actual couple relationship. If one can allow this kind of mating within oneself, it becomes more likely that one can allow it to occur between oneself and one's partner.
> (Morgan, 2005, p. 22)

Clinical examples

In presenting some clinical material to illustrate the theoretical intent of this chapter, I have encountered a dilemma. I am advocating considering Oedipal issues for all types of couples and families, including those not organized along heteronormative lines. But I do not want to imply that all couples and families are the same. As I have argued, all couples and families are beset with similar potential vulnerabilities, while bearing similar possibilities for healthy relating. A potential risk involved with making this claim is it may deemphasize other aspects of differences that are important.

For example, a couple with two partners who identify as same-sex *is dif-ferent* from a couple who identify as heterosexual. Whereas they may be similar in myriad ways, they are not the same in others. The multiplicity of ways in which particular persons, couples, or families may identify (e.g., as heterosexual, same-sex, bisexual, homosexual, queer, trans, polyamorous, etc.) are in themselves important signifiers intended to permit freedom for difference and to distinguish them from heteronormativity (or not).

Notwithstanding important distinctions in how particular couples and families identify, I want to emphasize the utility of contemporary Oedipal theory in clinical work. The following clinical vignettes illustrate some dynamics that might arise in couple or family relationships. Working with couple and family dynamics, from a psychoanalytic approach, requires thinking carefully about the complex conscious and unconscious anxiety/defense matrices that may be operative in the relationships between indi-viduals. I am presenting these cases without histories, complete dynamic formulations, or elaboration of technique and therapeutic interventions with two purposes in mind. First, I present these case examples, each dif-ferent from traditional heteronormative relationships, to demonstrate how an Oedipal lens and triangulation themes may be useful for understanding and working with a wide variety of modern couples and families. Second, I want to show how triadic structure is separate from, and not necessarily linked to, specific gender or sexual orientation. To further this aim, in these vignettes, I have highlighted the Oedipal dynamics and given them primary focus as independent of specific couple or family organizations or specific bodies (e.g., male or female or trans).

While the demands of the Oedipal situation have the potential to exert their presence in everyone, Oedipal issues will not necessarily be problem-atic, nor the most salient feature needing to be addressed in clinical work with couples or families. Moreover, Oedipal dynamics, when problematic, are rarely the whole story. They exist in a complex context in all relation-ships, within an array of multiple unconscious identifications, anxieties, defenses, and phantasies. As can be seen in the following cases, other important themes, such as separation issues or the inhibition of healthy expressions of aggression, play alongside and contribute to the relational dynamics. Rather than offering a full description of the totality of all the factors or possible dynamic formulations, I am privileging the Oedipal dynamics to emphasize the purposes of this chapter.

Emily and maria, a couple struggling with sexual boundary violations: triangulation as defense against separation issues

Emily and Maria, both in their mid-thirties, had been living together for two years. They said the beginning of their relationship was "incredibly romantic and perfect." They felt like they couldn't be apart and moved in with each other two months after their first date. In the beginning, they had sex "all of the time," and it was exciting and mutually satisfying for both of them. After committing to a monogamous relationship, and shortly after moving in together, the frequency of their lovemaking drastically diminished. They weren't sure what the problem was or how to remedy it, and after talking about it, they decided to try having an open relationship with the hopes this might revive their passion. They affirmed their love for each other, said they wanted to stay together, and decided to make the terms of their planned open relationship explicit to avoid hurting one another. They agreed they would each be permitted to have sex with other people, but this would preclude any emotional attachments. As long as it was just sex, it would be okay, but they were not to develop any strong feelings or attachments for anyone else. At first this went well, and they felt they had created something that felt exciting and expansive. Yet, about six months later, Emily felt Maria was growing more distant from her. She confronted Maria one morning, and Maria tearfully admitted she was falling in love with another woman. Maria said she felt terribly guilty, she didn't know how this had happened, she hadn't planned on developing feelings like this for another person, and she had kept this secret to avoid hurting Emily. Emily was devastated and felt Maria had betrayed her trust and their commitment to one another. They came to see me in a state of panic, wondering if there would be any way for them to salvage their relationship.

At the end of our first meeting, I said I could see they were both in anguish and facing a real crisis. I said it seemed they had initially tried to face the question of what happened to their sex life after they moved in together, but they had been unable to understand it. I said they may have jointly avoided the problem with the hope that expanding the boundaries of their relationship would solve their dilemma. While polyamory and open relationships can work out well for many couples, it had clearly complicated their lives. Instead of increasing their sense of freedom, erotic desire and enhancing their connection, they were now having to come to terms with the pain of jealousy, deception, betrayal and guilt. I said, contrary to their expectations, what they ended up with was something far more complicated and troubling, something that felt more like cheating, more like a betrayal or an infidelity. I thought this was something we might be able to understand together. I added we might be able to learn more about how the dynamics of their relationship contributed both to the diminishment of their sex life and to the dilemma they were now facing. With the hope of salvaging their relationship, the couple decided to begin couple therapy. Emily said she would not be able to stay if Maria continued to see her other lover, and she viewed this as essential to reestablishing trust. Maria said she was confused about what she ultimately wanted to do, but she understood that if they were going to try to stay together, she would need to stop the other relationship. As with most couples attempting to manage the crisis of an affair, I think one of the first steps involves helping them reestablish boundaries to promote some sense of psychological containment. On the one hand, this couple's capacity to do this was a hopeful sign that could indicate the strength of their commitment to one another, and an affirmation of the link between them. If they were going to work on their relationship, ending the triangulation seemed essential. But on the other hand, I thought this alone would not be sufficient, and that the risk of reuniting as a couple could potentially thrust them back into painful dyadic dynamics. We needed to understand the unconscious anxieties that had gotten stimulated in their relationship, and what had caused the dissolution of their former satisfying sex life together. Otherwise, wouldn't they likely be plagued again by the same problems they had attempted to solve by the failed transformation of their two-some into various three-somes?

In the throes of early romantic idealization, Emily and Maria had got along easily and without ruptures. However, as the honeymoon bliss waned, they were faced with a more complex experience of the actualities of one another and of the relationship. Like all couples, they learned there were aspects of one another they did not like and found to be problematic. Things went along smoothly as long as they both had the same idea, but when there was a disagreement, they couldn't talk about it, and felt pressure to give into the other for fear of hurting the other. I suspected they had unconsciously created a dynamic that required a disavowal of difference, a relationship that confused sameness with intimacy. I wondered if their relationship was founded on an unconscious pact of merger, an experience that was initially compellingly erotic, but one that had subsequently turned into something impossibly suffocating and claustrophobic. Instead of a relationship between two separate people, it had become more like a "duet for one" (Fisher, 1993). I suspected they might have tried to resolve this claustrophobic dilemma with the idea of opening up their relationship, and with the hope that freedom from the dyadic trap would solve the difficulty. I thought they had confused psychic separateness with physical and sexual separateness. They had traded entrapment for the exciting, yet tormenting agony of betrayal and exclusion. Because they had difficulty relating with psychic separateness dyadically, triangulation had been substituted for healthy triadic relating.

This vignette illustrates how triangulation may be used as a defense against dyadic anxieties. Ironically, instead of creating a stable sense of freedom and invigorating their erotic life, the solution they devised tragically confirmed the shared psychic belief that separation was threatening and posed a danger to the relationship. While this vignette exemplifies an unconscious defensive use of an open relationship, other couples may form open relationships that function well and serve more creative, non-defensive purposes. When polyamorous couples come to psychotherapy for help, it is important for clinicians to try to differentiate a primarily defensive use of triangulation from a more healthy, creative, and expansive form of relating in an open relationship — one that reinforces the emotional and erotic connection between the partners.

John and Patrick, a couple with whom rivalry, exclusion and primal scene anxieties emerge in the transference/countertransference

John and Patrick, a married couple in their early thirties, had been working with me in couple psychotherapy for about a year. One day, they arrived at my office with their 3-month-old infant in tow. As they had done upon entering my office every session since the baby had been born, John held their sleeping son while Patrick managed folding and guiding the stroller into the room. After they settled in, the baby awoke, and John asked if I would like to hold him. I accepted the offer and enjoyed a few minutes of holding and admiring a lovely, calm, and content infant. When I decided to return the baby to the couple, I held him out, deliberately not assuming which of them would take him. Patrick did not make a move. John hesitated, got up from his chair, and took the baby into his arms. In the following week's appointment, John looked anxiously worried, and Patrick had an angry, tense look on his face. Patrick said he was furious with John and me. He said he thought it was outrageously presumptuous of both John and me to "leave him out." When I asked for more details about why he was angry with me, he pointed to the moment when I handed the baby back to John and not to him. John said, "I told Patrick you didn't automatically give him back to me. You waited to see who would take him. You didn't get up, Patrick, so I did."

As it is often the case for many couples, including John and Patrick, the feelings accompanying many deeply painful interactions are often embedded in a repetitive dynamic. Like many unconscious enactments in couples, especially those driven by projective identification, these predictable experiences can feel both eerily familiar and, at the same time, incomprehensibly shocking in the disruption that usually ensues. There is a scripted quality to the interaction, a sense of being swept up in something that has its own momentum and cannot be immediately understood, because the experience is permeated with some mysterious mélange of shared unconscious contents (Nathans, 2009). The interaction between John, Patrick and myself can be understood as a manifestation of relational unconscious activity (Gerson, 2004; Ruszczynski, 1993), a process involving individuals being shaped simultaneously by both internal and real external objects (Hewison, 2019).

Because we had worked together for a year, and because I was familiar with this couple's history of competitiveness, jealousy, and tendency to triangulate, I was aware I could easily be conscripted into these problematic dynamics. I had known to be careful when handing the baby back to the couple and, as I described, I had hesitated and waited for them to decide who would hold the baby next. But despite my caution, we were all blind-sided. Instead of what I had consciously intended to be a sensitive navigation on my part, one designed to avoid difficulty, it felt like a threatening storm had gathered. A treacherous disturbance had entered the room, and the atmosphere became suffused with the painful feelings that arise when someone feels excluded, bearing witness to being left out.

In another couple, a couple not struggling with these issues, the very same sequence of events would not have had the same meaning and would not have created the same anxieties. But John and Patrick had been struggling with complex triangulated issues since the beginning of their relationship. I thought the three of us, John, Patrick, and I, were unaware, although at the same time unconsciously aware, of the unfolding triangulated dynamic before and during the enactment. On the one hand, John had offered the baby to me and not to Patrick. On the surface, he may have thought he was being kind and sharing the baby with me. But I think it registered with all of us, on some less than conscious level, that he handed the baby to me and not to his partner, John, the baby's other parent. From within the enactment, John's offering to me became an act of exclusion, a demonstration of a coupling between him and me, a primal scene coupling that painfully denigrated Patrick and left him on the outside. Similarly, my conscious caution about handing the baby back to the couple, and waiting to see who would take him, can be understood as a pre-conscious awareness not to fall into the triangulated trap of their competitive dynamics. It was a self-warning to avoid the implication that I was assuming who was the primary or better parent. Finally, Patrick's deferential stance, his failure to move forward and take the baby from me, formed the third side of the triangle.

This vignette emphasizes the Oedipal themes of competition and rivalry, primal scene anxieties, and the difficulty many couples encounter with the transition to parenting — when a two-some becomes a three-some. All groups of three encompass multiple couplings: There are always potential dyadic relationships in groups (e.g., John and Patrick; John and the baby; Patrick and the baby; John and me; Patrick and me; or the baby and me). As I have described, the flexibility to tolerate excluding, or being excluded, is crucial to mature forms of relating and rests on a psychic capacity for flexible triangulation that allows for a form of linked separateness (Britton, 1989; Balfour, 2005). Some couples may not possess these capacities at all, and others may simply need help to maintain stability. Clinical attention to these phenomena, as they wax and wane and manifest in the transference and countertransference, is often crucial in psychoanalytic couple psychotherapy.

Discussion of the clinical material

These vignettes illustrate three important points. First, the vignettes collectively exemplify the fictive presumption that there is a normative couple or family. Contemporary couples and families do not necessarily conform to the traditional heteronormative model of two biological parents, one female and one male, one father and one mother. Rather, they embody many shapes and sizes, and are sometimes constituted by shifting forms of relating over time. They have diverse relationship structures, with a variety of gender identifications and sexual preferences, new roles, creative divisions of labor, and novel forms of relating.

Second, Oedipal structure and Oedipal dynamics can be considered as separate from any specific gender or sexual preference and are not only applicable to heteronormative relating. Triadic structures in relationships can be theorized as distinct from specific biological bodies, gender identities, sexual preferences, or family configurations, and this conception is both theoretically and clinically useful.

Third, it is advantageous for clinicians to consider Oedipal issues, and their problematic impact, when working with all types of couple and family relationships. As the vignettes illustrate, Oedipal anxieties, and the defenses they engender, can potentially beset everyone. Clinical work will be enhanced by applying this lens to a broad array of relationships and attending to their manifestation.

It is beyond the scope of this chapter to comprehensively list the myriad symptoms and dynamics arising from Oedipal issues that may afflict couples and families. Instead, I have attempted to highlight just some of the more frequent clinical presentations of these types of issues. These may include anxieties and problematic dynamics involving feelings of inclusion, exclusion, jealousy, envy, competition, rivalry, boundary violations, and defensive triangulations. These dynamics are not problematic in all cases and will not necessarily be the focus of the clinical work. They may not be initially present in couples but can be triggered and flourish when a couple is compelled to integrate an actual third, such as a child, or when a couple decides to expand the sexual boundaries of their relationship. In these instances, Oedipal conflicts may be defensively projected into and onto others, forming a triangulation or triangulations. For example, a child may be experienced by one or both of the partners in a couple as an intruder, a rivalrous competitor, or as an object who threatens replacement. Correspondingly, a child may be the object of projections of extreme fragility with regard to exclusion or abandonment. Symptoms or enactments in couple relationships, such as some forms of infidelity, or the loss of sexual desire, may also rest on triangulations that require conceptualization in terms of unconscious Oedipal themes (Grier, 2005a; Nathans, 2012, 2016). This is certainly not an exhaustive discussion of the range of possible troubles that may manifest in all types of relationships. It is offered to orient clinicians to the benefit of taking Oedipal and triangular themes into account when working with couples and families.

Conclusion

These clinical examples serve to illustrate the value of revitalizing and reconceptualizing Oedipal theory, divorcing it from its historical heterosexist bias, and highlighting its relevance for working with all couple and family relationships, including LGBTQ and single-parent households. While the misguided use of Oedipal theory has been used to pathologize differences in gender identity and sexual preference, this same type of bias may also lead clinicians to neglect Oedipal themes in non-heteronormative couples and families.

In addition, as I have described, heteronormative couples and families do not necessarily fit into traditional, gender stereotyped roles: women as primary maternal figures; men as primary paternal figures. A contemporary psychoanalytic view affords us a refreshing, multidimensional perspective of gender in all people, even those who identify along heteronormative lines. Harris (2005) has described this idea of gender as a "soft assembly." This depiction offers a model of non-rigid, flexible sets of gender identifications within each of us, and accounts for the possible emergence of fluid, multidimensional aspects of self that are not restricted to the feminine/masculine dichotomy. This model has implications beyond the development of gender identification and sexual preferences in individuals. It can be usefully extended to describe the creative potential of aspects of gender and self that may flexibly emerge and adapt to the diversity of couple, family, and social arrangements.

This view is essential for contemporary clinicians because it helps us to examine our preconceived biases, and approach those with whom we work, from a non-moralistic, non-pathologizing stance. It opens our horizons by expanding our understanding of the creative possibilities of couple and family life and facilitates our attempts to help those we work with to do the same.

As clinicians working with modern relationships, we must strive to rethink our personal and theoretical biases. Stretching Oedipal theory, by employing its theoretical triadic structure beyond heteronormativity, offers the opportunity to understand the multiplicity of relationships found in modern couple and family life. The children and adults in many types of family structures must come to terms with the anxieties and demands of the Oedipal situation through the experiences of frustration, loss, and the relinquishment of the phantasy of omnipotent control. Some will falter, some will fare better than others, and none of us will ever completely resolve these issues. But, conceived through this contemporary lens, everyone, in all types of couple and family arrangements, may be considered to have the potential to gain from the struggle achieved by traversing this psychic terrain.

Note

i A previous version of this paper, entitled, Oedipus for Everyone: Revitalizing the Model for LBGTQ Couples and Single Parent Families, was published in *Psychoanalytic Dialogues*, 2021, 31(3): 312–328.

References

Abse, S. (2012). Commentary on Parents as Partners: How Parental Relationship Affects Children's Psychological Development, by G. Harold and L. Leve. In: *How Couple Relationships Shape our World,* A. Balfour, M. Morgan, and C. Vincent (Eds.). London: Karnac Books, 57–70.

Aron, L. (1995). The Internalized Primal Scene. Psychoanalytic Dialogues, 5:195:237.

Balfour, A. (2005). The Couple, Their Marriage, and Oedipus: or, Problems Come in Twos and Threes. In: *Oedipus and the Couple*, F. Grier (Ed.). London: Karnac Books, 49–72.

Balfour, A. (2009). Intimacy and Sexuality in Later Life. In: *Sex, Attachment and Couple Psychotherapy: Psychoanalytic Perspectives*, C. Clulow (Ed.). London: Karnac, 217–236.

Barden, N. (2011). Disruption Oedipus: The Legacy of the Sphinx. Psychoanalytic Psychotherapy, 25(4):324:34.

Benjamin, J. (1988). *The Bonds of Love: Psychoanalysis, Feminism, and the Problem of Domination*. New York, NY: Pantheon.

Benjamin, J. (1995). *Like Subjects, Love Objects: Essays on Recognition and Sexual Difference*. New Haven and London: Yale University Press.

Bertoldi, A. (1998). Oedipus in (South) Africa?: Psychoanalysis and the Politics of Difference. American Imago, 55(1):101–134.

Bion, W. (1962). The Psycho-Analytic Study of Thinking. International Journal of Psychoanalysis, 43:306–310.

Britton, R. (1989). The Missing Link: Parental Sexuality in the Oedipus Complex. In: *The Oedipus Complex Today*, J. Steiner (Ed.). London: Karnac Books, 83–102.

Butler, J. (1995). Melancholy Gender - Refused Identification. Psychoanalytic Dialogues, 5(2):165–180.

Chodorow, N. (1996). Reflections on the Authority of the Past in Psychoanalytic Thinking. Psychoanalytic Quarterly, 65:32–51.

Colman, W. (2009). What Do We Mean By Sex? In: *Sex, Attachment and Couple Psychotherapy: Psychoanalytic Perspectives*, C. Clulow (Ed.). London: Karnac, 25–44.

Corbett, K. (2001). Nontraditional Family Romance. Psychoanalytic Quarterly, 70(3):599–624.

Corbett, K. (2008). Gender Now. Psychoanalytic Dialogues, 18(6):838–856.

Davies, J. M. (2003). Falling in Love with Love: Oedipal and Postoedipal Manifestations of Idealization, Mourning, and Erotic Masochism. Psychoanalytic Dialogues, 13(1):1–27.

Davies, J. M. (2015). From Oedipus Complex to Oedipal Complexity: Reconfiguring (Pardon the Expression) the Negative Oedipus Complex and the Disowned Erotics of Disowned Sexualities. Psychoanalytic Dialogues, 25(3):265–283.

Elise, D. (2015). Reclaiming Lost Loves: Transcending Unrequited Desires. Discussion of Davies' "Oedipal Complexity." Psychoanalytic Dialogues, 25(3):284–295.

Elise, D. (2019). *Creativity and the Erotic Dimensions of the Analytic Field*. Abingdon, OX and New York: Routledge.

Ehrensaft, D. (2014). Family Complexes and Oedipal Circles: Mothers, Fathers, Babies, Donors, and Surrogates. In: *Psychoanalytic Aspects of Assisted Reproductive Technology*, M. Mann (Ed.). London: Karnac.

Fisher, J. (1993). The Impenetrable Other: Ambivalence and the Oedipal Conflict in Work with Couples. In: *Psychotherapy with Couples*, S. Ruszczynski (Ed.). London: Karnac, 142–166.

Fisher, J. (1999). *The Uninvited Guest*. London: Karnac.

Frisch, S. and Frisch-Desmarez, C. (2010). Some Thoughts on the Concept of the Internal Parental Couple. International Journal of Psychoanalysis, 91(2):325–342.

Gerson, S. (2004). The Relational Unconscious: A Core Element of Intersubjectivity, Thirdness and Clinical Process. Psychoanalytic Quarterly, 73:63–98.

Gonzales, F. (2009) Negative Oedipus Redux: Transfigurations of a Field. Unpublished manuscript. Psychoanalytic Institute of Northern California. May 9, 2009.

Green, A. (1995). Has Sexuality Anything to do with Psychoanalysis? International Journal of Psychoanalysis, 76(5):871–884.

Grier, F. (2005a). No Sex Couples, Catastrophic Change, and the Primal Scene. In: *Oedipus and the Couple*, F. Grier (Ed.). London: Karnac Books, 200–219.

Grier, F. (2005b). *Oedipus and the Couple*. London: Karnac.

Harris, A. (2005). *Gender as Soft Assembly*. Hillsdale, NJ: The Analytic Press.

Heineman, T. V. (2004). A Boy and two Mothers: New Variations on an old Theme or a new Story of Triangulation? Beginning Thoughts on the Psychosexual Development of Children in Nontraditional Families. Psychoanalytic Psychology, 21(1):99–115.

Hertzmann, L. (2011). Lesbian and Gay Couple Relationships: When Internalized Homophobia Gets in the Way of Couple Creativity. Psychoanalytic Psychotherapy, 25(4):346–360.

Hewison, D. (2019). Re-Visioning Creativity in Couple Psychoanalysis. Couple and Family Psychoanalysis, 9(2):167–180.

Klein, M. (1928). Early Stages of the Oedipus Conflict. International Journal of Psychoanalysis, 9:167–180.

Klein, M. (1946). Notes on Some Schizoid Mechanisms. International Journal of Psychoanalysis, 27:99–110.

Lingiardi, V. and Carone, N. (2019). Challenging Oedipus in Changing Families: Gender Identifications and Access to Origins in Same-Sex Parent Families Created Through Third-Party Reproduction. International Journal of Psychoanalysis, 100(2):229–246.

Loewald, H. W. (1979). The Waning of the Oedipus Complex. Journal of the American Psychoanalytic Association, 27:751–77.

Main, M. (2000). The Organized Categories of Infant, Child, and Adult Attachment: Flexible vs. Inflexible Attention Under Attachment-Related Stress. Journal of the American Psychoanalytic Association, 48(4):1055–1095.

Manning, W., M. N. Fettro, and E. Lamidi. (2014). Child Well-Being in Same-Sex Parent Families: Review of Research Prepared for American Sociological Association Amicus Brief. Population Research Policy Review, 33(4):485–502.

McCann, D. (2017). When the Couple is Not Enough, or When the Couple is Too Much: Exploring the Meaning and Management of Open Relationships. Couple and Family Psychoanalysis, 7(1):45–58.

Morgan, M. (1995). The Projective Gridlock: A Form of Projective Identification in Couple Relationships. In: *Intrusiveness and Intimacy in the Couples*, S. Ruszcynski & J. Fisher (Eds.). London: Karnac Books, 33–48.

Morgan, M. (2001). First Contacts: The Therapist's "Couple State of Mind" as a Factor in Containment of Couples Seen for Consultations. In: *Brief Encounters with Couples*, F. Grier(Ed.). London: Karnac Books, 17–32.

Morgan, M. (2005). On Being Able to be a Couple: The *Importance* of a "Creative Couple" in Psychic Life. In: *Oedipus and the Couple*, F. Grier (Ed.). London: Karnac Books, 9–30.

Morgan, M. (2019). *A Couple State of Mind: Psychoanalysis of Couples and The Tavistock Relationship's Model.* Abingdon and New York: Routledge.

Morgan, M. and Freedman, J. (2000). From Fear of Intimacy to Perversion: A Clinical Analysis of the Film Sex, Lies and Videotape. British Journal of Psychotherapy, 17(1):85–93.

Nathans, S. (2009). Discussion: "The Macbeths in the Consulting Room," by James Fisher. *fort da*, XV(2):56–65.

Nathans, S. (2012). Infidelity as Manic Defence. Couple and Family Psychoanalysis, 2(2):165–180.

Nathans, S. (2016). Whose Disgust is it Anyway?: Projection and Projective Identification in the Couple Relationship. Psychoanalytic Dialogues, 26(4):437–443.

Nathans, S. (2017). *Couples on the Couch: Psychoanalytic Couple Psychotherapy and the Tavistock Model.* Abingdon and New York: Routledge.

Nathans, S. (2018). *45 Years,* written and directed by Andrew Haigh. Sundance Selects, 2015; 1 hr, 35 min. *Fort da*, 24(2), 97–101.

Nast, H. J. (2000). Mapping the Unconscious: Racism and the Oedipal Family. Annals of the American Association of Geographers, 90(2):215–255.

Rosenthall, J. (2005). Oedipus Gets Married: An Investigation of a Couple's Shared Oedipal Drama. In: *Oedipus and the Couple*, F. Grier (Ed.). London: Karnac Books, 181–200.

Ruszczynski, S. (1993). *Psychotherapy with Couples: Theory and Practice at the Tavistock Institute of Marital Studies.* London: Karnac.

Ruszczynski, S. (1995). Narcissistic Object Relating. In: *Intrusiveness and Intimacy in the Couple*, S. Ruszczynski and J. Fisher (Eds.). London: Karnac Books, 13–32.

Ruszczynski, S. (2005). Reflective Space in the Intimate Couple Relationship: The "Marital Triangle". In: *Oedipus and the Couple*, F. Grier (Ed.). London: Karnac Books, 31–48.

Sehgal, A. (2012). Viewing the Absence of Sex from Couple Relationships Through the "Core Complex" Lens. Couple and Family Psychoanalysis, 2(2):149–164.

Seidel, E. (2019). *Queering the Psychoanalytic Family.* Unpublished manuscript.

Seligman, S. (2018). *Relationships in Development: Infancy, Intersubjectivity, and Attachment.* Abingdon, OX and New York: Routledge.

Shmueli, A. (2012). Working Therapeutically with High Conflict Divorce. In: *How Couple Relationships Shape our World*, A. Balfour, M. Morgan, and C. Vincent (Eds.). London: Karnac Books, 137–158.

Vincent, C. (2001). Giving Advice During Consultations: Unconscious Enactment or Thoughtful Containment? In: *Brief Encounters with Couples*, F. Grier (Ed.). London: Karnac Books, 85–97.

Winnicott, D. W. (1965). *The Maturational Process and the Facilitating Environment.* London: Hogarth Press.

Chapter 3

Family matters

The impact of family and sociocultural context on LGBTQ identities and psychodynamics

Andi Pilecki Eliza-Christie

Introduction

We need look no further than social progress toward lesbian, gay, bisexual, transgender, queer (LGBTQ) rights and representation to know the indelible role that culture plays on the inner lives of families and individuals. Family is the primary carrier of culture, with parents, consciously and unconsciously, transmitting dynamics, values, and beliefs to children, but the family itself is inextricably linked to wider sociocultural contexts. LGBTQ people are significantly impacted by cultural norms and biases concerning sexuality and gender which, for some, can lead to trauma associated with alienation and rejection from within the family of origin. Such trauma can have enduring effects on internal object relations, self-esteem, and interpersonal dynamics. As the scapegoats for culturally split-off longing and fears regarding gender and sexuality, LGBTQ people have suffered from negative stereotyping that characterizes them as immoral, mentally ill, and perverse.

Before the Gay Rights Movement, American dominant culture was so profoundly heteronormative that many LGBTQ people felt totally alone and alien in response to the dawning awareness of same sex attraction and/or emerging transgender identity. Heteronormativity supports representations of sexuality and gender limited to heterosexual, cisgender models of relating and, as such, renders the lived experiences of LGBTQ individuals and couples as invalid, invisible, and stigmatized. However, sociocultural progress catalyzed by LGBTQ activism has begun to widen this lens so as to include diverse sexual and gender identities, and we now have examples of LGBTQ lived experience in all major social institutions. This macro level change is impacting micro level change so that more LGBTQ people have greater access to support within the immediate spheres of family and community. In this chapter, I use a psychoanalytic perspective embedded within a psychosocial framework to address the impact of culture on the inner lives of queer individuals, couples, and families.

DOI: 10.4324/9781003255703-3

The link and intersectionality

It is important to remember that LGBTQ populations are not monolithic, and that there is significant diversity among queer people, where intersections of race, ethnicity, class, age, gender, family, and religion play a major role in social experience and psychodynamics. The link, or 'el vinculo', and intersectionality are two concepts that help to illuminate the role that diverse sociocultural contexts play in LGBTQ identity formation.

Pioneering psychoanalyst Enrique Pichon-Rivière developed the theory of the link, which addresses the myriad, intersecting forces that shape psychic, relational, and social life. Pichon-Rivière expanded Melanie Klein's notion of the internal world, and conceived of internal links as constantly informing and being informed by external links, so that there is a continual interplay between inner and external experiences and the broader social world. Links contain both vertical and horizontal axes; the former of which connects generations through unconscious transgenerational transmissions, and the latter, which connects persons to partners, family, community, and society (Scharff, Losso, & Setton, 2017). In American society, psychoanalysis has been an element in shaping cultural narratives of sexuality and gender on the horizontal axis, narratives that resonate within transmissions at the vertical level.

American lawyer and civil rights advocate Kimberlé Crenshaw (1989) first introduced the concept of intersectionality in her paper, "Demarginalizing the Intersection of Race and Sex", where she argued that by treating Black women as exclusively women or exclusively Black, the courts missed particular challenges Black women faced as a group. She has described intersectionality as "a prism to bring to light dynamics within discrimination law that weren't being appreciated" (Coaston, 2019, para. 25). In recent years, the concept of intersectionality has become almost ubiquitous within American culture, especially among social justice communities, where it is used to represent interlocking systems of power, oppression, and privilege, and to describe how sociocultural experiences intersect to inform the unique identity matrix of the individual.

Through the lens of intersectionality, we know that some LGBTQ individuals and couples are more vulnerable to systemic oppression than others. For example, Black trans women face greater stigma, discrimination, and violence than queer people with white and cisgender privilege (Human Rights Campaign Foundation, 2018). Intersectionality has also made its way into the psychoanalytic world (Belkin & White, 2020), as a means to more fully incorporating the sociocultural field into analytic formulations.

The culture of psychoanalysis

With its focus on intra-psychic and inter-psychic dimensions, psychoanalysis has historically failed to fully consider the real impact of sociocultural contexts on the inner and relational lives of individuals, couples, and families. One profound illustration of this tendency to block out awareness of external realities occurred during a meeting of the British Psychoanalytic Society, which took place in the midst of World War II. During a heated discussion, Donald Winnicott reminded his colleagues of the war raging outside, by announcing that, "there is an air raid going on" (Phillips, 1988, p. 61). Apparently, the meeting continued as though he had never spoken.

While there are notable exceptions such as the seminal work of Dorothy Holmes, Janice Gump, Adrienne Harris, Avgi Saketopoulou, Griffin Hansbury, Jack Drescher, Dionne Powell, Anton Hart, and others [see, for example, Altman (2010), Greene (2003), Hopper (2018), Vaughans (2015), White (2002), Belkin & White (2020)], it can seem as though the culture of psychoanalysis has ignored the symbolic air raids of white supremacy, misogyny, classism, homophobia, and transphobia within, and all around us. This is particularly noteworthy, as silence enshrouding social traumas like racism and homophobia within dominant groups (white and heterosexual people, in this case) is a significant factor in the perpetuation of those traumas on the horizontal axis, and their transmission at the vertical level. Karim G. Dajani (2020) asserts that the "collective dimension has been historically invisible or flatly denied" (p. 9) by many in the psychoanalytic field. Dajani expresses a perspective shared by an increasing number of analytically oriented clinicians, in stating that, "for many of us, traditional psychoanalytic theories delimited by a focus on instinct, impulse, defense and compromise without equal consideration of the individual's relation to wider dimensions of history, culture and society are felt to be lacking conceptually and clinically" (p. 7).

Whilst writing this chapter, the psychoanalytic world has been shocked out of complacency and into consciousness by the protests that were galvanized in response to the murders of George Floyd, Breonna Taylor, Tony McDade, and Ahmaud Arbery, all of whom were victims of institutionalized white supremacy that for centuries has normalized violence against Black, Indigenous, and People of Color (BIPOC). Psychoanalytic institutes across the country (such as the Psychoanalytic Center for the Carolinas, Boston Psychoanalytic Society and Institute, Washington Baltimore Psychoanalytic Institute, and the International Psychotherapy Institute) have released statements acknowledging the reality of systemic racism and the responsibility we have to examine our own embedded racism and to contribute to the movement for racial justice. We are seeing a surge of psychoanalytic conferences and town hall meetings organized around this very issue, which will hopefully lead to enduring changes within the field when it comes to more fully incorporating collective and sociocultural dimensions.

The analytic field benefits through receptivity to social change, becoming richer, more relevant, and more fully realized with the contributions of diverse writers and clinicians. Frankly, we see more clearly and honestly when we listen to voices on the margins. This has certainly been the case when it comes to the influence of queer theory and the movement for LGBTQ rights on psychoanalytic thinking and practice.

Historically, when psychoanalysts addressed sexual and gender differences, that is, any expression of sexuality or gender outside of heterosexual, cisgender identity, the focus was primarily on etiology, an exercise in understanding why those differences existed. The underlying assumption, based on heteronormativity, rests on a belief that heterosexuality is both the natural and normal expression of adult sexuality, and that deviations from this norm must be the result of some unresolved developmental difficulty. The institution of psychoanalysis conceived of homosexuality as a mental illness, pathology, or at the very least immaturity, embedded as it was in broader cultural attitudes and prejudice toward LGBTQ people. While psychoanalysis has come a long way, it is still important to reflect on the history and legacy that homophobia and heterosexism has had on our field.

Many in the American psychoanalytic community strongly objected to the American Psychiatric Association's (APA) decision to remove homosexuality from the Diagnostic and Statistical Manual (DSM-II) in 1973 (Drescher, 2008). While other major mental health professional organizations, like the American Psychological Association and the National Association of Social Workers, would soon endorse the APA's decision, the psychoanalytic community resisted the move toward the normalization of homosexuality and analysts continued presenting and writing about homosexuality as a mental disorder. It is also important to remember that until 1991, the American Psychoanalytic Association (APsaA) refused to allow openly gay and lesbian mental health professionals to train at affiliated centers.

Fortunately, much has changed within the culture of psychoanalysis in recent decades, and APsaA went from fighting the tides of social change to becoming a pioneer in the field. In 1997, eighteen years before the landmark Obergefell v. Hodges Supreme Court decision that required all states to recognize same-sex marriage, it became the first mainstream mental health organization to endorse gay marriage. In 2019, on the 50th anniversary of the Stonewall Riots, former APsaA president Lee Jaffe formally apologized for the role that psychoanalysis had played in the prejudice toward LGBTQ people, saying:

> "Regrettably, much of our past understanding of homosexuality as an illness can be attributed to the American psychoanalytic establishment. While our efforts in advocating for sexual and gender diversity since are worthy of pride, it is long past time to recognize and apologize for our role in the discrimination and trauma caused by our profession and say 'we are sorry'" (Drescher, 2019, para. 16).

Similar developments have taken place in the UK and other parts of Europe.

Family acceptance

Changes within the culture of psychoanalysis regarding perspectives of LGBTQ identities inform, and are informed by, broader societal progress. As the horizontal axis changes in favor of LGBTQ rights and representation, young queer people are more likely than in the past to find support and role models within their own families and communities, which may mean the difference between life and death.

We know that the mental and emotional health of LGBTQ youth is significantly impacted by the degree to which they experience acceptance and inclusion within the family (Ryan, Russell, Huebner, Diaz & Sanchez, 2010). All young people are vulnerable to suicide, which is the second leading cause of death among persons aged 10–24 (Centers for Disease Control and Prevention, 2013), but lesbian, gay, and bisexual youth are particularly at risk, being five times as likely as heterosexual youth to have attempted suicide (Centers for Disease Control and Prevention, 2016). In a national survey, 40% of transgender adults reported having made a suicide attempt, with 92% of those individuals reporting that the attempt was before age 25 (James, et al, 2016). In a national survey conducted by the Trevor Project (2019), LGBTQ youth who had undergone conversion therapy, or treatment based on the outdated premise that homosexuality is an illness that can be cured, were twice as likely to attempt suicide than those who did not.

Fearing rejection from family and peers, many LGBTQ youth learnt to take cover early in their lives through the development of a false, conforming self. Sadly, over-reliance on a false self can become deadening and deeply isolating, eventually leading to suicide as the only way out of such a suffocating trap. As Winnicott (1965) described, operated primarily from the false self can "lead many people who seem to be doing really well eventually to end their lives, which have become false and unreal" (p. 102), and that in cases where there seems to be no other option, suicide is used as the only defence against "betrayal of the true self" (p. 143).

James Baldwin (1964), in his unflinching essay on race in America, "The Fire Next Time", beautifully captures the dilemma of the false self when he says, "Love takes off the masks that we fear we cannot live without and know we cannot live within (p. 95)". Baldwin goes on to say that the white person's "unadmitted, and apparently, to him, unspeakable — private fears and longings are projected" onto the Black person (p. 96). Here, Baldwin captures the psychodynamic core of oppression; that is, that the dominant group projects split off, disavowed psychic content into the "other", and attacks its own "private fears and longings" through systemic and interpersonal violence toward that "other". Certainly, this is the case with homophobia and transphobia, as well as white supremacy and racism.

In every social movement, along with promoting structural and systemic change, marginalized communities are forced to fight for self-definition and determination against the vacuous pull of self-hatred and shame brought on by projective identification from an oppressive and annihilating culture. The isolation felt by the LGBTQ community explains why it is so important to celebrate "Pride" and to build queer affirming social and cultural spaces. Suicide among LGBTQ youth might be conceived as a malignant identification with the aggressor, through which introjected homophobia and transphobia are experienced to such a degree that self-hatred and shame result in brutal attacks on the self.

As LGBTQ communities and culture become more visible within the broader social milieu, many parents can feel less afraid of, and for, their queer children. Organizations like PFLAG (Parents and Friends of Lesbians and Gays), Gender Spectrum, and The Family Acceptance Project, have been invaluable in helping family and friends of LGBTQ people move from shock and fear, to acceptance and love. As progress is made toward maturing beyond institutionalized hetero and cissexism, it becomes possible to envisage a world where LGBTQ people are visible in schools, religious communities, politics, and media, and where parents can begin to imagine lives for their queer children out in the open with access to community support and family. Queer youth have more opportunities to find the role models, peer support, and recognition necessary to develop self-esteem, with much less pressure to hide behind a false self.

Even with significant social progress, it is important to remember that most LGBTQ patients have been affected by varying levels of heterosexism and homophobia, or cissexism and transphobia. Friedman and Downey (1995) distinguish between gay patients who grow up in relatively loving family systems, and those who suffer intrafamilial abuse and neglect. They posit that the former may present primarily with issues related to internalized homophobia, which can be addressed by supportive therapy, whilst the latter may require depth-oriented, exploratory therapy to uncover and modify hateful and ambivalent internal objects. Many LGBTQ people have adapted to family environments of relative deprivation, especially with regard to adequate mirroring and attachment needs, through the development of compensatory defenses and compromise formations, such as the use of a false self, splitting, and precocious self-sufficiency. By the time they seek therapy, many will look for clinicians who have experience and expertise with LGBTQ patients, with the hope of avoiding re-enactments of the implicit bias, shaming, and microaggressions to which they have already been subjected in their families and the wider social world.

I will now draw on case examples to illustrate the themes outlined above. All of the material has been disguised to protect patient identities.

Case material

Sarah

Sarah is a 24-year-old white, cisgender woman who identifies as bisexual. She first contacted me for therapy to deal with what she described as anxiety and self-worth issues. It was important to her to work with a therapist who had experience with LGBTQ patients. Sarah grew up in a community and family saturated in a religious fundamentalism, which was inherently and aggressively homophobic and heterosexist. Within this context, Sarah came to think of her sexuality as "a disgusting, horrible, filthy thing". She did not encounter positive representations of LGBTQ people until well into adolescence, when she began to meet other queer people and read queer narratives online. Internet communities are often used as transitional spaces for LGBTQ people, where initial contact and meaningful connections are formed, which support identity formation and self-acceptance, and where homophobic introjects can begin to be modified (Pilecki, 2015).

Sarah is 'out' as bisexual to her friends and community, but not to most of her family. She came out to her mother several years ago, but that did not go well and they now operate as if the conversation never happened. When her mother visits, Sarah hides books and other materials that pertain to her sexuality and is afraid that her mother will look through her things and find these hidden objects when she is not there. In my countertransference, I have felt angry with her mother for being so intrusive, particularly in moments where it seems Sarah is unable to maintain boundaries around her own mind or connect with her own anger.

Sarah fears the destructive power of her own rage, as well as her sexuality, which she has referred to as the "monster inside". Such anxieties have evolved within an identity matrix impacted by intersecting factors of family, religion, region, and race, as well as internalized homophobia, cissexism, and misogyny. Gender theorist Judith Butler (1990) articulated the links between cissexism and homophobia, stating, "Threats to heterosexuality become threats to gender itself. The fear of homosexual desire in a woman may induce panic that she is losing her femininity; that if she is not quite a man, she is like one and hence monstrous in some way" (p. 168). Sarah attempts to disguise her anger and sexuality with an almost overbearing politeness, which leaves her feeling detached and disgusted with herself. She developed a highly feminine, well-manicured, saccharine false self, which she has called a "sticky sweet, hard candy shell", designed to protect her true self, meet the needs of her parents, and provide a camouflage in a fundamentalist cultural context that demanded sameness and abhorred difference.

Sarah regularly heard her family deride "faggots" and equate AIDS with God's punishment for homosexuality. In the time of COVID-19, we can only imagine what it is like for some LGBTQ people who, like Sarah, already feel contaminated and as a result self-isolate for fear of outright rejection from others. Sarah is terrified that if she were fully 'out' to her parents, her fragile connection to them would be permanently severed. This terror leads to an impasse, where she is 'out' but not fully 'out', and the possibility of emotional intimacy and commitment within romantic relationships is therefore stifled. She finds herself trapped within a schizoid dilemma, where her longing to be truly understood is equally matched by an overwhelming fear of actually being known.

Max

Max is a 28-year-old Korean-American, transfeminine person, who uses "they/them" pronouns, and is married to a cisgender woman. Max contacted me for therapy related to gender identity issues. As with most patients, concerns about gender were embedded within other dynamics. A primary focus of therapy, along with gender, has been that of dealing with the impact of childhood abuse and neglect, which was inextricably linked with immigration stress and trauma.

Max was two years old when their family emigrated. In the United States, Max's family did not have the community support they had in Korea, and they recall from the age of five spending copious amounts of time alone. They remember feeling frightened and lonely, waiting for their mother to return from work. When their parents were home, Max recalls frequent fighting, and a family atmosphere that was tense, hostile, and cold. Patterns of isolation persisted into adulthood, as Max psychically retreats, and as a result they are often cut off from social connections and emotional intimacy.

Max's particular intersectional experiences leave them feeling alienated from Korean people, as they carry negative associations from intrafamilial trauma and did not grow up learning about or feeling particularly connected to Korean culture. In addition, they are also disconnected from the queer community because they are not out as trans to anyone other than their wife. Furthermore, Max feels invisible as a person of color in a country with deeply embedded white supremacy and privilege.

Max's wife is quite supportive and has encouraged them to make their own decisions regarding transition. Social progress has had a profoundly positive impact on the relational and family lives of many transgender people. In the past, the assumption and recommendation from medical professionals was generally that gender transition necessitated marital and family separation (Lev, 2004). Fortunately, this is no longer the case, and many transgender people transition, whether socially, medically, or some combination of both, with the support of partners and spouses. While there is still much work to be done, partners of trans people also have more access to their own supports, in the form of community groups, online forums, media and literature, and sensitive therapists and health-care professionals.

While Max has achieved a relative degree of marital security, they continue to feel isolated and ambivalent regarding other interpersonal connections. Like Sarah, Max has operated from a false self for many years, and has a tentative, fragile connection to their parents, fearing that their relationship would be completely severed if they were to come out as transgender. In the absence of adequate mirroring, LGBTQ people like Sarah and Max develop two selves as a compromise formation — one internal and the other external (Fraser, 2009). The internal, true self remains hidden and unmirrored, while the external, false self is seen and validated by others, creating a pattern of dependence on the false self for a pseudo security that is extremely difficult to break. To adapt, Max has learned to blend in, and is horrified by the attention that coming out as transgender could draw, from family and from the general public.

Unfortunately, there is no shortage of evidence on the level of the horizontal axis to validate Max's interior fears, which activates the rejecting objects transmitted through the vertical axis. For example, during a session in early 2020, Max lamented the "Vulnerable Child Protection Act" (HB 1057), legislation that would make it a misdemeanor for physicians or any other medical professional to perform gender reassignment surgery on minors or anyone who provides patients younger than 16 years of age with hormone therapy. Incidentally, in a testament to how far APsaA has come in the decades since homosexuality was removed from the DSM as a mental illness, the organization took a position of speaking out against this harmful South Dakota legislation, with Lee Jaffe making the following statement on February 4th, 2020:

> APsaA strongly opposes efforts to legislate appropriate medical treatments for transgender youth based on political ideologies that ignore both scientific research and expert clinical opinion. This law is fundamentally dangerous and if it becomes law would jeopardize the health and mental wellbeing of transgender youth in South Dakota.
>
> (*American Psychoanalytic Association, 2020*)

The Vulnerable Child Protection Act is a clear example of how the social and political world impinges on LGBTQ people and reinforces persecutory anxieties and rejecting internal objects. Max saw this as confirmation of being unwanted and feared as a trans person. The terrible catch-22 is that while LGBTQ people, like Max, remain closeted in order to protect themselves from external danger, they remain trapped within the hostile atmosphere of their own minds, where they are haunted by the ghosts of old objects and early attachment traumas, which cannot then be transformed into ancestors (Fraiberg, Adelson, & Shapiro, 1975).

Susan

Susan contacted me for therapy to work through issues related to self-esteem, past trauma, and gender identity. She is a 53-year-old white, transgender woman. Like Max, Susan is married to a cisgender woman, who supports her as a trans person, and to whom she came out early in their relationship, before marriage. Unlike Max, Susan is out to friends and some family, and has well-established relationships within the LGBTQ community. There is no single transgender trajectory, and at this point in life, Susan prefers to be out to most people in her life, but not to all.

Susan grew up in an economically depressed region, where there was little to no access to LGBTQ community or culture. Her first impressions of transgender people were the highly stigmatized, stereotyped guests on the Jerry Springer show. She became vaguely aware of gender dissonance in childhood, but did not come out to anyone until she was in her early 30s. Like Sarah and Max, Susan experienced relational trauma in her family of origin, and developed a protective false self to navigate through an unstable, volatile environment. She never felt close to her father, whom she has described as verbally abusive and withdrawn. She was a parentified child, and had an enmeshed relationship with her mother, for whom she felt significant emotional responsibility. Her parents were highly critical and quick to fits of anger. She remembers her mother chastising her for being too effeminate as a child, before she had any awareness of her transgender identity. In hindsight, Susan believes she internalized her mother's disdain and attempted to masculinize in order to ward off her disgust and win back her approval.

Lemma (2013), in writing about early developmental trends among transgender patients, has described the failure of primary objects to mirror experiences of incongruity between body and mind, and the related risk of forming an "alien self" in relation to the mis-attuned parent. Inadequate or faulty mirroring at foundational moments in development, and related compromise formations like false self-construction, have often been cited in the literature on LGBTQ patients (Devor, 2004; Lev, 2004; Fraser, 2009; McBee, 2013). In addition, some LGBTQ patients, like Susan, have been subjected to implicit or explicit negative reactivity from parents, who sense and reject their child's gender non-normativity. Alan Downs (2005), in his pivotal book on the psychological impact of homophobia and heterosexism on gay men, "The Velvet Rage", quite vividly described this dynamic:

> Along with the growing knowledge that we were different was an equally expanding fear that our "different-ness" would cause us to lose the love and affection of our parents. This terror of being abandoned, alone, and unable to survive forced us to find a way – any way – to retain our parent's love. We couldn't change ourselves, but we could change the way we acted
> (pp. 10–11).

Despite relative relational and career success, fears of loss and abandonment persist in Susan's internal object world, where she struggles with feeling un-loveable and inadequate. These attachment anxieties erupt at the slightest moment of marital conflict, when the shadow of Susan's chastising maternal object eclipses and distorts her perception of her wife. Such relational insecurities are not uncommon for many transgender patients, who grapple with persecutory, rejecting internal objects, and with internalized cissexism and related doubts about their worthiness as spouses, partners, and parents.

Intersections

While significant diversity exists among LGBTQ people, many can relate to the kinds of developmental and intrafamilial trauma experienced by Sarah, Max, and Susan. Intersections of class, race, nationality, religion, region, family, sexuality, and gender inform the unique shape and contour of each queer person's individual, couple, and family life. While cultural changes have made it possible for more LGBTQ people to come out within the context of a supportive family and community, many face bias and rejection within their families of origin, which can be compounded by broader, systemic discrimination and cultural trauma.

For marginalized communities, shared cultural identifications within the family can serve as a protective shield against the deleterious mental health consequences of systemic discrimination and social prejudice. Such early identifications can give meaning and historical links to experiences of oppression; something that many queer people will find out on their own, hence the importance of 'family of choice'. This is perhaps especially complicated for queer people with compounding experiences of marginalization. For example, some queer people of color (QPOC) may be afraid that coming out to family will lead to rejection by the very people with whom they share other vital cultural and racial links. This kind of dilemma can lead to profound anxiety in terms of identity and belonging, and pose the threat of feeling alienated from family of origin as a result of gender and sexuality biases, and from other LGBTQ people as a result of racism. Fortunately, QPOC have increasing access to networks and organizations that represent intersectional experiences (see, for example, The Brown Boi Project, National Queer Trans Therapists of Color Network, QLatinx, FIERCE!, UK Black Pride, Blackout UK, DesiQ, House of Rainbow).

As Sarah's case demonstrated, religion can have a profound impact on the quality and sustainability of family connections, as well as on identity development and self-esteem among LGBTQ people. Growing up within conservative religious contexts often leaves LGBTQ people with a sense that being gay, lesbian, bisexual, or transgender is morally reprehensible and sinful, and with profound internal conflicts. They are often caught in a terrible bind where they risk losing family and religious connections by coming out, but face self-alienation by remaining closeted.

Generational differences represent another point at which the horizontal axis intersects with and impacts the vertical axis. For instance, older LGBTQ people growing up in an era of extreme state sanctioned violence and discrimination may have suffered arrest, the loss of employment or family rejection simply for being gay. I have worked with some older LGBTQ patients who struggle with profound self-esteem and relational problems related specifically to the trauma of stigma and oppression. For these patients, early attachment relationships developed within the broader culture of severe homophobia and heterosexism often experienced parental and social rejection. According to Rohleder (2020), "early oedipal paternal rejection can lead many gay men to have difficulties with developing sustained intimacy in relationships" (p. 49). Intersections of the horizontal and vertical axis are profoundly impacted by cultural norms. The extent to which homophobia is embedded in the broader culture influences the degree to which it is enacted within the family, which in turn informs interpersonal experiences at the most intimate levels.

In 2015, the United States Supreme Court handed down the landmark decision that same-sex couples had the constitutional right to marry. In the final paragraph of his opinion, Justice Anthony Kennedy expressed his understanding of the undeniable impact that the right, or lack thereof, to marriage had on gay and lesbian individuals, couples, and families, stating:

> No union is more profound than marriage, for it embodies the highest ideals of love, fidelity, devotion, sacrifice, and family. In forming a marital union, two people become something greater than they once were. As some of the petitioners in these cases demonstrate, marriage embodies a love that may endure even past death. It would misunderstand these men and women to say they disrespect the idea of marriage. Their plea is that they do respect it, respect it so deeply that they seek it for themselves. Their hope is not to be condemned to live in loneliness, excluded from one of civilization's oldest institutions. They ask for equal dignity in the eyes of the law
>
> (Ehrenfreund, 2015).

It is impossible to imagine that exclusion from the foundational social institutions of marriage and family would not have enduring, profound psychological and emotional effects. While interpersonal connection and feelings of belonging cannot be guaranteed by the Supreme Court, this judgment represented a monumental decision that will continue to ripple out in innumerable ways for generations to come, impacting the experiences of gay and lesbian people in the broadest cultural, and deepest and most personal, relational realms.

Examining our own contexts and biases

Therapists, of course, do not live in a vacuum, and we are just as affected by sociocultural, intersectional experiences as anyone else. Even with all of the progress made toward LGBTQ equality, implicit and explicit biases regarding sexuality and gender are still deeply embedded within cultural institutions and dynamics, and are especially profound in areas of the country that have not been particularly affected by social change. Many therapists have grown up in a time or place where representations of queer lives in the cultural milieu were virtually absent. In addition, exposed to narratives that pathologized and demonized homosexuality as deviant and dangerous, and further reinforced through analytic training, it is hardly surprising that many therapists have embodied prejudicial attitudes.

Blechner (2006) argues that, "to do good clinical work we must be aware of how relative and subjective our judgments are". Lin Fraser (2009) suggests that when working with trans patients, "the therapist's examination of her own beliefs and assumptions about sex and gender is essential". This is also true when working with gay and lesbian patients, as most therapists, regardless of sexual orientation, hold an internal heterosexual parental couple, through which our unconscious, implicit perceptions are filtered, impacting countertransference to LGB individuals and same-sex couples and families (McCann, 2014). Hertzmann (2011) asserts that most therapists are impacted by early experiences of unmirrored sexuality, and that we are less likely to perceive and be able to work with these dynamics in patients if we do not address them within ourselves.

This raises the question of how to examine our unconscious biases and beliefs about gender and sexuality. We might begin by reflecting on implicit and explicit representations, or lack thereof, of LGBTQ people that we've absorbed, knowingly or unknowingly. For example, we might consider our earliest encounters with representations of LGBTQ people. How were they portrayed? What language was used to describe them? Did we know anyone who was gay, lesbian, bisexual, or transgender when growing up? How did we feel about them? How were they talked about? What can we recall about how LGBTQ patients have been described in psychoanalytic literature? What did we learn about homosexuality and gender variance in our training? Have we read articles on the subject that we knew were written by LGBTQ people?

In consideration of the kinds of questions LGBTQ people are often asked and, as a result of internalized hetero and cissexism often ask themselves, heterosexual and cisgender folks might consider the following: How did I know I was a man, or a woman, or heterosexual? Why am I a man, or a woman, or a heterosexual? Has anyone ever asked me those questions? Have I ever asked myself? Has a therapist ever asked me questions with the clear intention of trying to understand how I became cisgender, or heterosexual? Did I have to come out as straight or cisgender? If not, why not?

The queering of social contexts

In this chapter, I have attempted to address, from a psychoanalytic perspective, the impact of wider social contexts on the lives of LGBTQ individuals, couples, and families. Before concluding, I would like to consider the impact of LGBTQ people and cultures on wider social contexts. The benefits of LGBTQ social progress have not only been limited to queer people, but extend to the broader culture where norms and expectations regarding gender and sexuality are becoming less polarized and toxic. It is important to remember that heterosexual, cisgender women and men are also affected by the limitations of rigid gender roles.

As LGBTQ cultural expressions move from the margins to the center, we see a burgeoning of representations of queer people in politics (Pete Buttigieg and Andrea Jenkins), television (Ru Paul's Drag Race and Pose), education (there are at least 4,000 Gay Straight Alliances — school clubs for LGBTQ youth and allies — currently in the United States), and religion (a comprehensive list of LGBTQ affirming religious organizations can be found at the Human Rights Campaign website). This not only makes it possible for queer youth to grow up surrounded by more understanding communities, positive role models, and family support, but also leads to change in social contexts where all young people might better develop capacities for empathy, and thinking through and beyond fears of difference. Queer voices are absolutely vital in loosening the numbing grip of dominant culture, and in infusing vibrancy and color into the dull grey of complacent, deadening sameness.

In the field of psychoanalysis, with the help of LGBTQ and allied clinicians and writers, we are also growing and expanding beyond heteronormative notions of sexuality and gender, and more fully integrating social and cultural contexts into our understanding of psychic and relational processes. As we do, whole object relating becomes more possible, psychoanalysis more relevant and accessible, and Freud's concept of a "psychotherapy for the people" (Aron & Starr, 2013) is more realizable.

References

Altman, N. (2010). *The analyst in the Inner City: Race, class and culture from a psychoanalytic lens.* New York: Taylor and Francis.
American Psychoanalytic Association. (2020, February 4). *APsaA speaks out against harmful laws targeting transgender youth and healthcare providers.* Retrieved from: https://apsa.org/content/apsaa-speaks-out-against-harmful-laws-targeting-transgender-youth-and-healthcare-providers.

Aron, L., & Starr, K. E. (2013). *A psychotherapy for the people: Toward a progressive psychoanalysis*. Hove, East Sussex: Routledge.

Baldwin, J. (1964). *The fire next time*. Harmondsworth: Penguin.

Belkin, M., & White, C. (2020). *Intersectionality and relational psychoanalysis: New perspectives on race, gender, and sexuality*. Milton Park, Abingdon, Oxon: Routledge.

Blechner, M. J. (2006). Love, Sex, Romance, and Psychoanalytic Goals. *Psychoanal. Dialogues*, 16(6):779–791.

Butler, J. P. (1990). *Gender trouble: Feminism and the subversion of identity*. New York: Routledge.

Centers for Disease Control and Prevention. (2013, August 1). *Web-based Injury Statistics Query and Reporting System (WISQARS)*. Retrieved from: www.cdc.gov/ncipc/wisqars.

Centers for Disease Control and Prevention. (2016). Sexual Identity, Sex of Sexual Contacts, and Health-Risk Behaviors Among Students in Grades 9-12: Youth Risk Behavior Surveillance. Atlanta, GA: U.S. Department of Health and Human Services.

Coaston, J. (2019, May 28). *The intersectionality wars*. Vox. Retrieved from: https://www.vox.com/the-highlight/2019/5/20/18542843/intersectionality-conservatism-law-race-gender-discrimination.

Crenshaw, K. (1989). Demarginalizing the Intersection of Race and Sex: A Black Feminist Critique of Antidiscrimination Doctrine, Feminist Theory and Antiracist Politics. *University of Chicago Legal Forum, 1989*(1), 8th ser. Retrieved from: http://chicagounbound.uchicago.edu/uclf/vol1989/iss1/8.

Dajani, K.G. (2020). Cultural Determinants in Winnicott's Developmental Theories. *Int. J. Appl. Psychoanal. Stud.*, 17(1):6–21.

Devor, A. (2004). Witnessing and mirroring: A fourteen stage model of transsexual identity formation. In Drescher J. & Leli U. (Eds.), *Transgender subjectivities: A clinician's guide*. Binghamton, NY: Haworth Medical Press.

Downs, A. (2005). *The velvet rage: Overcoming the pain of growing up gay in a straight world*. Cambridge, MA: Da Capo Lifelong Books.

Drescher, J. (2008). A History of Homosexuality and Organized Psychoanalysis. *J. Am. Acad. Psychoanal. Dyn. Psychiatr.*, 36(3):443–460.

Drescher, J. (2019, June 21). Stonewall's 50th anniversary and an overdue apology: How the mental health professions evolved on LGBTQ rights. Retrieved from: https://apsa.org/content/blog-stonewall%E2%80%99s-50th-anniversary-and-overdue-apology.

Ehrenfreund, M. (2015, June 26). The one supreme court paragraph on love that gay marriage supporters will never forget. *The Washington Post*. Retrieved June 21, 2020, from https://www.washingtonpost.com/news/wonk/wp/2015/06/26/the-one-supreme-court-paragraph-on-love-that-gay-marriage-supporters-will-never-forget/.

Fraiberg, S., Adelson, E., & Shapiro, V. (1975). Ghosts in the Nursery: A Psychoanalytic Approach to the Problems of Impaired Infant-Mother Relationships. *J. Am. Acad. Child Psychiatry*, 14(3):387–421.

Fraser, L. (2009). Depth Psychotherapy with Transgender People. *Sex. Relatsh. Ther.*, 24(2),126–142.

Friedman, R. C., & Downey, J. (1995). Internalized Homophobia and the Negative Therapeutic Reaction. *J. Am. Acad. Psychoanal. Dyn. Psychiatr.*, 23(1):99–113.

Greene, B. A. (2003). What difference does a difference make? Societal privilege, disadvantage and discord in human relationships. In Robinson, J. D. & James, L. C. (Eds.), *Diversity in human interactions: The tapestry of America* (pp. 3–20). Oxford, UK: Oxford University Press.

Hertzmann, L. (2011). Lesbian and Gay Couple Relationships: When Internalized Homophobia Gets in the Way of Couple Creativity. *Psychoanal. Psychother.*, 25(4):346–360.

Hopper, E. (2018). Notes on the Concept of the Social Unconscious in Group Analysis. *Group*, 42(2):99–118.

Human Rights Campaign Foundation. (2018). Dismantling a Culture of Violence: Understanding Anti-Transgender Violence and Ending the Crisis. Retrieved from: https://assets2.hrc.org/files/assets/resources/2018AntiTransViolenceReportSHORTENED.pdf?_ga=2.208837522.1859914005.1593312083-1788481172.1593312083.

James, S. E., Herman, J. L, Rankin, S., Keisling, M., Mottet, L., & Anafi, M. (2016). *The Report of the 2015 U.S. Transgender Survey*. Washington, DC: National Center for Transgender Equality.

Lemma, A. (2013). The Body One has and the Body One is: Understanding the Transsexual's Need to be Seen. *Int. J. Psycho-Anal.*, 94(2):277–292.

Lev, A. I. (2004). *Transgender emergence: Therapeutic guidelines for working with gender-variant people and their families*. Haworth Clinical Practice Press.

McBee, C. (2013) Towards a More Affirming Perspective: Contemporary Psychodynamic Practice with Trans and Gender Non-conforming Individuals. *The Advocates' Forum*: 37–52.

McCann, D. (2014). Responding to the clinical needs of same-sex couples. In Scharff, D. & Scharff, J. S. (Eds.), *Psychoanalytic couple therapy: Foundations of theory and practice* (pp. 81–90). London: Karnac.

Phillips, A. (1988). *Winnicott*. Cambridge: Harvard University Press.

Pilecki, A. (2015). Transitional space: The role of internet community for transgender and gender non-conforming patients. In Scharff, J. S. (Ed.), *Library of technology and mental health series. Psychoanalysis Online 2: Impact of technology on development, training, and therapy* (pp. 53–66). London: Karnac.

Rohleder, P. (2020). Homophobia, heteronormativity, and shame. In Hertzmann, L., & Newbigin, J. (Eds.), *Sexuality and gender now: Moving beyond heteronormativity*. Abingdon, Oxon: Routledge.

Ryan C., Russell S. T., Huebner D., Diaz R., & Sanchez J. (2010). Family Acceptance in Adolescence and the Health of LGBT Young Adults. *J. Child Adolesc. Psychiatr. Nurs.*, 23(4):205–213.

Scharff, D. E., Losso, R., & Setton, L. (2017). Pichon Rivières psychoanalytic contributions: Some comparisons with object relations and modern developments in psychoanalysis. *Int. J. Psychoanal.*, 98(1):129–143. doi:10.1111/1745-8315.12496.

The Trevor Project. (2019). *National Survey on LGBTQ Youth Mental Health*. Retrieved from: https://www.thetrevorproject.org/wp-content/uploads/2019/06/The-Trevor-Project-National-Survey-Results-2019.pdf.

Vaughans, K. (2015). To unchain haunting blood memories: Intergenerational trauma among African Americans. In O'Loughlin, M. & Charles, M. (Eds.), *Fragments of trauma and the social production of suffering: Trauma, history, and memory* (pp. 277–290). Lanham: Rowman & Littlefield.

White, K. P. (2002). Surviving Hating and Being Hated. *Contemp. Psychoanal.*, 38(3):401–422.

Winnicott, D. W. (1965). The maturational process and the facilitating environment: Studies in the theory of emotional development. *The International Psycho-Analytical Library*, 64 (pp. 1–276). London: The Hogarth Press and the Institute of Psycho-Analysis.

Chapter 4

Cultural and intercultural considerations in working with same-sex couples

Patricia Porchat

Couples, culture and psychoanalysis

The types of conjugal interactions in each society vary according to how social and institutional relations regulate affective and sexual relations between people. However, given the history of marriage in the West, this claim itself is not without limitations, since love has not always been a part of conjugal relations (Duby and Perrot, 1990). Business agreements have also formed part of the relations between the families of men and women involved in a marital bond. Oftentimes, a spouse could not be chosen, as they were imposed by the family or by some authority to which the family itself was subject, and, as such, relations could be void of any affection. The autonomy in the choice of one's partner, and subsequently, the autonomy of women in relation to their husbands did not exist for many centuries. Indeed, even to this day, there are still countries in which this choice is not always permitted to certain social classes. For instance, future spouses only meet each other through pictures, and are fortunate enough if love sparks between them.

The history of women's dependence on men in the patriarchal system and the rigidity of their role as mothers and housewives have marked the history of heterosexual marriages. One could even argue that such dependence and lack of autonomy is one of the reasons, within relationships, which leads to acts of violence against women, or even to their murder. This could be related to the fact that men interpret any glimpse of autonomy as a violation of the right they have over their spouses. In this case, disrespect in itself already implies an offense or violation, and, as such, should be punished.

Cultural differences have often been a consideration when analyzing couples in which spouses come from different countries, religions or even different ethnicities. However, when it comes to the roots of a culture common to the partners of a couple, gender roles are usually naturalized, especially when the spouses themselves naturalize such roles, without realizing the problematic consequences of doing so. In other words, spouses try to adapt

DOI: 10.4324/9781003255703-4

to what are seen as natural roles, yet, throughout history, society has already endured the effects of the deconstruction of such roles and will continue to do so.

Moreover, psychoanalysis being a relatively new subject in the history of humankind — 120 years old if one takes into consideration the publication of Sigmund Freud's *The Interpretation of Dreams* — tends to focus on couples' relationships within this timeframe. Furthermore, given that psychoanalysis tends towards the universalization of the psychic subject, it could be argued that it does not adequately consider the importance of the effects that culture has on a couple's relationship, and particularly in regard to the performance of roles within those relationships. However, at one and the same time, psychoanalysts evidently perceive the changes that have occurred in conjugal relations, i.e., there are more women in the job market, more men are actively participating in childcare, and the blurring of gender roles and behaviors has never been greater. In addition, psychoanalysts know that these changes must be affecting and shaping the relationship between the parties of a couple.

Psychoanalysis has also begun absorbing the contributions brought forth by feminist, queer and decolonization theories and their impact on our understanding of, for instance: the roles of femininity and masculinity within relationships; on the possibilities of gender beyond binary definitions; on the legitimacy of same-sex marriages; and on the importance of understanding the position from which knowledge and theories are devised, developed and imposed as universal. A number of authors both within and beyond the field of psychoanalysis have also sought to support the importance of Freudian thinking, whilst also suggesting that certain psychoanalytical concepts and assumptions should be reviewed. In this regard, it is worth acknowledging the works of Gayle Rubin (1975), Judith Butler (2006), Eve Kosofsky Sedgwick (1973, 1993), Grada Kilomba and Thamy Ayouch (2018). These contributions have forced psychoanalysts to look further into the changes affecting all couple relationships, thereby questioning the limits imposed by certain theoretical assumptions that have become too conservative for our purpose. In other words, psychoanalysis requires further innovation in both the interpretation and understanding of its theory, especially when faced with gaps and ambiguities relating to lived experience.

Despite the changes observed in conjugal relations and despite the changes that have occurred in psychoanalysis, we must admit that analyzing the impact of culture on a heterosexual couple shines a particular light on the limitations that are still placed around spouses in certain forms of expression of femininity and masculinity, thus making it clear that it is very difficult to abide by gender norms without placing a toll on the singularity of each member of the couple. When the members of the couple limit themselves to playing stereotyped roles, such as women-wives or men-husbands, the different possibilities of being a woman and being a man get lost and the diversity that exists within and between spouses is also lost. Likewise, analyzing same-sex couple relationships means taking into consideration how the parties of the couple are confined to heterosexual marriage models, and how much those conducting such analysis are biased by common-sense perceptions on femininities and masculinities that are allegedly present in female and male homosexuality. But, are these same-sex couples really trapped in heterosexual marriage models, or is this idea part of the common-sense perception that many analysts hold? It might help to reflect on the psychic effects that emerge from the organization of the daily life of same-sex couples, especially with regard to the division of household chores in order to obtain the answers to our questions.

Traditionally, we have conceived an understanding of this division of tasks based primarily on our knowledge of heterosexual couples, but we know that there must also be a comparable version of this in same-sex couple relationships. The analysis that follows is based on examples of same-sex couples in Brazil, a country in which the influence of a sexist and patriarchal culture creates substantial inequalities in the gendered politics of relationships between men and women, relating to the organization of money and social status. How then do same-sex couples manage gender inequality in their daily lives? Do they replicate the gender inequality we see in heterosexual relationships, by imposing the notion that there is a superior, dominant member, who has authority over the other, rooted in one's financial inferiority or linked to masculine entitlement such as the chauvinistic male, or do these couples construct their relationships differently? How do partners in same-sex relationships reflect on and manage these roles? For instance, does one of the partner's adjust to a female condition of dependency, inferiority, docility and obedience, whilst the other takes on more masculine traits? What does each member of the couple expect from the other? In addition, how do psychoanalysts work with same-sex couples embedded as they are in heteronormative constructions of couple relating?

Same-sex couples

In Brazil, due to the substantial conservatism with respect to same-sex unions, lawmakers continue to resist drafting specific laws that would allow for the legal recognition of same-sex couples and homo-parental families (LGBT parenting). Unsurprisingly, this conservatism is also seen in the families of gay and lesbian couples, who, to this day, fail to represent or legitimize the same-sex union to family or indeed to those in the outside world. With this in mind, it is not unusual for gay men to hide their partners in the presence of family; in other words, the partner becomes invisible and simply does not exist for the family. And for lesbians, the couple is represented and viewed as nothing more than a friendship, i.e., the family has a relationship with their daughter and "her best friend". However, the initial — and often ongoing — rejection eventually causes hardships for the couples. As a consequence, many same-sex couples choose to expand their family through the inclusion of a network of friends. However, this does not necessarily assuage the feelings of loss, a grief that is difficult to realize given that there is no death, but rather an abandonment caused by the rejection of the family of origin. According to Waseda et al (2016), the subsequent family recognition of their children's same-sex relations is considered essential by the couples, as a means of strengthening or even to establishing their identity as a couple. In Brazil, this rarely if ever happens in certain conservative environments.

The support and acceptance of the family of origin for members of a same-sex couple relationship may be somewhat different from the kind of support and acceptance experienced by heterosexual couples, even if the latter undergo family rejections triggered by differences in religion, ethnicity, social class or political ideology. The couple's identity is weakened whenever the relationship is not accepted by the family of origin, thus hindering the projection of a life together. Moreover, even where there is recognition, we may assume that the families of origin, in general, will tend to limit their understanding of the possibilities and challenges brought forth by same-sex arrangements within a heteronormative tradition. Therefore, it is likely that same-sex couple relationships would be perceived as a close version of heterosexual couples, with similar patterns of behavior linked to the expectation that one of the partners will display greater masculine behavior and the other more feminine traits. In this regard, adopting gendered roles normally associated with heterosexual couples in Brazil affords greater legitimacy and recognition to same-sex couple relationships as a family unit? However, at one and the same time, the distinction between heterosexual and same-sex couple relationships is lost, which limits the analysis that these relationships offer, both as a form of criticism to and transformation of the family institution (Santos, Scorsolini-Comin and Santos, 2013, p. 580). Therefore, working psychoanalytically with same-sex couples poses particular challenges in regard to the ways in which these couples construct meaning and identity within the given culture. How then might the analysis of such couples help to legitimize their uniqueness and freedom to operate outside the confines of heteronormativity?

Sex and gender in Brazil

According to Silva et al (2016), gender identity in Brazil is often confused with sexual orientation, because they are seen as one and the same, implying that one of the members of the couple will usually be seen as more masculine and the other as more feminine. It is taken for granted that if a person identifies as a man, then one has masculine traits and will be attracted to women, or at most to feminine men. Similarly, if someone claims to be a woman, then that is because she has feminine traits and will be attracted to men, or, possibly, to masculine women.

Unfortunately, a number of health professionals in the city of Brasília, the capital of Brazil, endorse these beliefs and in turn confuse homosexuality with transsexuality, for instance, viewing *travestis* or trans women as gay men because they dress or cross-dress as women (Santos, Shimizu and Merchan-Hamann, 2014)[i]. This confusion is also evident in other Brazilian regions, such as in the inner state of São Paulo. Sadly, this misunderstanding and confusion between transsexuality, travestility and homosexuality has negative implications for same-sex couples who are perceived as *"manqué"*, a fake or incomplete version of a heterosexual couple.

Moreover, when considering the relationship between *travesties*, or trans women and cisgender men, one can see clearly the reproduction of stereotyped roles based entirely on the traditional heterosexual couple relationship. Whilst subverting the notion that gender stems from biological sex, i.e., the identification with all that is feminine whilst having a penis, the *travestis* interviewed by Pelúcio (2006) reinforced the binary notion and ideology of what it means to be a "man" and a "woman". For example, *travestis* demanded that their partners adhere to strict and stereotyped gender roles with the husband expected to behave as the breadwinner, while taking upon themselves the domestic responsibilities normally associated with that of the female. Even in a marriage between two *travestis*, they also reproduce the gender stereotypical roles associated with that of cross-gendered couples.

In addition to the division of household chores, sexual positions also seem to play a key role in maintaining the gendered relations of *travestis* and trans women with cisgender men. Sáez and Carrascosa (2016), for example, argue that heterosexual women are socially built as penetrable, but never as the penetrator, in contrast to the heterosexual man who is built as the penetrator and whose anus must never be penetrated, even without consent. A man who allows his anus to be penetrated becomes "girly" or a *fag*. Therefore, from a very young age, anus related vigilantism is aimed at building the identity of the heterosexual man. Needless to say, the same type of vigilance is seen in same-sex couples, manifest in the strict division of roles relating to one being seen as the active/dominant/masculine partner and the other as the passive/submissive/feminine partner (also played out in the positions partners take sexually) as a means to making coupling intelligible.

Household Work, Types of Conjugality and Gender

The history of the division of household work in Brazil is best understood in relation to the country's colonial background. According to DeSouza, Baldwin and Rosa (2000), Portuguese settlers enjoyed substantial sexual freedom. Considering the absence of Portuguese women in colonial Brazil, the settlers maintained sexual relations, first with indigenous women and then with enslaved African women. The Portuguese women who arrived in Brazil during the colonial period, which extends to 1822 when Brazil was no longer a colony, suffered stereotyping: they were fragile, submissive, passive and had no power in the public realm. They had no access to formal education and were groomed for marriage, in order to take care of the household and the children. According to Costa (2004), during the colonial period, household chores were almost entirely conducted by enslaved black people, and especially women, in regard to cleaning and preparing the household.

From the eighteenth century onwards, a number of enslaved people were gradually dismissed from household services, deemed to be the source of disease, and were gradually replaced by foreign, mainly European, white servants. This heralded the tradition of the white woman-wife taking care of the children, thus reinforcing the image of woman-mother, especially by means of breastfeeding, an act that only women were able to perform. This movement contributed to maintaining women in domestic confinement and further strengthening male domination of women. Women's emancipation and their engagement in work outside the household were strongly resisted in order to maintain a relationship of domination and gender hierarchy. The strengthening of the bourgeois nuclear family and its domestic confinement in regard to the outside world also intensified identification and loyalty among family members. For instance, children became entirely dependent upon their parents, and given the strict division of gender roles within the family, children especially identified with their respective same-sex parents (Reis, 2012). It therefore becomes possible to see the way in which household work reinforces and further develops the production of masculinity and femininity within heterosexual couple relationships and by default within the family environment. Apart from confirming the subordination of women by men, this narrative also suggests that household work is not only an undervalued activity, but that it also undervalues those responsible for it. What then can we expect to find in regard to the division of labour for same-sex couples, and especially when it comes to the production and maintenance of gender and gender roles?

Same-sex couples: different paradigms

Nico and Rodrigues (2011) suggest that same-sex couples tend to employ strategies in the division of household chores, linked to the likes and dislikes of relevant tasks as the main criteria for defining household work that will be undertaken by each of the partners. Skills and affinity with respect to the task, the complementarity of roles, delegation to the other person (when only one of the spouses does not like the chore), and the fact that one of the spouses is the owner of the house, all play a part in decisions concerning who does what within the couple relationship. We can also observe the gender-based heritage in gay male couple relationships, since they tend more often than their lesbian counterparts to resource outside help, i.e., employing female domestic help. Upon comparison, the division of household chores is generally less equal among gay couples than among lesbian couples, perhaps due to the fact that in their family of origin, household chores were attributed to women. That means that they often try to rid themselves of the task and instead delegate it or even deny the need of it. In Brazil, the work of Meletti and Scorsolini-Comin (2015) also suggests that the division of housework among same-sex couples is neither defined nor based on gender binarism, in that personal tastes and skills prevail over the determination of roles in the relationship. However, although Carvalho (2020) found that the division of household chores among gay couples in the inner state of São Paulo was based on companionship and the need for the task to be performed on a given day and the availability of one of the partners to carry out the task as well as the roles derived from one's family of origin, traces of gender-based heritage were also identified in at least one of the members of the couples who frequently tended to reproduce gender stereotypes in the organization of household chores.

When further investigating the differences between lesbian couples in Brazil and Canada, Zauli (2011) noted that in the latter, lesbian women, much like heterosexual women, increasingly invested in their careers, although lesbian couples organized housework on a more equal basis than their heterosexual counterparts. This particular organization of household chores afforded lesbians the possibility of focusing more on their professional careers in contrast to heterosexual females. The relationship of lesbian couples is seen as a space for the negotiation of housework between two people, in this case between "equal women, *de jure* and *de facto*" (p. 173). Both members are *de facto* women who have equal rights. This translates into a relationship with greater solidarity, conciliation and partnership. To be lesbian or gay in Canada is to be a citizen like any other. Canada is a pro-minority country whose anti-discrimination laws are severe. Civil rights are accessible both to same-sex and to heterosexual couples. The support and safety offered by the government and consequently by most of the society actually affirms and promotes the affective and sexual relationships of same-sex individuals and couples.

Unlike lesbian couples in Brazil, it seems that lesbian couples in Canada are not necessarily perceived or indeed perceive themselves as a couple in terms of one of the partners identifying as feminine and the other as masculine. If this were the case, perhaps they would not see themselves as "*de juri* and *de facto* equal women*"*, and would easily tend to reproduce heteronormative standards based on the so-called masculine woman being cast in the role of breadwinner and the other carrying the so-called feminine role dedicated to housework. This reflects the unconscious appropriation of the heteronormative regime in Brazil, or, in other words, the way in which sexist patriarchal power is shaped in the psyche and manifest in the structures of couple relationships.

Based on the aforementioned studies, one can conclude that by recognizing themselves as same-sex couples, be they male or female, and by perceiving themselves as equals, this allows members of these couple not to reproduce the gender-based stereotypes of the heteronormative regime. In any case, these studies suggest that same-sex couples have the potential to disrupt the strict gender roles seen in heterosexual couples in Brazil. The organization of housework demonstrate that these couples use criteria other than gender to structure their relationships. Therefore, when thinking about and comparing the nature and division of housework in heterosexual relationships with that of same-sex relationships, it is important to understand that the gendered nature of undertaking these tasks is somewhat different for gays and lesbians who, generally speaking, appear to share a more equal and indeed broader definition of the organization, management and administration in the performance of household chores. Unfortunately, in Brazil, the strict division of labour along gender lines in heterosexual couple relationships remains a reality. In light of these differences, it seems important to consider how the couples themselves represent the gendered nature of their relationships in therapy and how their psychoanalytically minded therapists think about and work with these disparities. It therefore remains a problem if therapists continue to draw on heteronormative assumptions linked to the gendered nature of relationships. In this regard, scholars such as Corbett (2009), who further explore masculinities, or studies that deconstruct gender roles, such as those by Preciado (2013), Butler (2006) and Miskolci (2007), encourage an analysis of our gender assumptions when working with same-sex couples.

New paradigms imply new possibilities of complaints and conflicts. Or would those be the same old complaints and conflicts a same-sex couple takes to the psychoanalyst? Gay couples that open their relationship, for instance, oftentimes seek therapy, as they have trouble determining the boundaries in this type of relationship, which seems to cause discomfort and hurt for one or both partners. Sexual relations, which many times are the starting point of a gay relationship, tend to decrease in frequency over time, leading to disappointment and a break in the expectations of living in some sort of sexual paradise. In turn, lesbian couples, may at times experience a real fusion, in that each of the members might lose their individual identity. Nonetheless, this does not mean that the heterosexual model should be considered the ideal relationship.

Working with same-sex couples highlights the importance of deconstructing gender norms, the acceptance of difference and the possibility of opening new pathways that allow for a relationship of trust and creativity. Although this may seem obvious, in a country in which gender binarism — framed by sexism and patriarchy — results in the objectification and devaluation of all that is feminine, it is vital that same-sex couples and those working with such couples avoid the re-inscription of gender stereotyping, since it assists in promoting the emergence of new and more healthy forms of relating that transcend the restrictions imposed by the existing gender hierarchy. Butler (2006) also draws attention to the creative power of those occupying an outside, or alien position, through the transformation in everyday relationships of same-sex couples — beyond the limitations of gender binarism.

Homophobia

Sedgwick (1990) and Castañeda (2007) draw our attention to the impact of homophobia, in terms of rejection, exclusion and violence against homosexuals and the impact that this has on their lives and relationships. In that regard, it is also important to acknowledge the impact of internalized homophobia with some lesbians and gay men living their lives in social isolation. Even when they partner with other lesbians and gay men, it is still possible that these couples also struggle to integrate their relationship into the wider society. Sedgwick (1990) references the closet as the "defining structure of gay oppression in the twentieth century", for even when it is possible to 'come out' in certain social circles, many will remain in the closet to family, friends and work colleagues. It is also possible that couples will experience the tensions of stage discrepancy, where, for example, one of the partners is more 'out' than the other, resulting in conflict relating to the differential needs of the partners as they work out what to say to families, friends and to their therapist. Because of the shame associated with being lesbian or gay, individuals and couples often take time to find a comfortable place within Brazilian society. Castañeda (2007) reinforces the point by highlighting other impacts of being raised and living in a society that eschews homosexual relationships. For instance, this environment will often trigger difficulties in social relations and issues relating to self-esteem, manifested in a belief that one is not capable of doing certain things, or, alternatively, showing a tendency towards overachievement as a means of managing the so-called 'defect' of homosexuality in its many guises (Castañeda, 2007, p. 152). It is also argued that a homosexual person will (unconsciously) do his/her best in order to try and prove that he or she is 'acceptable' according to the criterion of heterosexual society (Castañeda, 2007). The same may also be true of same-sex couples who struggle to prove their 'normality' both socially and psychologically. In fact, this is what society demands of such couples, since any sign of 'abnormality' is perceived as a weakness or deficit linked to that individual or couple being seen as gay or lesbian with the attendant risks of being labelled as perverted, unstable, promiscuous, immature, etc.

Finally, Castañeda (ibid) argues that gays and lesbians internalize the homophobic violence (whether physical or emotional) suffered throughout

Cultural and intercultural considerations   69

their lives, which in turn triggers depression and self-destructive behaviours. The overbearing feeling of anger that stems from such violence is either repressed or turned against others or oneself. One's history is marked by several events of violence, in the form of mockery, jokes, humiliation, name-calling, rejection, exclusion and even physical aggression (Castañeda, 2007, p. 149). It is therefore important to pay particular attention to references of repressed anger or rage. We might also wonder how these feelings are managed between partners within the couple relationship and between the individual, couple and their psychotherapist. It is worth noting that the unconscious hate that comes forth in psychoanalysis cannot be exclusively interpreted as the result of aggressive impulses/instincts, since our understanding of the effects of homophobia in terms of psychological development was not properly taken into account in the formulation of psychoanalytical theory. To that end, Butler's (2006, 1997) works relating to the notion of "gender melancholia" and "gender trouble" pushes the theory beyond the limits of outdated paradigms of individual and couple development rooted in heteronormative models of relating.

The impact of social, economic and cultural conditions on same-sex couples in Brazil

Brazil is a continental country and Brazilian society is very complex. In thinking about lesbian and gay couples in Brazil, it is also important to consider race, class, education and geography, i.e., whether one lives in large cities (São Paulo or Rio de Janeiro) or in smaller rural areas, since these intersections also affect the lived experience of homosexuals as well as heterosexuals. For instance, São Paulo has approximately twelve million inhabitants, and Rio de Janeiro seven million inhabitants, and so one sees a greater diversity of traditions and cultures influenced by immigration, tourism, etc. Such a melting pot produces a permanent conflict between conservative and more flexible family organizations, less visible in other parts and regions of Brazil. Being the richest region, social inequality is also present in these larger cities, visible in the sharp contrast between high-income neighborhoods and *favelas*. Lesbians and gays who wish to enjoy greater freedom in their affective and sexual lives generally move to cities such as São Paulo and Rio de Janeiro. In a country marked by so much social, economic and cultural inequality, and operating on outdated assumptions relating to gender, it is unsurprising that being 'out' and confident as a same-sex couple is a privilege few lesbians and gay men come to share. Working with same-sex couples in a culture such as Brazil requires a deep understanding of the impact of the ways in which culture shapes gender, sexuality and psychological and mental wellbeing, in order to provide a therapy that responds to the particular needs of this population.

A vignette

Gabriel and Ricardo first arrived to our session a few years ago. Ricardo is the one who insists that they go to couple therapy. He knows Gabriel loves him but is aware that his husband struggles to define theirs as a homosexual couple relationship per se. Gabriel is unable to assume the designation "husband". When he visits his parents, he tells them that Ricardo is his "best friend", despite their living together for four years. Ricardo has always had and been in gay relationships, and previously lived for a number of years in Berlin with his partner Martin, whom he referred to as his husband. In that context, he felt free to live his gay relationship publicly, whereas in São Paulo, he worries that he and Gabriel will become the target of homophobic attacks. Despite this, Ricardo believes that their lives together would be better if Gabriel had less difficulty with his own homosexuality.

Gabriel was in a heterosexual marriage for nine years, from which he has two small children, an eight-year-old girl and a six-year-old boy. He was accused by his former wife's family of being gay, a pedophile, and promiscuous. He lost custody of his children as a result of an obscure lawsuit brought by his ex-wife and believes that there was a homophobic bias on the part of the judge, a bias that was also shared by his ex-wife and her family, since they obstruct Gabriel's contact with his children. Because of this, he is unable to authorize himself as a gay parent, a privilege that is really only afforded to heterosexual fathers. As a consequence, he believes that being gay makes him a less worthy father and he is suffering because of the loss of contact with his son and daughter.

Ricardo can see that Gabriel's feelings about his sexual orientation are also affecting his ability to be confident and comfortable about his same-sex relationship with Ricardo. For instance, in their everyday life, Gabriel does not fully engage in the relationship with Ricardo, claiming that he is depressed because of the situation with his children. The two men are also in conflict because of Gabriel's feelings about housework. After returning from work, he likes to sit on the sofa watching football and drinking beer and when Ricardo points out that he needs help with housework, Gabriel says that he was not born to be a "housewife". Although Ricardo is sympathetic to Gabriel's emotional distress, he does not accept Gabriel's premise that engaging in housework renders him feminine. Ricardo also reflects on his previous life with Martin, where both men had a more collaborative relationship, and believes that Gabriel is struggling to adjust to life outside the confines of a gender-determined heterosexual marriage.

It is noticeable that Gabriel has not fully authorized himself as a gay man, holding tight to social mandates that have been internalized as psychic mandates. A parental and social superego has become an impediment of living a fuller and more truthful existence. Unable to feel that his wishes are consistent with what he believes is his anatomic destiny, the interdiction

Cultural and intercultural considerations   71

of loving himself or of loving another man have become the core of his sense of self, which renders him unworthy. In cities such as Rio de Janeiro and São Paulo, where gay life is socially more openly accepted, Gabriel is freer to love and live with Ricardo. However, unconsciously and under imaginary social mandates, he, like many gay men who are fathers and a great number who are not, find themselves placed in a lower social order. Many will be viewed as pedophiles and Gabriel seems to function under these premises. He loves his children but cannot claim his right to be near them.

It is evident, as seen through this clinical vignette, how difficult it is to break loose from patriarchal biases and allow oneself to live a fuller, and more gratifying life, detached from the power of cultural and social paradigms.

Conclusion

In this chapter, I have highlighted the different ways in which models of heterosexual marriage in Brazil come to exert an influence on and shape the ways in which many same-sex couples conduct their own relationships. To some extent, we seem to witness in same-sex couple relationships patterns of behaviour similar to those seen in heterosexual relationships, particularly in regard to gender roles. Yet, same-sex couples have the potential for constructing their relationships differently, and some may even look to their psychoanalytically minded therapists to assist them with this developmental task. It is therefore beholden upon psychoanalytic practitioners working with same-sex couples to ask themselves whether the models of relating that inform their practice are relevant to these couples and the extent to which they feel comfortable opening themselves to dynamics that require a non-heteronormative stance and approach. Furthermore, it will also be necessary that practitioners recognise and work with the importance of internalised homophobia, especially since this may be contributing to the presentation for therapy, as these couples battle notions of pathology, perversion and immorality. Until same-sex couples encounter a more accepting society in which to conduct their relationships, they will continue to struggle to reclaim their relationship from the grip of heteronormativity and notions of gender-determined behaviour within the confines of such couplings.

Note

i The English word transvestite does not fit exactly with the translation of the meaning of Brazilian *travestis* as a gender category. The difference between *travestis* and trans women is controversial in Brazil. Unlike in medical psychiatry, psychology and psychoanalysis have worked on a closer basis with social movements, in order to accept self-identification as the more respectful way of understanding who are the *travesti* women and who are trans women, or simply, "trans". According to psychiatric medicine, *travestis* are often seen as people who suffer from a psychological disorder — transvestic fetishism — which consists in the sexual interest in cross-dressing, especially regarding undergarments. To the extent in which they come closer to the theories on gender and queer theory, certain psychologists and psychoanalysts were able to understand the fluidity in how one experiences gender and one's body, and have chosen to accept how the person sees their self. In this sense, there are *travestis* who wish to undergo or have undergone sex reassignment surgery (SRS) and who have never identified as transsexuals. There are transsexuals who do not want SRS, who like their penis, and wish to maintain it, but neither identify or see themselves as *travestis*. Nowadays, there are certain youths who identify as trans and therefore free themselves from the traditional classifications of psychiatry, which have long been used by psychology and psychoanalysis.

References

Ayouch, T. (2018). *Psychanalyse et hybridité: Genre, colonialité, subjectivations*. Leuven: Leuven University Press.
Butler, J. P. (2006). *Gender Trouble: Feminism and the Subversion of Identity*. New York: Routledge.
_____ (1997). *The Psychic Life of Power: Theories in subjection*. New York: Stanford University Press.
Carvalho, M. A. de. (2020). *Lugar de homem é na cozinha? Um estudo sobre a organização do trabalho doméstico em uniões gays*. Dissertação de Mestrado apresentada ao Programa de Pós-Graduação em Educação Sexual da Faculdade de Ciências e Letras – Unesp/Araraquara.
Castañeda, M. (2007). *A experiência homossexual: explicações e conselhos para os homossexuais, suas famílias e seus terapeutas*. São Paulo: A Girafa.
Corbett, K. (2009). Boyhoods: Rethinking masculinities. New York: Yale University Press.
Costa, J. F. (2004). *Ordem médica e norma familiar* (5ª ed.). Rio de Janeiro: Edições Graal.
DeSouza, E.; Baldwin, J. R.; Rosa, F. H. (2000). A construção social dos papéis sexuais femininos. *Psicologia: Reflexão e Crítica*, 13(3), 485–496.
Duby, G.; Perrot, M. (1990). *História das Mulheres (vol. 2): A Idade Média*. Porto: Edições Afrontamento.
Meletti, A. T.; Scorsolini-Comin, F. (2015). Conjugalidade e expectativas em relação à parentalidade em casais homossexuais. *Revista Psicologia – Teoria e Prática*, 17(1), 37–49.
Miskolci, R. (2007). Pânicos morais e controle social: reflexões sobre o casamento gay. *Cadernos Pagu* (28), 101–128.
Nico, M.; Rodrigues, E. (2011). Organização do trabalho doméstico em casais do mesmo sexo. *Sociologia, Problemas e Práticas* (65), 95–118.
Pelúcio, L. (2006). Três casamentos e algumas reflexões: notas sobre conjugalidade envolvendo travestis que se prostituem. *Revista Estudos Feministas*, 14(2), 522–534.
Preciado, P. B. (2013) *Testo Junkie: Sex, Drugs, and Biopolitics in the Pharmacopornographic Era*. New York: Feminist Press.

Reis, J. R. T. (2012). Família, emoção e ideologia. In: Lane, S. M. T.; Codo, W.G. (Eds.) *Psicologia Social: o homem em movimento* (14a ed). Sao Paulo: Brasiliense. 99–124.

Rubin, G. (1975). The Traffic in Women. Notes on the "Political Economy" of Sex. In: Reiter, R. (ed.) *Toward an Anthropology of Women*. New York: Monthly Review Press.

Sáez, J.; Carrascosa, S. (2016). *Pelo Cu: Políticas Anais*. Belo Horizonte: Grupo Editorial Letramento.

Santos, A. B.; Shimizu, H. E.; Merchan-Hamann, E. (2014). Processo de formação das representações sociais sobre transexualidade dos profissionais de saúde: possíveis caminhos para superação do preconceito. *Ciência e Saúde Coletiva*, 10, 4545–4554.

Santos, Y. G. S.; Scorsolini-Comin, F.; Santos, M. A. (2013). Homoparentalidade masculina: revisando a produção científica. *Psicologia: Reflexão e Crítica*, 26(3), 572–582.

Sedgwick, E. K. (1990). *Epistemology of the Closet*. Berkeley: University of California Press.

_____ (1993). *Tendencies*. New York: Duke University Press.

Silva, G. W. S.; Souza, E. F. L.; Sena, R. C. F.; Moura, I. B. L.; Sobreira, M. V. S.; Miranda, F. A. N. (2016). Situações de violência contra travestis e transexuais em um município do nordeste brasileiro. *Revista Gaúcha de Enfermagem*, 37(2), e56407.

Waseda, D.; Lofego, L.; Feijó, M.; Chaves, U. H.; Valério, N. I. (2016). Casais homoafetivos femininos: demandas do ciclo vital familiar e aceitação social. *Pensando famílias*, 20(2), 115–131. Acesso em 20.jul.2020.

Zauli, A. (2011). Famílias Homoafetivas no Brasil e no Canadá: um estudo transcultural sobre novas vivências de gênero e nos laços de parentesco. *(Tese de Doutorado)*. Brasília, Brasil: Universidade de Brasília.

Chapter 5

Exploring unconscious anxieties for couple psychoanalytic psychotherapists working with same-sex couples

The same or different?

Kate Thompson

Introduction

In this chapter, I describe my work as a psychoanalytic couple psychotherapist working with same-sex couples. As a heterosexual and cisgendered woman, I'm interested in unconscious censorship and internalised heterosexism, associated with the difficulty of straight therapists thinking about the intimate world of same-sex couples. Do fears of hurtful discrimination and the expression of politically incorrect views hamper discussion of the differences and similarities that need to be thought about in relation to the psychoanalytic stance? Is there a danger that anxieties associated with the fear of 'getting it wrong' result in side-stepping issues unique to same-sex relationships and of responding to these as universal couple difficulties and dynamics?

Considering the burden of unconscious blame and shame, central to all human experience but potentially more potent for same-sex couples, I will focus on the likely countertransferences for therapists, drawing particular attention to the importance of supervision as a safe space for opening discussion and of processing countertransference material. It is important to add that this chapter is written not from an expert position, but more as a reflection on hurdles encountered and knowledge gained during many years of clinical practice with same-sex couple dynamics.

In an effort to provide the necessary context for the exploration of sameness and difference, I will outline some key principles of couple psychoanalytic psychotherapy, developed at Tavistock Relationships. This will inevitably touch on object relations theory, Kleinian concepts of unconscious phantasy, projective processes and the idea of the 'couple state of mind' and 'creative couple' processes (Morgan, 2001).

DOI: 10.4324/9781003255703-5

The task in couple psychotherapy

Couple psychoanalytic psychotherapy aims its focus at the couple system, the bridge between two intimate partners, a central space made up of the two individuals and a creative extension of them both, symbolising their union. An important boundary for couple psychotherapy necessitates acknowledging 'the relationship as patient' as in 'their shared internal world, projective system and interactional field which is the therapeutic focus and area of treatment, rather than either or both the individuals' (Hertzmann, 2011).

When couples present for couple psychotherapy, something in their relational system has gone awry; a 'fault' has blocked the healthy affect flow across this bridge, halting or hampering both individual and relational development. Simply put, this relational 'fracture' may arise from external pressures, such as unemployment being processed and experienced differently by the two halves of the couple. Internally, more unconscious anxieties may be weighing down a relationship, such as fears of being unloveable or treated unjustly, often linked to earlier attachment experience. Or there may be a combination of the two, as in the relationship struggling to emerge from one or both partners suffering traumatic loss or illness, but triggering divergent reactions in both partners.

Psychoanalytic couple psychotherapists are trained to identify familiar relational patterns, linked to early attachment experience. The central tenants of attachment theory saw Bowlby echo Freud's hypothesis on the infant-parent relationship creating the prototype for intimate adult relationships. These relational currents are often replicated, as unconscious attempts to either recreate what is familiar or to react against it.

The couple psychotherapist's job is essentially to enter into the unconscious defensive system of both partners and that of their shared relationship, in order to better understand the control it exerts on their functioning as a couple. Whilst, at times, therapists will be required to *move towards* the relationship, utilising transference and countertransference to inform what might be at play unconsciously within the couple dynamic, they still need to maintain the ability to *stand outside* the affect states of both the two individuals and the organisation they create together. This movement to-and-fro enables a metaperspective on the strengths and vulnerabilities of the relational system as a whole. In thinking about the relationship from both the inside and the outside, the therapist symbolises the possibility of a third space, one which represents the shared relationship. The presence of the therapist as an attentive external observer of their relationship may facilitate a sense of connection for the couple that has never been present, whilst at others it seeks to recreate a combined sense of their lives together that has been temporarily lost. It's a complex process, involving retracing of the two individuals' impressions of their parents' intimate coupling; a chance to revisit childhood experience.

Working alongside the couple, the therapist uses transference and countertransference processes that pass between the couple and herself as a tentative guide to internal workings of the relationship presented before her. And finally, not to be overlooked, the consulting room is inevitably inhabited at times by the therapist's own internal relational world, formulated as a product of her own attachments. In the case of a heterosexual therapist working with same-sex relationships, the difference in sexual orientation and natural bias carried by the therapist, influencing the countertransference, will need overt exploration in supervision.

Throughout this chapter, I shall illustrate couple psychoanalytic theoretical concepts through the discussion of two case studies. First, Billie and Dan, a male same-sex couple in their late 30s, together for 8 years, who were contemplating separation and, second, Suz and Susannah, a lesbian couple in their mid-30s, who were facing a crisis whilst deciding whether to have a child. These relationships have been anonymised and are an amalgam of cases to illustrate key areas whilst protecting confidentiality.

Containment to steady the pull between intimacy and autonomy in couple relationships

Bion's ideas of containment linked to his theory of thinking underpins psychoanalytic couple psychotherapy. Containment encapsulates both the provision of a sanctuary and the sense of being inside something good, where meaning can be found. It's key in understanding the frame which encompasses the work for couple psychotherapists and mirrors the necessary boundary around an intimate relationship. Understanding a couple's primitive defence mechanism of splitting and projection, tolerating the transference, managing the countertransference, whilst maintaining a thinking state-of-mind and containing couple anxieties, are the 'bread and butter' of couple psychotherapy as clinicians attempt to shift a couple in distress from more paranoid-schizoid states of mind to a more depressive way of thinking.

The push and pull between the desire for couple intimacy and connectedness and the need for space and individual development is a familiar psychic tug-of-war encountered in the consulting room. A desire for tolerance of difference and autonomy and a magnetism towards the safety of psychic sameness when vulnerability is acute, is an aspect of all intimate relationships. This attraction to *being of the same mind* is perhaps something that needs deeper examination when working with same-sex couples, since gender difference isn't an easily identifiable demarcation and may represent additional pressure. This seems particularly important given the historical references that continue to abound in regard to the idea of merging in lesbian couple relationships and questions of intimacy associated with gay male couple relationships.

Exploring unconscious anxieties **77**

For instance, when I met with Suz and Susannah, they told me that they were attempting to get pregnant by the same sperm donor, at exactly the same time. They described this as normal for lesbian couples. It took several months of us working together before it became possible to think with them about alternate meanings for what was happening, alongside their understanding. Could there possibly be envious and competitive parts of themselves that feared being 'left out' of the chance to experience motherhood? Or did they yearn for a more traditional and delineated maternal gender role in order to counteract feelings linked to being regarded as outside the mainstream? As therapeutic trust developed between us, I was able to be curious as to whether this drive to become mothers at the same time was also connected in some way to their lifelong and exhausting struggle with the experience of being different, and the wish to be the same as an unconscious reaction to this.

During the work with this couple, my own relationship had ended. As a single woman in her early 30s, I found myself reflecting on aspects of my femininity that had been secured within my heterosexual relationship with a male partner. In that regard, I found myself thinking about Suz and Susannah's gendered relationship and wondered if they might have to work harder to maintain a clear, boundaried sense of self in the absence of difference. Was this something I could discuss with my supervisor, was I being naive or, worse still, might my thinking be seen as discriminatory.

The necessary ability to maintain a secure enough self-identity within an intimate coupling is linked to the achievement of tolerating being both inside an intimate relationship and being an observer of it; of being dependent on it whilst maintaining a degree of self-agency. This process begins in the course of infantile development, where each individual must traverse the Oedipal situation to reach a position where they can be in an intimate relationship with an other and, where together they can create a third, in which they can experience their relationship as a shared resource. The template for this originates in the infant's secure enough experience of at once being welcomed into the parent-couple relationship and being excluded from it, whilst still being kept in mind. "The working through of the early Oedipal situation and the creation of what Britton (1989) describes as a 'triangular space' in which we can see ourselves in interaction with others, entertain another point of view, and also retain our own, is one of the important steps towards achieving a satisfying intimate relationship with another" (Morgan, 2010).

Life events can get in the way of development and result in an Oedipal 'stuckness', as became clearer when Suz was able to think about her relationship with her mother:

Suz was raised in South Africa and was the only child of white parents who spent large tranches of their married lives apart, due to her dad working for an oil company based in South America. As a by-product of this enforced isolation, Suz's British-born mother tended to over-rely on her daughter and, as she became a teenager, relate to her in an intrusive way. Suz could identify the day that she stopped telling her mum that she had been praised at school, as she realised her mother absorbed this information as if it was happening to her, rather than her daughter. Suz described her own feelings as being appropriated by her mother; her defence was to shut-up and emotionally shut-down. She explained that "If I was feeling sad and would try to explain why, it somehow morphed into her sadness, that was much bigger and more terrible".

Later, when Suz was bullied by classmates for being 'butch', her mother got to hear about it from a neighbour and was outraged. The sense of injustice that started to obsess her mum left Suz and her own feelings as some kind of adjunct or side-show to the more important event, namely, how it was affecting her mother. Later, Suz was able to think more sympathetically about her mother's loneliness which may have contributed to this over-identification with her daughter. This difficulty in separating Suz's experience from her mother's, however, left emotional scars that made adult intimate relating more challenging for her and I noticed she seemed to switch-off when Susannah talked about her feelings. In an early session, when Susannah remarked, "when Suz is happy, I'm happy", Suz seemed distracted and started to look out of the window. Whilst by no means the preserve of same-sex couples, this mother-daughter dyad and its vacillation between being separate and of one mind gave me some context for understanding the couple's 'too close-too distant' dilemma.

Couple fit

Individuals encompassing all manner of difference, be it sexual identity and orientation, ethnicity, age, religion and socio-economic status are drawn to pair up for both conscious and unconscious reasons. It is the latter, the unconscious couple fit, that primarily concerns the couple therapist, since it is in navigating the terrain of unconscious phantasy and unconscious defensive mechanisms that acts as a prompt for couples to seek help.

Billie described being drawn to Dan because they both liked doing-up houses and shared a love of karaoke. Billie's previous relationship with a much older man had ended abruptly, and it had taken him a couple of years to be able to contemplate any kind of committed relationship again. He envied Dan's seemingly carefree attitude towards life, it felt like a healthy contrast to his experience as a child with a depressed mother and violently aggressive father.

Conversely, Dan liked the steadiness that Billie seemed to represent with his spreadsheets and savings accounts, well-thought-out plans for the future and open desire for a committed, exclusive relationship. Raised in Ireland, alongside 5 siblings, by an over-anxious mother, Dan was infected by his mother's shame at the failure of her marriage, reflected in the eyes of her staunchly Catholic family.

One layer of this couple's unconscious 'fit' might see Billie attracted to Dan's supposed laidback personality, in contrast to his own. After the traumatic end of his previous relationship and a neglected childhood watching over his depressed mother, deep within himself he carried a fear that he was emotionally leaden, even lifeless. Conversely Dan is drawn to what he believes to be the secure base represented by Billie's embrace of all things adult and planned, an imagined safe haven from the chaos and confusing shame of his Irish family which he had hitherto denied through a none-stop social life and multiple sexual partners.

Another perspective might emphasise Billie finding a receptacle in Dan into which he could project his sadness and depression whilst being in receipt of Dan's anxiety and dismissiveness.

Klein's (1946) theory of projective identification, which begins from birth as a means of managing infantile fears for survival, is an important tool for understanding projective processes between couples, regardless of gender or sexual orientation. Bion suggests that working to understand the patient's anxious projections, the therapist bears and contains them and they become detoxified. If the distressing aspect of the self that is defensively projected can be identified and thought about by the therapist, then the complex job of how to help these disavowed aspects of the subject be reintroduced and thought about as part of the self can begin. The disavowed aspects, carried over from early childhood, of the two partners in a same-sex relationship may be overlaid by defence mechanisms developed as a result of being different. It may be harder for a straight therapist to identify and disentangle more infantile defences within the couple she is seeking to help from those justifiably erected to counter fears of discrimination.

Whilst Suz's mother related to her daughter in an over-intrusive way, in reaction to an absent husband, Susannah's upbringing appeared very different. Her parents were caught up in a tempestuous union, always on-and-off and lacking consistency. As a little girl, Susannah felt on the outside of this 'folie a deux' and described not being allowed into the sitting room, banished to the doorway from where she could watch her parents either bicker or passionately 'make-up'.

In the therapy, as time wore on, I began to register an internal sense of injustice which seemed to hook itself to both the couple and my supervisor failing to realise just how hard I was working. I could interpret this in two ways. It either reflected a somewhat over-stretched therapist or was part of my countertransference, originating from Suz and/or Susannah, who both had problematic relationships with their primary caregivers and expressed anger at having to work so hard at living within a heteronormative world, the equivalent perhaps of Susannah not being allowed into the sitting room.

As the therapy progressed, I noticed my sense of injustice settling somewhat and there seemed to be enough space for us all to work hard and mostly feel its value. I made the assumption that somehow the two individuals in the couple had been contained by my attentiveness to their distress. I, in turn, continued to work hard but found myself looking forward to the sessions and being 'fed' by the learning and developments within it.

Projective processes

Linked to a couple's unconscious fit, unconscious projection into the other is another important part of relating: we all do it with friends, partners, family and colleagues. In its most desperate form, however, which may be the 'fight or flight' state of mind of distressed couples, excessive projective processes can be akin to psychic annihilation, persecution or abandonment. Klein described 'the violent splitting of the self and excessive projection having the effect that the person towards whom the process is directed is felt as a persecutor' (Klein, 1946). The receiver of projections suffers their own mind and affect states rendered insignificant or besieged, and at its worst, their identity can be jeopardised. Working to understand the defensive nature of a rigid couple projective system, the therapist often experiences psychic space in the consulting room as being restricted. In addition, fixed yet curiously interchangeable boundaries can confuse relational dynamics, attributes and characteristics belonging to one half of the couple are suddenly present within the other.

One reason Billie and Dan came to couple psychotherapy was because Dan had been recently diagnosed with depression. Dan's depression confirmed the couple's worst fears about him — and what was 'wrong' with him became a major focus for them both. Through defensive projection and introjection, there was a split with one viewed by both as 'good' (Billie) and the other 'bad' (Dan). This good-bad split was manifest in many areas of their intimate relationship with 'bad' Dan exorcising his depression with hedonistic parties, leaving a 'martyred' Billie to clear-up his mess, yet again. This split ensured that neither had to tolerate mixed feelings; that there might be a part of Dan wondering about monogamy and, similarly, a side of Billie that wanted to raise hell or be irresponsible. As it was, Billie said, 'living with Dan was like raising a child' and Dan seemingly complied with Billie's view. Any difference of opinion between them, such as Dan objecting to this 'adolescent' persona, caused a massive row.

The splitting was mirrored in their relationship with me and ensured their primitive fears initially remained misunderstood, as everyone in the consulting room was caught-up with the 'battle'. I was either with them, or against them, there was no middle ground. Billie would look contemptuously if I suggested that he might need his relationship with Dan, defensively citing Dan's incompetence as evidence of his utter dependence on him. For Dan and Billie, their projective gridlock, a pseudo-dominating of or being taken over by the object, was an echo of Oedipal anxieties and contributed to their difficulties in conceiving a third position, a psychic space in which the creative couple can think objectively about what passes between them. Though unsatisfying, Dan's apparent compliance with Billie's way of seeing him was a well-trodden and safer path, despite the pain of being wiped out by Billie's increasingly rigid state of mind and becoming depressed. After all, as one, you can't be abandoned, as two, there's the chance of real separation.

Mutual understanding was yearned for but feared by both Dan and Billie; to be seen and understood required reintrojecting the projected parts of themselves, the pain and knowledge of which they shied away from. Without knowing it consciously, it began to emerge that Dan feared getting in touch with the more serious side of himself, his intellectual 'agency' or executive functioning. The therapy traced back in time to where this separation from thinking might have begun and Dan wondered about his young-self witnessing his mother's shame and resentment towards his father, her family and the church. Together the couple also wondered how his aversion to and misunderstanding of her was developing alongside his sexual identity and how his mother's shame may have got tangled up with his fears about acceptance within their narrow-minded community.

The process of mourning plays a crucial role in the recovery of lost parts of the self as described by Steiner, 'The process of regaining parts of the self lost through projective identification involves facing the reality of what belongs to the object and what belongs to the self, and this is established most clearly through the experience of loss. It is in the process of mourning that parts of the self are regained, and this achievement may require much working through.' (Steiner, 1993).

Therapist stance and a couple state of mind

The couple therapist undertakes to maintain a central stance, which Morgan (2001) describes as having a 'couple state of mind'. This way of thinking hopefully holds the worker secure in her task, providing another therapeutic gear within which to work and prevents straying too far and tending to one individual over the other or over the relationship as a whole. Therapists are required to receive communication on multiple conscious and unconscious levels; between the two individuals, the two individuals and their therapist and the couple relationship and the therapist. The hope is that the therapist's 'couple state of mind' is, in time, internalised by the couple, and enables the development of a secure relationship base within them.

The practitioner occupying this central space is an important factor in creating a safe framework, and the therapeutic role and stance may at times be quite active. By 'active', I don't mean verbally, it is more in the dance of their psychic stance and working minds, moving back, forth and around the two individuals and their relationship.

'In applying the concept of the creative couple in therapeutic work with lesbian and gay couples, I have found that there can be a mirroring of the societal indictment of homosexuality reflected in the couple's relationship. This can interfere with the couple's capacity to inhabit a creative couple state of mind' (Hertzmann, 2011). Therefore, maintaining a 'couple state of mind' for gay couples inescapably faces us with a necessary awareness of how wider society's 'outside' views and judgements on gay relationships impacts the 'inside' working mechanisms of the two individuals and their therapist, and perhaps also involves some adjustment in thinking and practice.

Societal indictment may also manifest as part of internalised homophobia, 'the gay person's direction of negative social attitudes toward the self, leading to a devaluation of the self and resultant internal conflicts and poor self-regard ...' (Meyer & Dean, 1998, p. 161). With this in mind, the place of historical and current discriminatory practices in working therapeutically with same-sex couples and the existence of internalised homophobia in both therapist and client needs to remain uppermost in the therapist's mind, and central in supervision. Well-meaning protestations from supervisees over the years, 'well, I've not got a problem with it', minimises the importance of open dialogue in supervision and the therapy itself, shutting down thinking around unconscious phantasy and takes no account of historical and current context for same sex relationships.

Understanding and tolerating the couple's repeated judgement of their friends was not straightforward on my part. In one session, I was surprised by what seemed like Dan and Billie's rather sneering reference to a particular friend being 'too camp for words' and another couple as 'such queens'. Although perhaps fuelled by the need to distance themselves from their gay friends in front of me, I also was able to reflect on my own relationship's capacity to judge our friends as ridiculous or flashy; so why shouldn't same-sex couples be able to do the same without it being classified as internalised homophobia? On the other hand, I wondered if the couple were trying to work something through for themselves or connect to me because these issues were bought to the session quite often.

Therapists working with same-sex couples may need to take on board a world of disillusionment related to being part of a minority group, whilst simultaneously realising how strongly these couples may identify with their difference, all of which may be affecting their internal development. There may be a weariness for gender and sexual minority individuals and couples at 'not being got', as well as a wariness of 'being got' that therapists need to recognise. This slight at growing up 'on the outside' of society is as confusing as 'being on the inside' of an intimate relationship. This is not how they have come to see themselves, and coming to couple therapy, long regarded as a heteronormative practice, may well act as a trigger. Many same-sex couples have endured a real or imagined lack of understanding and have erected a defensive shield to mitigate this pain, which is likely to be hampering the intimate relationship they are attempting to repair. The straight therapist working with same-sex couples needs to think about and work with this potential barrier to the therapeutic relationship in order to reduce its ability to silence creative discourse and exploration.

Thinking about sexual intimacy as a straight therapist working with gay couples

Writing nearly 20 years ago, Michael Butler and Jeremy Clarke observed, "Sadly gay couples hoping to improve their relationship are still likely to find themselves in therapy which exacerbates their problems rather than resolves them. 'The sexual side of our relationship, or lack of it, was not mentioned, it was skated over' is an example of comments which not infrequently come our way at the Albany Trust" (Butler & Clarke, 1991, p. 197).

Whilst many believe that things have moved on in terms of acceptance and celebration of gay relationships, nevertheless, the issue of therapists, perhaps because of heightened sensitivity, failing to explore the psycho-sexual needs of same-sex couples, is something that needs consideration. Inevitably, there are pressures that arise from drawing on heterosexism as the basis for a straight therapist's curiosity when working with LGBT couples, and this may in part account for the lack of enquiry with differently gendered or sexually orientated couples. Similarly, sidestepping the sexual domain in same-sex relationship therapy may also be replicated in the supervisory domain, given that both parties may be anxious to avoid ignorance or discomfort. Masters (2008), for instance, highlights the fact that when gay patients describe their sexual activities in sessions, it can create a host of countertransferences regardless of the gender or sexual orientation of the therapist. "At times we may find ourselves intrigued, disgusted, envious, and, yes, even sexually excited (Masters, 2008, p. 376).

As shame associated with sexuality, again not the preserve of same-sex couples, is an aspect of many gay relationships, therapists may need to work harder to understand that which needs to be understood:

Eight months into the therapy, Billie arrived on his own and described in some detail an impulse when Dan was away with work to seek out unprotected sex in clubs. Having never been inside a gay club, Billie's description of dark rooms and the exciting, risky encounters found me genuinely curious about this unfamiliar world.

After failing to resist temptation and seeking sexual freedom from the confines of the closed relationship he insisted upon with Dan, Billie talked about an almost unbearable tension that propelled him to attend the sexual health clinic, whilst awaiting test results for a sexually transmitted disease. I realised that up until now the couple hadn't focussed on their physical relationship. Billie now seemed open to thinking with me about this repetitive pattern and the anxiety associated with hiding this aspect of his life from Dan and the intense shame that he was holding. Together we wondered what he was doing to himself and, despite the pleasure it momentarily gave him, if it might be a form of self-harm.

84 Kate Thompson

Transference, countertransference and therapeutic relationship

In offering the couple an interpretation rooted in transference and countertransference material, a deeper level of understanding can be offered, perhaps helping to identify the mutual trap of unhelpful projections the couple sets up, comprising a malign cycle between them. The therapist's ability to recognise and reflect on their feeling states, largely but not exclusively in the here and now of the therapeutic encounter, can be diagnostic. 'The patient is somehow able to induce in the analyst a state of mind very similar to one he was more or less successfully attempting to eliminate in himself' (Carpy, 1989). The therapist's task is to identify and differentiate between affect induced as part of the couple's dynamic, separate to their own feelings aroused by the material.

This main area of productive work requires the therapist to tolerate levels of confusion, inside and out, before her hypothesis can take shape. (Pick,1985) described 'having recognised countertransference feelings and having avoided acting them out in a destructive manner, the analyst must attempt to undo the inevitable tangle in his mind between what is more directly patient produced and what is more a function of his own personal responses to that production'.

Suz and Susannah had been in couple psychotherapy for 6 months and it was the week before Christmas. In hindsight, I realised my omission in not providing them with the dates that I would be away in advance, as I would normally do, telling them with only the week before I would be away. It was only later could I see what an act of 'neglect' that had been; that I'd been pulled into not being able to look after them properly. I was alerted to this by the fact that the couple left the session on 21st December with absolutely no reference to the Christmas break, perhaps punishing me for failing to reference my holiday. I felt wiped out at the end of the session and only in supervision was I helped to think about the lack of maternal psychic space that was set aside for them as they grew up and, the subsequent rejection they had felt at almost every life stage. I could see that I had unintentionally replicated this rejection and then experienced it myself, as part of my countertransference.

Morgan describes the concrete nature of a couples' unconscious shared belief and the particular emotional experience and tone of the countertransference for the therapist when exposed to these kinds of shared defences. She describes the unconscious belief as feeling like a fact, with the dialogue in the room sounding like a script. The difficulty centres on the couple's ability to move from this belief as fact to understanding the defensive function that the belief serves. Suz and Susannah were defending against confronting aspects of themselves that related back to a time in their lives when they were indeed helpless and their survival was at stake.

Supervision

"The processes at work currently in the relationship between (patient) client and worker (analyst) are often reflected in the relationship between worker and supervisor" (Mattinson, 1975, p. 11).

A few months into the work with Billie and Dan and presenting the case in supervision, I described the couple as always busy, renovating their house, eating out and taking numerous trips abroad for long weekends. This had begun to irk me as the couple had negotiated a low fee at assessment, linked to fluctuations in their self-employed income. However, I had started to feel resentful whenever I heard them approaching my consulting room, the familiar sound of a small suitcase being wheeled along, as the couple were either returning or leaving for a weekend break abroad. I confessed to this growing resentment in my supervision, along with an inability to raise the low fee with the couple.

Enactment in supervision of dynamics between the therapist and the couple and between the couple themselves gives more material within which to helpfully identify unconscious bias and internal judgement:

My clinical supervisor wondered if the couple felt guilty at 'getting away' with paying a low fee for couple psychotherapy and questioned why I had felt unable to raise this with them. I found myself blushing in the face of my supervisor's open curiosity and identified a defensiveness within myself as I began to reel off all that was getting in the way of broaching this subject. Fortunately, my supervisor noticed this and commented on my difficulty in being curious with myself and her, something that I would normally be open to doing.

As we explored this 'blocking' in thinking, my supervisor recognised her reluctance to explore the couple's fantasies linked to me. Together we wondered if something was being side-stepped in both supervision and the therapy itself, linked to a concern that the couple avoided persecution, not only about the fee but also in regard to their sexual orientation. In a way, as long as sex and difference had been named in supervision, that seemed to be enough, it was a relief to move on to more familiar territory. However, it threatened to lead to a paralysis within the supervisory alliance; a tacit agreement to 'leave it there', perhaps relating to the couple's own experience of avoiding intimacy in their relationship. My supervisor recognised her fears of getting something wrong as a possible countertransference reaction between supervisee and supervisor and this possibly being a parallel process between Billie, Dan and me.

Hertzmann (2011) describes how internalised homophobia obstructs couple development and can cause a paralysis or stuckness in the couple presenting for therapy. Moss also talks of how some gay men live out a conflicted relationship with their desired objects linked to internalised homophobia. While simultaneously desiring the same-sex object, they also hit up against an internal repulsion and hatred of their own desire. According to Moss, "the founding opposition between desire and repulsion collapses, and the result is a fundamental statis" (Moss, 2002, p. 7). Perhaps aspects of the stuckness within the supervisory process was in some ways an echo of Billie and Dan's internalised homophobia; a pull towards but rejection of their sexuality which led to the unconscious stalemate between them and subsequently between them and me, which needed to become part of the work.

Parallel processes in supervision are to be expected. Working with therapists embroiled in couple psychoanalytic psychotherapy may well leave a supervisor reacting against what may be perceived as judgemental, critical observations of a supervisee's work. "Collusive crossed transactions are more noticeable; both participants may feel irritated, and a 'judgemental' supervisor may be left full of self-criticism at having yet again been so intolerant" (Hughes & Pengelly, 1997, p. 149). When supervising same-sex couple psychotherapy, there is the added possibility that this perceived judgement could be linked to unconscious homophobia both within the supervisee and her couple clients and needs to be explored in the safety of the supervisory alliance. Only it first needs to be identified.

Conclusion

In thinking about this chapter, one gay friend I spoke to ruefully explained, 'Kate, I still have to come out every day'. Why this should be necessary when the heterosexual community are reticent to broach the subject of their sexuality in the main, except in the privacy of their own bedrooms, alerts us to an enduring imbalance within contemporary British society. This difference is further highlighted with the blunt reality that, in many countries, being gay can result in imprisonment, torture and sometimes death, and the psychic burden of a public denigration of homosexuality that many same-sex couples carry, underlines the necessity of the therapeutic space being one of acceptance and safety.

Scanning art, film and television, there is scant evidence of same-sex couple relationships enduring lifetimes and providing both partners with enriching lives together, raising children and allowing for individual and couple development. Hollywood isn't hot on same-sex coupling as its mainstream offering and the impact of this for gay couples and, increasingly, for their children, still can't be underestimated despite real change in the last few decades.

Despite a growing inclusivity in Britain, school children can still be heard taunting one another in the playground with 'you're gay'. The weight carried by many young people in 'coming out' to friends and family is testament to this. Heterosexual young people are not under such perceived or imagined judgement by their peers or family. They don't feel compelled to discuss their emerging sexuality with their parents. This simplistic comparison is perhaps echoed in the later struggle that same-sex couples may encounter when contemplating parenthood and resenting the lack of privacy in the begetting of children for many gay couples. Exploring these struggles in more detail in couple therapy and in the parallel process of supervision is vital, and I wonder if the avoidance of the detail of the strife, for both therapist and supervisor, replicates in some way the internal process for the same-sex couple.

It could be argued that Bion's working 'without memory, desire or understanding' (1967) has never been more apt for working with LGBTQ clients and patients, although it relies to some extent on an openness to the process on the part of both the therapist and those with whom they work. I can own a fair share of clinical reticence and, indeed in writing of this chapter, and I wonder how my words will be received. In this regard, I fall into the unhelpful, hampering anxiety about 'getting it right'.

In many respects, the suggestions I am putting forward for further thinking are the same for all therapeutic work with couples. As therapists, we model and promote open benign curiosity and the kinds of communication and connectedness that encourages understanding and growth in both patients and practitioner. As a straight therapist working therapeutically with same-sex couples, I recognise a need for greater use of supervision and self-reflection to spot what might be being glossed over through my own ignorance, anxiety about causing offence and working inevitably through a heteronormative lens.

It strikes me that working with same-sex couples is both the same and different to working with the dynamics of heterosexual relationships. The difficulties in thinking about difference that many clinicians find themselves tussling with or oblivious to, are rooted within unconscious cultural bias and avoidance of the struggle associated with it. By that I mean an avoidance of unfairness, inequality and being insufficiently validated. This places a responsibility on clinicians and supervisors alike to know that difference is there, alongside what is the same, and so to seek it out — rather than remain afraid of it being 'outed'.

References

Bion, W. R. (1967). Notes on Memory and Desire. *Psychoanalytic Forum*, 2: 346–360.

Britton, R. (1989). The missing link: parental sexuality in the Oedipus complex. In: J. Steiner (Ed.), *The Oedipus Complex Today: Clinical Implications*. London: Karnac.

Butler, M., & Clarke, J. (1991). Couple therapy with homosexual men. In: D. Hooper & W. Dryden (Eds.), *Couple Therapy*. Buckingham and Philadelphia: Open University Press.

Carpy, D. V. (1989). Tolerating the Countertransference: A Mutative Process. *Int. J. Psycho-Anal.*, 70: 287–294.

Hertzmann, L. (2011). Lesbian and Gay Couple Relationships: When Internalized Homophobia Gets in the Way of Couple Creativity. *Psychoanal. Psychother.*, 25(4): 346–360.

Hughes, L., & Pengelly, P. (1997). *Staff Supervision in a Turbulent Environment*. London: Jessica Kingsley Publishers.

Klein, M. (1946). Notes on Some Schizoid Mechanisms. *Int. J. Psycho-Anal*, 27: 99–110.

Masters, D. (2008). Homosexuality and Psychoanalysis 111: Clinical Perspective. *J. Lesbian Ment. Health*, 14(4): 373–378.

Mattinson, J. (1975). *The Reflection Process in Casework Supervision*. London: Tavistock Institute of Marital Studies.

Meyer, I. H., & Dean, L. (1998). Internalized homophobia, intimacy, and sexual behaviour among gay and bisexual men. In: G. M. Herek (Ed.), *Stigma and Sexual Orientation: Understanding Prejudice Against Lesbians, Gay Men and Bisexuals* (pp. 160–186). Thousand Oaks, CA: Sage.

Morgan, M. (2001). First contacts: the therapist's 'couple state of mind' as a factor in the containment of couples seen for consultations. In: F. Grier (Ed.), *Brief Encounters with Couples*. London: Karnac.

Morgan, M. (2010). Unconscious Beliefs about Being a Couple. *Fort Da*, 16: 36–55.

Morgan, M. (2019). *The Couple State of Mind: Psychoanalysis of Couples and the Tavistock Relationships Model*. Abingdon, Oxon: Routledge.

Moss, D. (2002). Internalized Homophobia in Men: Wanting in the First Person Singular, Hating in the First Person Plural. *Psychoanal. Q.*, 71(1), 21–50.

Pick, I. B. (1985). Working Through the Countertransference. *Int. J. Psycho-Anal.*, 66: 157–166.

Steiner, J. (1993). A theory of psychic retreats. In Elizabeth Bott Spillius. (Ed.) *Psychic Retreats: Pathelogical Organisations in Psychotic, Neurotic and Borderline Patients*. (p.9.) London: Routledge.

Chapter 6

Bisexual people and their partners in relational psychoanalytic couple therapy
Aesthetic conflict, multiple selves and the uncontainable

Esther Rapoport and Irit Kleiner Paz

Introduction: Bisexuality in society, individual mind and couple relationship

Bisexuality is a complex sexual identity that has become increasingly visible in recent decades. Despite the substantial accomplishments that the bisexual community has made, this identity continues to challenge many contemporary subjects. Defined as a potential to be attracted to more than one sex or gender, the bisexual identity marks its bearers as people whose sexual and romantic trajectories are unpredictable. Far from being the only people whose trajectories may zigzag and whose futures are unknowable, self-identified bisexuals and people with bi- or pansexual interests are nonetheless likely to evoke anxieties in those around them, since bi-identified people wear unknowability on their foreheads (Rapoport, 2019). Bisexuality as a concept represents a position that is "both-and" or "neither here nor there", which Rapoport terms "bi-valent" (Rapoport, 2019). Such a position is epistemologically challenging, and conflicts with the universal human needs for certainty, clarity and predictability. At the same time, however, grappling with bisexuality, be it one's own or one's partner's, is an opportunity to expand and enrich both the partners' individual selves and their emotional communication as a couple.

The idea of loving or being attracted to many genders has been constructed in the social discourse as a paradoxical statement made to reconcile contradictory facts. On the societal level, bisexuality is, to a large extent, accurately perceived as a threat to the heteronormative, patriarchal ideal of monogamous marriage based on unequivocally defined gender roles (Charles, 2002). Philosophically and psychoanalytically speaking, bisexuality may be experienced as illogical and excessive of one's mental capacities. We believe that it is not only the sexual indetermination of bisexuality but, more pertinently, the sense of contradiction and unpredictability commonly arising in the encounter with the signifier of bisexuality, as the signifier at the edge of the signifying system that is difficult for the mind to contain

DOI: 10.4324/9781003255703-6

(Rapoport, 2010). Two minds in a close couple relationship, reflecting and magnifying one another's anxieties, can drive each other mad as they attempt to grapple with bisexuality.

"Methods of escaping doubt": philosophical perspectives

The philosopher Charles S. Peirce (1955 [1868], p. 57–60) argued that the need for certainty was a universal human need. Knowledge, according to Peirce, is mediated through senses and, therefore, cannot be proven true. Human babies learn facts about their environments and absorb them without questioning. For children and adults alike, doubt and uncertainty appear only when it is no longer possible to maintain the unquestioned belief. Doubt is a painful experience, Peirce maintained, whereas certainty and clarity produce pleasure. Peirce and later pragmatist philosophers saw the evolution of thought and reason mainly as driven by the need to escape the pain of not knowing: "The only cause that we plant ourselves in reason is that other methods of escaping doubt fail" (Peirce, 1955, p. 58, Struhl, 1975).

Wittgenstein takes a similar path, suggesting that belief is a relief. Certainty is a psychological need, and human minds prefer being in the calm zone of knowing (Wittgenstein & Anscombe, 1969). Our "system of convictions" allows us to picture the world in a particular way and that is accompanied by the pleasurable feeling of understanding. We inquire and struggle with the pain of uncertainty only after sufficient evidence has shaken up our worldview.

Freud thought along the same lines when he based the etiology of neurosis in conflict and ambivalence. He saw contradicting motives, thoughts and ideations as sources of tension that the organism sought to alleviate. Contrasting emotions, like loving the Oedipal father yet also hating him for being the partner of the mother, were seen in his texts as a source of great pain. Freud did not see reason as a tool to escape ambiguity; conversely, skeptical about the reach of rational thought, he postulated that in their efforts to avoid the pain of uncertainty, people utilize defense mechanisms that lead them to think irrationally (Freud & Strachey, 1964 [1909]; Freud & Strachey, 1963 (1916-1917)).

In contemporary cognitive science, the mind's tendency to prefer simple explanations over complex ones has been termed "the simplicity principle" (Chater, 1997; Chater & Vitányi, 2003). Researchers find that in multiple areas of cognition, human thought appears to be profoundly impacted by a bias towards simplicity (Feldman, 2016).

Uncertainty and bisexuality

Why is bisexuality associated with uncertainty? In patriarchal societies, binary gender categories of unequal social status serve as a chief organizing principle. Many social and legal mechanisms keep in place binary oppositions between the categories "male" and "female" because the clarity of these oppositions is vital to the preservation of patriarchy (Bordieu, 2002; Dimen, 1991). In liberal/neoliberal patriarchies, women are lured into accepting gender inequality primarily through economic rewards and social sanctioning, rather than the more direct methods of control such as physical punishment. The maintenance of the patriarchal status quo in such societies depends on the population's "buying into" the idea that differences between men and women are significant and unbridgeable. The current upsurge of the global neo-conservative anti-gender movements testify to the great threat that critical and fluid concepts of gender and sexuality present to the social order (Kuhar & Paternotte, 2017). Stereotypical binary notions about male-female distinctions remain popular in part because they satisfy individuals' yearnings for simplicity.

Numerous bisexual theorists have reflected on bisexuality's propensity to be perceived as a threat to patriarchal social order (e.g., Ault, 1996; Daumer, 1992; Garber, 1996). Bisexuality interferes with category-making in sexual politics: bisexuals appear not to believe in firm distinctions between women and men, or between homosexual/queer and heterosexual lifestyles. While not all bisexuals are revolutionaries aiming to change social structures, all are likely to be perceived as such, hence evoking anxiety and abjection affects (Dimen, 2003; Oliver, 2004; Rapoport, 2019). Often not recognizable visually, bisexuals cannot easily be identified or ousted. In patriarchal social contexts, where one's status is determined by how one is positioned in relation to powerful men (Connell, 1995), attraction to multiple sexes, genders and lifestyles make an individual appear unknowable: if someone is rumored to be bisexual, little can be assumed about that person's romantic availability, preferred erotic position(s), political outlook or socioeconomic status. Furthermore, because many bisexuals are well-integrated into the mainstream, this unknowability cannot easily be dismissed as a property of a marginal group.

We suggest that in couples in which one or both partners practice bisexuality and/or identify as bisexual, there is often a tendency to relate to the bisexual partner's bisexuality as the signifier for what is uncertain about the partners' sexualities and erotic trajectories. The bi- (or pan-) sexual partner's identity or behavior becomes the portal through which the couple is made to face the unbearable unknowability of the other's (and ultimately, one's own as well) desire. Bisexuality threatens relationships insofar as it disobeys heteronormative logic and signifies openness to change. It stands for the non-normative, idiosyncratic and enigmatic aspects of desire, which are elusive and difficult to grasp. Engaging with content related to bisexuality makes present and inescapable for the couple the fact that their yearning for certainty cannot be satisfied: binary thinking and role-based shortcuts have failed to safeguard their relationship. It is only by talking to each other, out of the chaos of their emergent otherness, that a sense of security and the possibility of relating may be co-created.

Tolerating erotic otherness: Sara and Jacob

Sara and Jacob, both Jewish Israelis in their 40s, raised by socially conservative families, sought couple's therapy at the height of a crisis in their relationship with adult children. They had been married for 18 years and had two adult children. The partners enjoyed a close and passionate connection, yet throughout their years together, difficulty in emotional regulation persisted. They described a highly co-dependent relationship, where Sara tended to position as the sensitive, attentive caregiver, while simultaneously demanding intense communication and closeness. Jacob appreciated Sara and acknowledged his dependency on her wisdom and warmth while at the same time comforting Sara as she struggled with her mood swings. Despite Jacob's many years of experience in soothing Sara's anxieties, at the time when the couple presented for therapy, he felt helpless in the face of her distress.

For a few years, as Sara began to notice some changes in Jacob's clothing style and behavior, a suspicion crept in for her that Jacob was hiding a homosexual orientation. This led to heightened tension, in the form of quick oscillations between moments of erotic and emotional symbiosis and harsh confrontations, during which Sara grew more suspicious and rageful. Jacob sought individual therapy, and a year later, he shared with Sara that he did indeed feel some attraction to men, which he was not interested in putting into practice. He decided to share those fantasies with Sara so as to be honest and "clear the air" in their relationship.

What happened next shook them both. Sara's mental condition deteriorated and the couple arrived at my (I. P.) office in a confused and anxious state. Sara could hardly work or concentrate on anything besides her urgent need to interrogate Jacob again and again about his sexual desires. She felt that her world had been shattered and needed his soothing constantly. Jacob found her reactions bewildering and felt unsure how to proceed. After some inquiry, we were able to identify aspects of their family histories that seemed to contribute to their unconscious dynamics. Sara's mother had felt sexually and relationally betrayed by her husband; while choosing to continue the marriage, she displayed anger and vengefulness towards her husband till the day he died. We linked the escalation of Sara's anxiety to her fear of finding herself in her mother's position, betrayed and humiliated by the man.

Jacob was the only son of a mother who engulfed him with love and possessiveness. We understood his new sexual fantasies as part of his developmental thrust to construct boundaries, both in his marriage and his relationship with his mother. Being attracted to men was for him a sanctuary from the engulfing and highly conflictual relationships with both his mother and wife. His bisexual fantasies were a source of great excitement yet at the same time revealed his wish, which he experienced as shameful, to differentiate himself from his mother figure. Moreover, Jacob was struggling

Bisexual people and their partners 93

to differentiate himself, not only from the female object but also from his heteronormative upbringing. He could no longer stand being bound to his socially approved role as a dutiful family man and was rebelling against the taboos on male femininity and pleasure-oriented sexuality.

Despite Jacob's insistence that he had no intention to act upon his homosexual desire until he found a way to make it palatable for Sara, her depression and anxiety were exacerbating and I worried about her emotional stability. In a particular session, Sara talked about the breast cancer from which she had recovered a few years earlier, and which has undermined the pillars of her self-esteem and identity. I suggested that her worries about Jacob's bisexual fantasy might be related to her feelings about her mastectomy: "Perhaps you are talking about something that you cannot give Jacob. That you are incomplete..." She immediately uttered tearfully: "I will never have a penis! He needs a penis and I don't have one to give him". As the therapy progressed, the theme of Sara not having a penis received additional meanings, becoming a symbol of the couple's deep symbiotic wish to penetrate each other and become one, but also of Sara's wish for agency, for her own separate power and for the recognition of her worth. Aging, the loss of one of Sara's breasts, and Jacob's bisexual thoughts revived deep anxieties and wishes related to separation and loss.

The oscillation between passionate attractions to different genders could be seen on the transference level as well: the therapist became aware of being a "bisexual object" for both of them — symbolizing the possibility to be attracted to both women and men. Working with Sara's self-esteem, I realized that she saw me as a "woman with a phallus", to whom much knowledge and power were being attributed. When we were discussing the threat of the therapy to their symbiotic bond, I experienced myself in the transference as the Oedipal father precluding the fulfillment of the symbiotic wish. As Jacob wished to have his bisexual feelings accepted, I strove to become the accepting object and tried to create a "bisexual container" (Mukamel, 2018), where his wishes and anxieties could be faced and worked through. Unfortunately, this couple could not contain the threat of ambivalence and uncertainty. Sara's condition deteriorated into a major crisis, and she filed for divorce.

This and other clinical work with couples where one or both partners expressed some bisexual interests made us think about bisexuality as a unique signifier for a more general issue in love relationships: the inevitability and tremendous difficulty of tolerating erotic otherness. The monogamous cultural ideal emphasizes security and permanence: one's partner is represented as one's better half and is therefore knowable. Yet, sexual fantasies and practices engage raw bodily senses and can therefore never be made to fully answer to the cultural norms. Sara's difficulty accepting her partner's emergent sexuality revealed her fear of uncertainty and her deep worry that in some ways, she may never be enough. These fears and worries had to be faced, for indeed, as a subject, one can possess neither completion nor certainty. In Lacanian terms, subjects are ethically required to face their constitutional lack (Lacan, 1992). For many couples, bisexuality works as an irritator that reveals the unsustainability of normative ways of relating as well as a portal through which the potentially transformative emergent qualities of (inter)subjectivity, curiosity, dialogue and playfulness can enter the relationship.

Aesthetic conflict in the couple relationship

Donald Meltzer developed the concept "aesthetic conflict" to designate painful, conflictual and potentially unbearable affective states that plague the infant, who is attracted to the visible beauty of the mother's body, yet cannot know what hides inside it, much less so predict or control the mother's emotional states or her comings and goings (Meltzer & Williams, 1988; Meltzer, 1987). The insides of the mother's body, which cannot be known directly, can be engaged with indirectly by means of creative imagination. Yet the capacity to imagine evolves only gradually, and in turn requires the capacity to delay gratification. Frustrated by the enigmatic beauty of the mother and its overwhelming emotional effects on the nascent self, the infant resorts to violence towards the mother, in an attempt to uncover her essence, but the impulse to know cannot be gratified through violence. Alternatively, the baby may defensively withdraw from the mother.

The regressive effects of adult couple relationships (Balint, 1979) often lead to the reemergence of the aesthetic conflict. Insofar as the other is loved, and therefore experienced as beautiful, the unknowability of her/his inner essence may become difficult to tolerate. Defensive attempts are then made to control or conquer one's partner by knowing her/him: the partner is questioned and interrogated about what is intuitively felt to be the core of her or his subjectivity (Balint, 1979). Alas, the aesthetic conflict can only be resolved by developing the capacity for transitionality, and not by forcefully securing an answer. And more so than in primary relationships, in adult relationships, attempts at control, especially when accompanied by blunt disrespect for the other's boundaries, are likely to cause the "enigmatic" partner to withdraw, further disrupting emotional regulation in the couple.

Object relations and the couple

Clinicians in the field of psychoanalytic couple therapy seek to understand the shared unconscious mechanisms that operate in a long-term couple relationship. In conflictual relationships, one can often track pervasive dynamics of projection and projective identification. Various aspects of the self and of one's internal objects are split off and assigned to the partner, leading to a pathological process of polarization between the partners. The projecting partner treats the other as if the other were an unwanted part of the self, and the receiver of the projection feels coerced into a role she or he experiences as alien (Klein, 1947; Bion, 2013; Scharff & Scharff, 1991).

Collusion is a specific pathological mechanism in long-term relationships, where both partners' unconscious representations are split off and projected onto the other, while the receiver of the projections identifies with it (Dicks, 1967; Willi, 1982). Couples where one or both partners identify as bisexual or practice bisexuality may collude in an unconscious dynamic related to the "superego" function of the couple. Kernberg (1993) suggests that couples sometimes create a "shared superego" as an unconscious intersubjective system. The more severe the superego pathology of one or both partners, the more restrictive the couple superego functions, leading to jointly agreed-upon narrow definitions of what is tolerable.

As bisexual practice is subject to social condemnation, a partner's desire to explore bisexuality can trigger an identification with a forbidding and punitive aspect of a parental object, which functions as an archaic superego, aggressively punishing forbidden urges and inducing shame, guilt, and/or anxiety. For example, Sara saw Jacob's homosexual curiosity as a destructive threat to their boundaries and social status as a couple, as well as a personal attack on her. In fact, she was identifying with both her own and Jacob's persecutory superego functions and expressing fear, shame and biphobia on both their behalf. As Jacob first mentioned his attraction to men, feeling guilty and ashamed, he projected onto Sara his expectation to be punished, with which Sara colluded in the extreme. The unconscious shared superego function of this couple could not allow such a scandalous deviation from their conservative upbringing and values.

When conditions are favorable, the mutually regulated mechanism of the couple's superego function may enable a healing process, in which the partners may be able to help each other overcome the restrictions of their harsh archaic superegos. Colman (2014) describes the couple's shared container as a system of object relating challenged by the tensions between oneness and separation, identification and otherness. Bisexuality is a signifier of otherness and is seen by the heteronormative "superego" as a threat. Bisexual people and their partners need to become aware of the social pressures to reject bisexuality and learn to consciously dialogue with their personal superego contents that make them vulnerable to such pressures. In therapy, a container may be created within which the partners can experience containing one another and tolerating each other's otherness. The relationship can thereby become a vehicle of healing from self-condemnation and anxiety (Hewison, 2014).

Multiple self, couple relationship and bisexuality

Relational psychoanalytic theorists have developed a conception of the self as multiple and fluid (Bromberg, 2001, 1996; Mitchell, 1991, 1988). According to this view, a stable unitary self is an adaptive illusion, whose function is to maintain a sense of unity over time. No stable or central "self" can be found anywhere in the brain, body or mind; subjective experience and manifestations of self in relational contexts are seen as streams of shifting, and often co-existing, self-other configurations originating at different developmental stages, in relationships with various others. Harris coined the term "soft assembly" to describe the impermanent and idiosyncratic nature of self-assemblages (Harris, 2009). Adaptive functioning requires some measure of integration in the self, but excessive integration results in rigidified personality and the inability to own important aspects of oneself.

The multiple-self model relies on a revised understanding of dissociation. Bromberg expanded the scope of this concept far beyond its traditional understanding as a posttraumatic defense mechanism, situating it as a primary organizing principle of the personality, which makes it possible for incongruous self-aspects to all be part of the individual's affective and behavioral repertoire (Bromberg, 2001). The normal functions and healthy "voluntary" uses of dissociation include the possibility of affective immersion in one self-aspect, with no intrusions from others, in order to fully experience enjoyment or play, and the freedom to express different aspects of the self in different social-relational contexts (Bromberg, 2001; Goldman, 2016; Howell & Itzkowitz, 2016). These functions of dissociation markedly differ from its defensive function of keeping outside the awareness memories of painful traumatic experiences — yet, as with other psychological functions spanning unconscious and unsymbolized aspects of self-experience, some overlap between the healthier and the pathological uses is unavoidable.

The multiple-self model allows for acknowledging aspects of the partners' selves that cannot be encountered or known in any direct, uncontroversial way. In fact, the conception of the self as softly assembled of multiple incongruous self-aspects makes for a friendly way to gently introduce to the contemporary couple the idea of the dynamic unconscious. This model normalizes the individual's inability to know oneself, or the other, fully. Learning to tolerate unknowability may reduce the impulse to withdraw or become violent in the face of one's partner's enigmatic qualities.

Biphobia abounds in our society in part because bisexuals make it difficult to neatly categorize people based on their identity or to predict their behavior. Bisexual people bear the burden of embodying and representing much of what is perceived as unclean and improper about sexuality — its excesses (hypersexuality, non-monogamy), its fluidity and uncertainty, its non-goal-directedness (immaturity, playfulness, polymorphous perversity), its femininity (confusion, indecision, multiplicity) and its stench (Charles, 2002; Dimen, 2003; Rapoport, 2019). In couples, partners' bisexual identities and practices produce a sense of disquiet, and at times, evoke abjection affects, including hatred and disgust (Oliver, 2004). Often, *dissociative collusion* becomes the couple's way to deal with these uncomfortable affects.

Bisexual people and their partners 97

It can be understood as an unconscious cooperation to avoid intimidating aspects of life, feelings, thoughts or behaviors (Kleiner-Paz & Nasim, 2020). The couple's helplessness and distress in the face of bisexuality can reveal an unconscious relationship contract according to which, only that which is predictable and knowable can be "allowed" in. Once dissociative collusion is eased, bisexuality can become a doorway through which otherness can be apprehended and, eventually, inspire curiosity, awe and aesthetic enjoyment.

Whose desire matters? Dani and Ayala

Dani and Ayala, a couple in their late 30s, contacted me (E.R.) requesting help managing persistent tensions in their relationship. It was important to them, they stated, that the therapist be experienced in working with "sexually diverse, non-normative" couples. They had been dating for close to three years. Within this time period, they had broken up five times. Four out of the five breakups were initiated by Dani, but the time before last, it was Ayala who said she could not take it anymore. She came back after a few days, unlike Dani, who would typically let weeks pass by before suggesting getting back together.

Before I knew much else about their relationship, the story of their repeated separations already pointed me in a particular direction. Dani and Ayala seemed to have some self-aspects that they were only able to access while apart from one another. Perpetually left outside the relationship, these dissociated self-aspects (his indecisiveness? her rage?) kept returning to haunt them. Whatever it was that they enacted by breaking up and spending time apart was, I assumed, uncontainable for them as a couple. They needed help expanding their shared emotional container.

Ayala enjoyed a successful career as an academic but felt pessimistic about her ability to build a satisfying personal life for herself. She was not sure what she wanted, she confessed. She knew she would feel like a failure if she never had children, and imagined that she could make a pretty good mother, but she did not feel ready. Recently she had had some eggs extracted and frozen so as to maintain the possibility of getting pregnant later in life. The partners were also discussing among them the possibility of creating, and freezing, some embryos, but were not able to reach a conclusion about the meaning of this act — would this mean they would later raise shared children? Would they be parenting partners even if the romantic relationship between them ended? Or was Dani acting as a donor for Ayala? What made this matter all the more difficult to think about was that Dani knew — despite Ayala's protestations that he did not owe her anything unless he formally committed — that he would feel obligated to act as the father even if he never chose to commit to the relationship or to parenting.

Dani, a co-founder of a small hi-tech company, was not sure Ayala was the right life partner for him. He was sexually attracted to men, something all his friends knew. He would participate in gay pride marches and sometimes went to work wearing rainbow-colored t-shirts or pink lacquer, to make public his affiliation with the gay community. He regularly met other men for sex and occasionally dated some for a week or two — but he had given up, he said, on the idea of a primary relationship with a man. He had spent many years in intensive individual therapy trying to figure it all out, and this was the understanding that he gradually reached. He was not disinterested in women — in fact, some women sexually excited him. Those tended to be women who were a bit vulgar, hypersexual and crude in their manners. Ayala, who was quite the opposite, knew all about these dilemmas. She even knew that Dani had contemplated gender transition. He had additionally learned in his individual therapy that he had a hard time integrating sex and intimacy. He was not sure what to do with all this self-knowledge, however. Was he to commit to being in a primary relationship with Ayala, and hope that his doubts would go away gradually? He had been trying that for three years — wasn't this enough? Or, should he keep trying to find someone, of one or another gender, who was more his type? Yet he felt that no one could understand him as well, or love him as deeply and unconditionally, as Ayala did.

Ayala seconded these feelings. She both understood Dani and felt understood by him. He had a far greater emotional intelligence, she added, than the other men she had dated. She felt that he alone managed to draw her out of her defensive withdrawals, her intellectual pursuits, which kept her interested and occupied but all the while served as means of escape. She cherished the genuineness of their connection and admired his inner freedom and insistence on living authentically. Her feelings about their non-monogamous lifestyle were mixed, however. She understood Dani's versatile attractions and felt relieved on some level that he had his own life, leaving her plenty of space. But she would probably not have chosen non-monogamy herself.

Dani had been raised on a kibbutz, the third in the family of four children. His youngest brother was born a year after him, and when he was four, the mother went back to work full time. His parents were distant and, in his mind, emotionally handicapped. As a child, he was angry and moody. As a young adult, he had used recreational drugs. After graduating high school, Dani came out as gay to his family but even after coming out, he continued to date girls. All his siblings were married with children.

Ayala was born and raised in Tel Aviv. She was an only child. Her father, an army pilot, had been killed when she was three. She had no memory of him. Her mother had another partner after her husband's death, eventually separating from him when Ayala was eight. She described her mother as loving and generous but overprotective and intrusive in ways that annoyed Ayala. Before meeting Dani, Ayala was in a long and stable marriage-track relationship, which she had experienced as superficial and boring, and

Bisexual people and their partners   99

eventually ended. She had been depressed a number of times, in high school and college.

I found myself, in that initial session, feeling confused and slightly annoyed. What was ailing this couple? Why did Ayala stick with Dani, despite the hurtful things he said about his lack of attraction to her and the many times that he had left her? Was she avoidant, withdrawing when her needs were not being met, instead of demanding their fulfillment? Was it beneficial for Dani to be in this relationship? Did either of them have a choice about staying or leaving, or were they hopelessly stuck in their "I can't live with you and I can't live without you" limbo? How central was Dani's struggle with his sexual identity — was this what his commitment difficulties were all about, or was it more of an excuse? What did it mean that they were able to communicate with each other honestly and articulately — yet at the same time, the merger persisted, with neither one of them capable of reaching a decision and enforcing his or her own will? What did they need from me?

After a short while, I realized that I was already letting in the enormous complexity, and indeterminacy, that defined (or, perhaps, undefined) their relationship. The rules of engagement were not clear, for better or worse, and I felt annoyed because my role, too, had not been spelled out for me.

In the second session, a rift occurred. Ayala was sulky at the beginning and was not eager to talk. When I suggested that her facial expressions were saying a great deal even when she was silent, and encouraged her to try using words, she expressed hurt and anger towards Dani, who had chosen to schedule a sexual encounter with a casual partner on an evening that had been designated as their "time together". Dani did not try hard to disguise his anger. He felt guilty, he said, but he did not really believe that he was guilty. His meeting a guy that evening was something that Ayala had knowingly agreed to, and she had no right to guilt-trip him after the fact. In general, the non-monogamous structure of the relationship was consensual, he insisted. From his point of view, he said, addressing me, and avoiding looking at Ayala, that was not the issue. The real question was — was she the right partner for him or not?

"You're both very angry now", I said. "You are angry because there is conflict. You (addressing Ayala) would like for Dani to want to spend his Saturday nights with you and not with his fuck buddies. You, Dani, would like to be the one who decides whether or not the relationship continues. At least, when you're fighting, each of you assumes one position — one, and not a dozen. The question is, how do you each decide which position to assume?"

Both were silent for a moment. Dani said, "I think you're saying that my not being sure if I want to be in this relationship is something I do in reaction to something she does... that I want to feel that it's my own thing, but it's not. I don't know. I still experience it as my own dilemma, that's independent of anything she says or does". Ayala said, "I don't know why I choose to act hurt. He is right — I am choosing to be with him, and I am realistic that it cannot be monogamous with him. Maybe I am just acting like my mother would — a martyr, a woman who can complain but takes it for granted that she is not going to get what she needs — and so complaining, or blaming, is part of the acceptance. I don't know why I do this. I don't like it".

As I explore with Ayala the meanings of her attraction to Dani, she articulates her perception of him as liberated and self-directed. His bisexual sexual expression means, to her, that he is a person who is able to desire and enjoy himself as a free agent. Gradually, she learns that by being with him, she is trying to gain access to her own personal freedom and authenticity — properties that she so admires in Dani, yet simultaneously denies herself. Why is this not happening for her, she wonders, why does she find herself acting like a martyr instead? It is too frightening for her to inhabit the "liberated" pole of the self-other configuration in which one person is free and the other attached, relationship-oriented and self-sacrificing. If she were to allow herself to identify with her father — the pilot who took off and crossed the skies — the guilt she already feels in relation to her mother would become even more severe. Ayala cannot yet, I suggest, imagine relational freedom — in practice, she is giving up on some of her most basic relational needs, such as her need for safety. Fearing abandonment and not ready to face her vulnerable self-aspects as the child multiply abandoned by a father who died, a mother who succumbed to grief, and a step-parent who disappeared, she finds herself trying to prevent Dani's feared abandonment of her, by angrily blaming and guilt-tripping him. She is trapped in a version of the aesthetic conflict, magnetized to the beauty of Dani's freedom, yet all the while hating him for being free. She is deeply conflicted about her wish to tie him to herself. Her clinginess and thinly veiled attempts at control confirm Dani's expectation, based in his self-other configurations, that committing to a partner will inevitably limit his freedom.

I wonder out loud if Ayala is clinging to Dani on behalf of her own abandoned-child, or because she is caught up in her identification with the punitive, limiting super-ego function that Dani is projecting onto her? Ayala anxiously rejects the idea that she may be performing a super-ego function for Dani. She seems to experience this idea as dangerously at odds with her politically progressive aspiration to be a supportive partner for her LGBT boyfriend.

A discussion ensues about Ayala's perception of her mother's lack of sexual and emotional satisfaction as a widowed, single woman. I suggest that her need to ensure that Dani is sexually fulfilled in his secondary relationships may be related to her guilt for her mother's lack of personal fulfillment. We identify her guilty self-aspect, one that wishes to compensate the other by setting him free, at the expense of her ability to accept her own needs and demand their fulfillment. As she gets acquainted with this self-aspect, Ayala learns to dialogue with it, instead of anxiously compensating for her "badness" by enacting her ideal of a good LGBT-supportive partner, at the expense of her own authenticity.

Dani, meanwhile, is profoundly conflicted about his sexuality. He understands rationally that it is OK to be bisexual but emotionally, feels that his needs are too complex, and simultaneously feels tormented by his guilt about the suffering he inflicts on Ayala. He admits that he felt the same way towards his parents — that he was a bad, difficult child for them, that his different sexuality was an excessive burden for the emotionally handicapped parents who had other children to look after. Ayala is, indeed, letting him know that she is suffering, confirming his worst fears. I suggest that they have jointly appointed Ayala to be a prosecutor: "There is simply too much guilt that the two of you are jointly carrying, for either of you or your relationship to have a degree of freedom that you both desire. You don't deserve to be playful, or for your needs to be met. Rather, you deserve to be punished, and you had better sacrifice all your vital needs — only then will you be acquitted". Both Dani and Ayala laugh at my intentionally hyperbolized pronouncement. By playfully taking on the prosecutor function, I have invited both partners to acknowledge and engage with their self-aspects as both the "bad child" needing too much from the parent and the "starved healthy child", whose needs are healthy and legitimate even if they cannot be met by the caregiver.

Dani is pessimistic about the possibility of both his sexual and emotional needs being met. He knows he needs Ayala's love and believes he can only enjoy it if he sacrifices his sexual freedom. His lost-and-needy-little-boy self-aspect assumes that he has to adjust to a mother who has no ability to adjust to him, while his angry-self-sufficient-boy self-aspect has given up on the hope of ever being loved and resolved to make do without needing anyone.

While these partners are younger and politically progressive people, city dwellers who have been exposed to post-modern ideas about sexuality, they are nonetheless trapped in the patriarchal model of relating, according to which only one of the partners can be a desiring subject, while the other is resigned to being an object (Benjamin, 1998, 1988). Overwhelmed by the complexity of their lives, they attempt to evade the unbearable feelings of rage, pain and grief and to organize their experiences by assuming stereotypical gender roles. They gravitate, within their couple relationship, towards simple, binary positions, enacting that which is socially and familially known, in pursuit of simplicity: a free, sexual man who won't be tied down and a woman who has no choice but to accept him as he is — or, alternatively, a family man restraining his sexual impulses to please a woman, whose self-fulfillment presumably rests on stable family life.

Bisexuality, for both, symbolizes the desired freedom and agency, while also representing a threat associated with the otherness of their unacknowledged needs and desires. This couple needs to deal with affective and cognitive challenges that exceed the partners' processing capacities and produce overwhelm. The various defensive solutions they tried before pursuing couples therapy — including adopting stereotypical roles and temporarily separating at times of crises — made matters worse. They need the therapist to help them expand their shared emotional container, so that the formerly uncontainable, complex and excessive relational situation may be partially contained. Facing bisexuality requires the partners to confront their various self-aspects and encounter each other as complex multi-faceted subjects, beyond what they have projected onto each other and beyond the stereotypical roles that society assigns to men and women. Through intersubjective dialogue, both eventually develop their capacities to face complexity and to voice their own emergent desires and needs, instead of reacting to their guilt or unreflectively identifying with one another's projections.

Conclusion

Bisexual identity marks its bearers as unpredictable both in the public discourse and in the privacy of couple relationships. In couple relationships, grappling with bisexuality often involves facing severe anxieties that arise when the needs for certainty and simplicity are not met. Mutual defensive enactments like distancing, projections and unconscious collusions between partners are common reactions to such anxieties. We term this relational situation "the uncontainable" and suggest that couple therapists working with bisexual people learn to recognize the complexity and potential explosiveness of these dynamics. Bisexuality as a practice, fantasy, self-identity or ideation can have unique conscious and unconscious meanings for each partner. Those need to be explored and owned. Couples faced with the uncontainable relational situation need the therapist's help in processing relational meanings, softening shared superego prohibitions on non-normative choices and creating conditions for an ongoing intersubjective dialogue about emergent desires, vulnerabilities, wishes and needs. A therapeutic process of this kind can facilitate expansion in both the partners' individual selves and in their shared emotional container function as a couple.

References

Ault, A. (1996). Ambiguous identity in an unambiguous sex/gender structure. *The Sociological Quarterly, 37(3)*:449–463.

Balint, M. (1979). *The Basic Fault: Therapeutic Aspects of Regression.* London/ New York: Tavistock Publications.

Benjamin, J. (1988). *The Bonds of Love: Psychoanalysis, Feminism and the Problem of Domination.* New York: Pantheon.

Benjamin, J. (1998). *Shadow of the Other: Intersubjectivity and Gender in Psychoanalysis.* New York: Routledge.

Bion, W. R. (2013). Attacks on Linking. *The Psychoanalytic Quarterly*, 82(2):285–300.
Bordieu, P. (2002). *Masculine Domination*. Trans. by R. Nice. Stanford. CA: Stanford University Press.
Bromberg, P. (1996). Standing in the spaces: the multiplicity of self and the psychoanalytic relationship. *Contemporary Psychoanalysis*, 32:509–535.
Bromberg, P. (2001). *Standing in the Spaces: Essays on Clinical Process, Trauma and Dissociation*. London and New York: Routledge.
Charles, M. (2002). Monogamy and its discontents: on winning the Oedipal war. *American Journal of Psychoanalysis*, 62(2):119–143.
Chater, N. (1997). Simplicity and the mind. *Psychologist*, 10(11):495–498.
Chater N.,& Vitányi P. (2003). Simplicity: a unifying principle in cognitive science. *Trends in Cognitive Sciences*, 7(1):19–22.
Colman, W. (2014). The intolerable other: the difficulty of becoming a couple. *Couple and Family Psychoanalysis*, 4(1):22–41.
Connell, R. W. (1995). *Masculinities*. Cambridge, UK: Polity Press.
Daumer, E. D. (1992). Queer ethics; or, the challenge of bisexuality to lesbian ethics. *Hypatia: A Journal of Feminist Philosophy*, 7(4), 91–105.
Dimen, M. (1991). Deconstructing difference: Gender, splitting and transitional space. *Psychoanalytic Dialogues*, 1:335–352.
Dimen, M. (2003). *Sexuality, Intimacy, Power (Relational Perspectives Book Series)*. New York/London: Routledge.
Dicks, H. V. (1967). *Marital Tensions*. London: Routledge & Kegan Paul.
Feldman, J. (2016). The simplicity principle in perception and cognition. *Review of Cognitive Science*, 7(5):330–340.
Freud, S., & Strachey, J. E. (1963). Theories of Development and Regression—Etiology. *The Standard Edition of the Complete Psychological Works of Sigmund Freud, Volume XVI (1916-1917): Introductory Lectures on Psychoanalysis (Part III)*, i–vi. London: The Hogarth Press and the Institute of Psychoanalysis.
Freud, S., & Strachey, J. E. (1964). Notes upon a Case of Obsessional Neurosis (1909). *The Standard Edition of the Complete Psychological Works of Sigmund Freud III*. London: The Hogarth Press and the Institute of Psychoanalysis.
Garber, M. (1996). *Vice Versa: Bisexuality and the Eroticism of Everyday Life*. New York: Touchstone.
Goldman, D. (2016). "A queer kind of truth": Winnicott and the uses of dissociation. In: Howell, E., & Itzkowitz, S. (Eds.). *The Dissociative Mind in Psychoanalysis: Understanding and Working with Trauma*, pp. 97–107. New York: Routledge.
Harris, A. (2009). *Gender as soft assembly*. New York: Routledge, Taylor and Francis.
Hewison, D. (2014). Shared unconscious phantasy in couples. In: Scharff, D., & Scharff, J. S. (Eds.). *Psychoanalytic Couple Therapy*, pp. 25–34. London: Karnac.
Howell, E., & Itzkowitz, S. (Eds.). (2016). *The Dissociative Mind in Psychoanalysis: Understanding and Working with Trauma*. London/New York: Routledge.
Kernberg, Otto F. (1993). The couple's constructive and destructive superego functions. *Journal of the American Psychoanalytic Association*, 41:653–677.
Klein, M. (1947). *Envy and Gratitude and Other Works, 1946-1963*. UK: Vintage.
Kleiner-Paz, I. & Nasim, R. (2020). Dissociative collusion: reconnecting clients with histories of trauma in couple therapy. *Family Process*, X:1–10.
Kuhar, R., & Paternotte, D. (Eds.). (2017). *Anti-gender campaigns in Europe: Mobilizations against equality*. London: Rowman & Littlefield.

Lacan, J. (1992). The Seminar of Jacques Lacan: Book VII. *The Ethics of Psychoanalysis (1959-1960)*, *ed.* Miller, J.-A., transl. Porter,D. New York: Norton.

Meltzer, D. (1987) On Aesthetic Reciprocity. *Journal of Child Psychotherapy*, 13:3–14.

Meltzer, D., & Williams, M. H. (1988). *The Apprehension of Beauty: The Role of Aesthetic Conflict in Development, Art, and Violence*. London: Karnac.

Mitchell, S. A. (1988). *Relational Concepts in Psychoanalysis*. Harvard, MA: Harvard University Press.

Mitchell, S. A. (1991). Contemporary perspectives on self: toward an integration. *Psychoanalytic Dialogues*, *1(2)*:121–147.

Mukamel, M. (2018). The Bisexual Container. Lecture given on December 26th, 2018 in Tel Aviv, as part of the lecture series "Gender and Sexuality from Relational Standpoints" produced by the Israeli Forum of Relational Psychoanalysis and Psychotherapy.

Oliver, K. (2004). *The Colonization of Psychic Space: A Psychoanalytic Social Theory of Oppression*. University of Minnesota.

Peirce, C. G. (1955). *Philosophical Writings of Peirce*. New York: Dover Publication.

Rapoport, E. (2010). Bisexuality: the undead (m)other of psychoanalysis. *Psychoanalysis, Culture, & Society*, *15(1)*:70–83.

Rapoport, E. (2019). *From Psychoanalytic Bisexuality to Bisexual Psychoanalysis: Desiring in the Real*. London/New York: Routledge.

Scharff, D. E., & Scharff, J. S. (1991). *Object Relations Couple Therapy*. New York: Jason Aronson Book.

Struhl, Paula R. (1975). Peirce's Defense of the Scientific Method. *Journal of the History of Philosophy*, *13(4)*:481–490.

Willi, J. (1982). *Couples in Collusion*. Lanham, MD: Jason Aronson Inc.

Wittgenstein, L., & Anscombe, G. E. M. (1969). On certainty (Vol. 174). Oxford: Blackwell.

Chapter 7

Queer relationships: unmapped intimacies

Iggy Robinson and Alice Kentridge

> Heard a gay therapist on a talk show, explaining how gay men are "searchings" who search all the time, all their lives. That even with a monogamous relationship, they search for new ways of defining relationship because there are no role models, as in the het scene. I like the idea of being a "searcher". We are always searching — we see many things and absorb much and look for more.
>
> *The diaries of Lou Sullivan*

Introduction

As queer therapists, our clinical work (and our lives) hold a range of relationship constellations: open, polyamorous, monogamous couples, couples where one or more partners are trans, partnerships of both same and opposite sex where gender expression and sexuality are multi-layered and in flux. These are relationships that move from friendships to lovers and back again, where community and "queer family" are formed but not fixed, and where intimacy seeps across boundaries and pools around a range of experiences. Here, we explore ways of thinking about and supporting these relationships as they unfold or expand in unexpected ways.

This chapter is an invitation to embrace the playfulness and creativity of stepping into unfamiliar territories, while being aware of the anxieties that walking this uncertain ground can produce in both therapist and client. To begin, we turn to queer theory for what it provokes, rather than what it clarifies. We also draw on our personal experiences, as well as conversations with clients and interviews with members of our communities, to explore how the idea of queerness serves in structuring identity and shaping relationships. In that spirit, the quotes we use are an attempt to bring an evolving conversation into the text. Presented without context or biography, we invite the reader to eavesdrop at an imagined house party where friends, lovers, colleagues, queer theorists and psychoanalysts mingle, debate or hook up in corners.

We bring a focus on relationships that "search" beyond the borders of conventional relationship models, because we see this variety of relationships and queer negotiations of intimacy in our work, because we live them in our partnerships, and because they are so easily erased by the clear-cut categories that exist around us. What is beyond the nuclear or biological family, or the long-term monogamous relationship? We know that when psychotherapy continues to erase the variety of queer relationships, or relates to them only through existing theoretical paradigms, it does harm to those forging relationships, families, and communities on this margin, and misses out on the richness queer relating has to offer.

Who is in the room?

What do we mean by the term queer, and what do "queer relationships" look like? We would like to set off on solid footing, to provide some clear definitions, some typical examples — but the word resists, contradicts, overflows. To take Eve Kosofsky Sedgwick's famous description: "Queer is a continuing moment, movement, motive-recurrent, eddying, *troublant*" (1993, p. xii). The evasive, liquid quality of queerness is invoked in queer theory, the academic tradition that emerged in the 1990s to examine the radical potential of sexuality and gender on the margins.

In this chapter, we are in a world of identity and relationships in flux, on the move, unsettling, provoking, and evolving. Rather than attempting to fix and clarify, we are invited by our queer clients and our queer community to swim in this water and feel the pull of conflicting currents. To find a psychoanalytic notion that similarly evades and overwhelms, perhaps we can think of Freud's description of "the dream's navel", "the tangle of dream-thoughts which cannot be unraveled... the spot where it reaches down into the unknown" (1900, p. 525). Queerness might be seen as another disappearing centre. As when working with a dream, queerness offers a tangle of meanings that slip away the more we try to look at it directly. So instead, we will look at it askance, in fragments.

> *All my life I was told that I can't have the other side at all, and I have these specific roles to fulfil. Now I've been able to get past those binaries I was caught in. I'm so happy that I didn't let my sexual trauma, all the bad things that have happened to me, define me. That is queerness for me — that no one can actually define queerness and say this is what it should look like or sound like. It allows play, and that play has saved my life.*

As well as articulating an individual identity, it is helpful to think about how queerness asserts a set of connections with others on a critical margin. For some, "queerness" might offer connections to parts of their identity that are othered or attacked, linking up with experiences around race, class, or ability.

I feel like I understand my queerness not just in terms of sexuality but also in terms of just being strange, in my body. Being dyspraxic, I'm quite awkward in my body and I think that ties into not feeling I can perform butchness or femininity in a particular way. Another aspect is being mixed race, growing up not being part of a black community, being white but not white. There were lots of ways that I felt outside of things, not fitting in this world, growing up.

Queer theory shifts us from thinking about being queer as something one *is* (in the way being gay, bisexual or lesbian might function as a label of identity) to a verb, something that is *done to* stable categories or relationships when the certainty around them is unsettled. Queer theorist David Halperin (1995, p. 112) encourages us to "conceptualize queer identity as an identity in a state of becoming rather than as the referent for an actually existing form of life... preserving queerness as a resistant relation rather than as an oppositional substance".

At their core, queer traditions, both academic and activist, hold a deep suspicion of the purity of categories, labels, and binaries. In her influential work *Gender Trouble*, Judith Butler (1990) makes clear how the gender binary, while socially constructed, sets out rules and labels that make us "intelligible" to ourselves and others; and that to function outside of these categories comes at a cost, exposing people to violence, censure, or invisibility.

To expand Butler's thinking to a queer perspective on relationships requires us to question the foundational binaries we use to make sense of the messy variety of human intimacy and connection. Binaries such as friend/lover, sexual/platonic, casual/long-term, or family/community. This chapter looks at some of those more "unintelligible" relationships that disturb these binaries. Here, the language of "queerness" might be used to assert an expanded set of sexual practices, relationship structures or ways of expressing or subverting gender.

What's at stake in queer relationships?

Many of our clients, regardless of their sexual or gender identifications, will find themselves falling outside of what Gayle Rubin (1984) termed the "charmed circle" of socially sanctioned sexualities deemed "good, normal and natural", and will consequently experience varying degrees of marginalisation, social, legal and medical ostracism, and cultural erasure. The function of societal prejudices as a defence against the anxieties provoked by difference has been richly explored in psychoanalytic literature, and there is much to be said about how these dynamics play out in reactions to sexual and gender diversity. Here, we invite reflection on the specific anxieties that are provoked by the destabilizing, *troublant* qualities of queerness, and how those anxieties impact queer relationships.

The violence of mainstream heteronormative and gender-normative scripts are inevitably internalised by many lesbian, gay, bisexual, transgender, and queer (LGBTQ+) people, creating an obstacle to intimacy and authentic relating. This structural violence particularly excludes those unable, or unwilling, to "fit the mould"; those whose queerness stands for the unnameable, the boundary-crossing, for that which defies familiar categorisations.

> *So many times, I've been called an 'it' and a 'thing', treated as subhuman by gay men for showing femininity, for something as small as wearing a necklace. Once I invited a man to meet me at a cocktail bar, instead of the grimy pub he'd suggested. He replied, "I'm not that kind of gay", and immediately blocked me.*

This all-too-commonplace experience suggests a fear of being somehow contaminated by proximity, or intimacy, with a more fluid identity — an anxiety that one's own more normative identity may be destabilized by an encounter with one who exists outside those norms. This fear leads R. D. Hinshelwood (2017, p. 204) to protest that "society could permit fluid sexualities, rather than oblige people to be more fluid". This belief that queer people are policing and oppressing normative sexualities is a startling inversion of the reality of marginalisation and violence to which queer people are subject.

When identities, and relationship structures, are queered, there may be a disquieting sense of loss — the loss of a history to bolster or legitimise us; the loss of a script for the future; the loss of a comforting, and often hard-won, category to place ourselves within. There are many ways this loss of a stable frame might play out in relationships. When we enter into a non-monogamous relationship, how might this uproot our expectations for the future path that our relationships will follow? When a partner comes out as trans, how might this destabilize our ideas about our own sexual orientation? If the identity of our relationship changes, how might that impact our sense of belonging to, and our acceptance by, a particular community?

> *Sometimes women would start dating me with an expectation that I was butch, and I'd find myself trying to fit into that mould that wasn't really me. It felt to me like there was an attempt to replicate an idea of lesbian culture, to create a sense of continuity, and fit each other into that. Which is understandable — I think people just feel much more secure when they have a script they can follow. It's much more scary to just explore what your desires are, who you are, without all of that.*

Of course, as therapists we also depend on certain "scripts" and theoretical frameworks to ground ourselves in the therapeutic relationship. These frameworks lend us confidence that we can work competently and safely.

The therapist may find their anxieties roused when working with clients whose gender identities, relationship styles, or sexual practices appear to challenge foundational psychoanalytic underpinnings. Some analysts have defended themselves against this perceived threat to the framework by pathologising and objectifying non-normative genders and sexualities as narcissistic, paranoid, fetishistic, incapable of mourning, infantile, or psychotic (see Bergeret 2002, Green 1973, Wiederman 1962, Withers 2015). Experiences of oppression can be similarly disavowed by this defensive manoeuvre — for example, when trans and gender non-conforming people's accounts of society's unease with their appearances are interpreted by therapists as paranoid or psychotic projections (as in Lemma 2012 and Quinodoz 1998).

This defensive response is also marshalled against the more abstract threat of queer theory, leading to the unproductive standoff in which "feeling attacked, perhaps outnumbered, the analyst perceives difference through an imaginary schema that frames the queer and the psychoanalytic as enemies" (Dean 2017, p. 355). We suggest that if therapists are able, instead, to sit with and inquire into the anxieties raised in them by their queer clients, we might fruitfully expand our psychoanalytic frameworks further beyond the strictures of their white, heteronormative and gender-normative twentieth-century foundations.

At the other end of the spectrum are therapists whose defence against the anxieties of not-knowing, and the fear of "not knowing enough" to work with the queer client, is to shut down curiosity and uncertainty with flattening affirmation. While surely preferable to pathology, this denies queer clients access to the full richness of the psychoanalytic encounter.

> *One of the things I wanted to be able to explore in therapy was my own complicated feelings around masculinity, and therapists have reacted to that by just trying to "support my gender" in a very simplistic way. My most recent therapist told me, "you're a proud, able trans man" — well firstly that's not my gender, but there are so many things about that statement that felt wrong. I think he was trying to be reassuring, but it felt like he was shutting me down, and really not seeing me.*

Such reductive affirmations may also miss the opportunity to explore the complex effects of prejudices (such as homophobia, transphobia, whorephobia, and misogyny), inevitably internalised by both therapist and client, on the therapeutic relationship.

Both the pathologising and "reassuring" responses to queerness point to an impulse to defend against its destabilising qualities by grasping more desperately for certainties. The predomination of paradox, ambiguity, fluidity and transition in queer relationships invites us to remember the crucial value of the therapist's ability to sit with not-knowing. Perhaps here more than ever, we hold in mind Bion's famous invocation of Keats' striving for "negative capability" which celebrates the psychoanalytic capacity for "being in uncertainties, Mysteries, doubts, without any irritable reaching after fact and reason" (Keats 1970, p. 43).

In "Crossing Over", Melanie Suchet (2020) illuminates both the anxieties that may be roused, and the possibilities that can open up in the therapeutic relationship, when we allow ourselves to really sit with our psychoanalytic not-knowing around queer identities and ways of being. At the start of the analysis, Suchet and her client share a lesbian identity; Suchet tracks their relationship's turbulent journey from this common ground into "unfamiliar territory" as her analysand, Raphael, moves towards a new identity and embodiment as a trans man. Bion (1980) offers guidance for the exploration of such unknown places when he commands:

> *Discard your memory; discard the future tense of your desire; forget them both, both what you know and what you want, to leave space for a new idea. A thought, an idea unclaimed, may be floating around the room in search of a home (1980, p. 11).*

With refreshing humility, Suchet maps the doubts, resistance, and ultimate transition she undergoes through her work with Raphael. At first, she struggles to discard her own desires for her client's body, her impulse to shape his identity in a direction that is comfortable for her. As their work nears its end, she reflects:

> *I have discovered that my psychoanalytic training had not prepared me for the kind of relationship to a body that Raphael has. I am aware of a need to revise our theories […] I start to allow myself more space to think openly, more fluidity in myself (2020, p. 229).*

Once Suchet has reached this space of holding her theory more loosely, of opening up to internal fluidity, she is able to come into contact with the personal anxieties stirred in her by Raphael's changing body and gender expression:

> *Now that I have made large conceptual leaps in understanding his need to transition, I find that what is asked of me in the room as he begins his transformation is a different process altogether. If intersubjectivity is an embodied process (Reis, 2009), a way of knowing each other through our bodies, how will his changing body affect my own? Perhaps I am afraid that his transitioning will rock my own gender stability. Will it open options I have never contemplated? Do I fear opening up new realms of possibility? (2020, p. 229).*

This illuminating account of their therapeutic relationship in transition echoes a familiar experience in queer romantic relationships, in which one partner's dis-identification from a fixed role or identity can release the relationship from its established dynamic, and unsettle our own internal model of self-in-relation. Can we mourn such changes in ways that allow us to open up to new potentialities? What might we discover when we come into intimate contact with identities that we experience as destabilising — with clients, with friends, with lovers, who implore us to "leave space for a new idea"?

> *The more that I've become open to, and intimate with, other people's trans identities, gender creativity, and sexual fluidity, the more I've let go of my fixed ideas about my own gender and sexuality. Now I see my identities not as the final destination or ultimate "truth" about me, but as things that feel true right now — in this or that relationship, or social context, or phase of my life. There has been a feeling of unravelling which is freeing, while also being a kind of loss. If we want to be truly open to the queerness of others' identities, I think we have to be open to the potential for our own identity to shift, to come undone — and to be curious about that potential.*

Stepping sideways

In many ways, queerness opens things up — from a line to a field, from a couple to a community, from a well-trodden path to a network or maze of possible routes. In Ron Britton's (2004) exploration of Oedipal development, he contrasts the blinkered frustration of the dyadic — a to-and-fro relation which can only "move along a single line and meet at a single point", fixing our roles and restricting our knowledge — to the opening up of perspective and possibility that occurs through lateral movement in a linked-up, triangular space (2004, pp. 47–50). When we can "step sideways" into new places in our minds, we can access our curiosity about our identities and our relations to others.

The oppositional dichotomy of identity and desire that underpins developmental psychoanalytic models of sexuality is one that pervades our cultural consciousness — shorthanded by the equation that "opposites attract" (Kuzniar 2017). This equation is reliant on a view of our gender identities and the vectors of our desire as fixed and unchanging.

> *At the beginning of a relationship, someone will often want me to be "the boy", and to top, and then I don't always feel entitled to ask for what I want sexually. And it can take longer for me to open up emotionally, which also makes me seem like "the boy". When I've been fitted into that box of being "the boyfriend", it's quite hard to get out of it sometimes. And when I can't keep it up, I sometimes feel like I'm letting people down.*

Esther Rapoport (2019, p. 56) challenges these rigid structures in her account of "bisexual subjectivity" as a playful approach to the erotic, in which lovers' bodies are encountered as "transitional objects with both/and qualities rather than stationary objects with set, essential properties". In this expansive sexual subjectivity, participants creatively experiment with idiosyncratic, mixed and changing roles, acts, and uses for sexual organs. In this process, one's own and one's partner's bodies can take on new, previously unexplored roles and meanings, facilitating access to unknown or less known aspects of the self.

Rapoport focuses on the potential for such self-discovery through bisexuals' diverse sexual encounters with partners with different "sexed anatomies". We would add that the queer challenge to fixed, binary and essentialised identities shows how such experiences become available with partners of any gender identity or expression; with multiple partners of the same sex or gender; and indeed, through different encounters across time with the *same* partner. A partner's transition is just one example of how queer disidentification from a fixed role or identity can release the relationship from a fixed dynamic and unsettle our own internal model of self-*in-relation*. The experience of our gendered selves as "ongoing events, not discreet endpoints" (Corbett 2020, p. 247) undermines our ingrained cultural fantasy of the happily-ever-after relationship that will fix our identity in orbit around our partner's, setting us off together on a clear life trajectory.

Lee Edelman (2004) coined the term "heterofuturity" to describe our society's insistence on a narrow path from which successful relationships will not stray — a path which our parents walked down before us, and down which our children will follow in our footsteps. Psychoanalytic developmental models have often been used to bolster the view that generational repetition and replication is the mark of a healthy relational life, delegitimising relationship styles and patterns which do not follow this "distinctly Oedipal regularity and repetitiveness" (Sedgwick 2003, p. 147). Rather than being crushed by the failure to meet these pervasive standards of success, queerness offers strategies for embracing the potentialities of this failure.

In *The Queer Art of Failure*, Jack Halberstam (2011) offers up the idea that failure to meet these pervasive standards of success is not a dead end, but an opportunity to uncover new forms of knowledge: "The queer art of failure turns on the impossible, the improbable, the unremarkable. It quietly loses, and in losing it imagines other goals for life, for art, and for being" (2004, p. 88). Taking up this idea in a relational context, we suggest that the queering of failure can allow relationships to grow sideways, taking on new and unexpected forms.

What might this sideways growth, which is commonplace in our communities, look like? A relationship might begin as a conventional monogamous partnership, before shifting into a polyamorous configuration that

Queer relationships: unmapped intimacies   113

supports explorations of sexuality and identity beyond the couple. If this breaks down, the pair, having mourned the loss of their early relationship and its projected future, may shift again into a supportive friendship, or perhaps into a platonic, domestic partnership within the framework of queer kinship. The ability to co-create adaptive new models of partnership and family contrasts strikingly to conventional responses to relationship breakdown, in which the meaning and value of the relationship is frequently negated, and the possibility of continued intimacy in new forms is foreclosed.

> *I used to be looking for this one person, a partner who I could find everything in, be my authentic self and be understood — and I didn't have that expectation from friendships. Now I allow myself to prioritise intimacies and connections that don't have to resolve in sex or romance.*

In questioning normative hierarchies around partnership, family, and intimacy, we might also question the "authenticating notion of longevity" that underpins such hierarchies, and which gives "permanent (even if estranged) connections precedence over random (even if intense) connections" (Halberstam 2011, p. 72).

> *With someone I don't know, I can have wild and spontaneous experiences, and you can't do that with your regular partner in the same way. You can kind of be whatever you want; I find it much more possible to say, "This is what I want now; what do you want now? Are we compatible in this moment?"*

Queer ideas such as chosen family, queer kinship, and platonic partnership make space for recognising the value of the relationships that are in our lives right now, instead of always giving precedence to the ghosts of blood-tie relationships (Weston 1995), or to potentially reproductive romantic partnerships.

> *When I stopped being in contact with my parents, it was really important for me to say that my queer houseshare was my family. People have come and gone, but this house still feels like home — my biological family has never had that feeling of closeness, of being loved or understood. The people I've loved and lived with here are my most important relationships and these are my closest people, and there's a way in which they are my chosen family; but I also know that people will move on, and that's okay. So much rests on the idea of family, and people can't always meet those expectations — but part of queer community is that they don't have to, because there are so many people who can have different roles in your life and support you in different ways.*

These practices sidestep the paths to relational success set out by the discourse of heterofuturity, and may present a challenge to traditional psychoanalytic assumptions about which relationships matter. Such assumptions are grounded in a set of values that are heteronormative, white supremacist and often anachronistic. Normative models of family structures and relationship styles are historically enmeshed with the construction of race and of scientific racism, and continue to pathologise kinship structures that do not replicate the nuclear family model. Post-colonial queer theorists such as Ranjana Khanna (2003), Mel Y. Chen (2012) and Siobhan Somerville (2000) work to address the intersectional violence of treating this model as normal, natural, or neutral.

At the same time, increasing numbers continue to live in shared houses long into adulthood, especially in crowded megacities like London, and the proportion of single adults continues to rise. Culturally ingrained fantasies about what intimacy, family and home look like, then, often fail to accurately reflect lived experiences — and queer kinship models suggest the potential value for many, both within and beyond the LGBTQ+ community, of questioning static relationship hierarchies.

> *When we think of love and relationships, we often think of romance or sex, and I think there are so many other kinds of love. Before I met other people like myself, I really wanted to die — friendships have been so important to me. Even people who aren't friends, but are just part of my community — having that space in which we have different kinds of bodies, different sexualities... it's difficult to properly articulate what unites us, but we are here in this space and we feel united.*

Queerness, with its expanded boundaries of intimacy and kinship, shows us potential routes to interrogate our unconscious assumptions about the meaning and mattering of our relationships. There can be great value in helping our clients to mourn the fantasies of these unattainable (and often undesirable) normative ideals; to no longer foreclose the potential of queerer alternatives under the mark of "failure", but instead to embrace the possibilities that their real relationships offer them.

Queering the consulting room

> *I have this significant memory of hooking up with someone on Grindr; going to his house and really needing some intimacy and affection, and realizing my nails were painted. And standing on his doorstep and quite painfully chipping away at my nails, in order to not be rejected, and to be held. And what was really sad, was that person turned out to be super femme, and super embracing of that aspect of me — and then I felt doubly shit for having broken, for conforming to that external pressure, when this could have been someone who could have held me and seen all of me in that way.*

Perhaps we might transpose this scene to the doorway of the therapist's room. We imagine our clients chipping away at parts of themselves, in need of care, and in expectation of hurt. In many of the conversations that informed this chapter, people spoke of the desire to feel "seen" and "held". "Seen" in their complexity and contradictions, "held" in their transforming, changeable, exciting, and wounded bodies and identities. What does this require of us as therapists? How do we work towards an embracing form of seeing and an expansive holding? And how might these general therapeutic qualities meet specifically queer concerns?

Informed by our clinical work, and drawing on conversations with queer people in our communities about their experiences of therapy, we propose three areas of particular therapeutic focus: learning from and supporting a sense of queer community; recognizing the context of oppression; and developing a capacity for play in ourselves, our clients, and their relationships. These conversations and informal interviews come out of a specific context — queer life in a large urban centre, London — and represent a range of perspectives, rather than a unified view.

The value of queer community, as a space of healing and acceptance, recurred strongly in our conversations. This connection is found with partners, in hook-ups, friendships and a wider sense of belonging.

> *Queerness has given me a sense of deep empathy; being in a queer community where there is more acceptance, more holding, between all these people with such different lives and experiences, has allowed me to be more accepting. I've been able to articulate my experience for myself, and not judge myself before speaking. So for me one of the most important things about queerness is that it builds community through empathy.*

This relationship to community is a resource we can learn from and support clients to deepen. This might include thinking with clients about joining queer support groups or social groups, or getting involved with volunteering or activism. We can hold a perspective that wonders: do our clients have a sense of community and is this an affirming space? For clients who do not feel a sense of community, why is this? Perhaps this might reflect internalized queerphobia, or a rejection of parts of the self; we might also consider how broader toxic pressures, for example around gender and relationship scripts, fatphobia, and racism play out in painful ways within this community. To hold in mind questions about queer community can allow clients space to explore the fears and potentials it may bring.

Alongside these direct conversations and engagements with queer culture and community, we may also wonder where we, as therapists, are positioned in our clients' narratives of community. The integrating experience of being able to bring multiple and contradictory parts of the self into the therapeutic relationship may serve as a precursor that enables clients to step into community. Equally, we can notice ways in which we recreate for clients the experience of being with straight parents or family, leaving them separated from a sense of queer kinship or feeling isolated in the therapeutic relationship. It can be productive to acknowledge these moments of rupture and disconnect, not only in terms of the client's transference, but also as the client being affected by the real differences present in the consulting room.

> *There was a period when I was really struggling with my friendship with one of my housemates — we were close but kept arguing, I found him very emotionally volatile — and I was talking about it a lot in therapy. Eventually my therapist questioned why I was putting so much time and energy into this relationship with this difficult person, and she said well, "It's not as if he's your brother". In that moment I realised how my therapist saw the world, what she thought our lives should look like — and I felt so far away from her understanding.*

Working to support queer relationships may require us to rethink our own relationship to community, and find ways to integrate the therapeutic relationship into a broader network of meaningful connections. From our clients' and interviewees' descriptions of what they value or long for in their community, we might also draw an alternative model of the therapeutic relationship. A relationship not exclusively mapped onto the monogamous and enclosed couple, but one which seeks a community in the room, allowing both the therapist and the client multiple positions, voices, and selves.

The second quality that we have found to be important in the therapeutic relationship is the therapist's capacity to recognize experiences of oppression. There is a desire among many queer clients for therapy to help situate the inner world in the outer, to bring deeper thinking and attend to the way experiences of homophobia, transphobia, and racism are shaping relationships.

> *I went to see a therapist to talk about relationships, and how I struggle with rejection. When I would tell her about negative experiences I had with men, she reacted as though these were exceptional moments of people behaving badly, rather than my real norm. It's like, no, this is the culture... Even though what I wanted to work on was me — how am I choosing these people, why is this a pattern — I did also want to acknowledge that I was working within that material reality of gay culture. She wasn't able to take that on board. So it ended up feeling like I was being blamed for my experiences, without having her recognize that there was this oppressive system around me.*

When therapists use language that recognizes structural inequalities — for example, wondering about how heterosexism or transphobia has shaped an encounter — it can offer clients powerful moments of care and recognition, and give context and clarity to individual experience. There can also be value in the therapist making links to broader histories, and seeking out rich narratives of queer experience, for example in theory, memoir, or media. These voices help us to hear our clients' experiences within a broader context of oppression and resistance. We also might support clients to expand and develop a relationship to aspects of queer culture and history as a source of validation and mirroring.

> *When I first saw Paris is Burning, that was revelatory — it was such a window into what a camp, femme, gay, male, black sexuality was. I was drowning at that point in toxic masculinity... and it was like that moment as a child of being given the word "gay" and being like, I can channel myself through that. Watching this film, I felt very held by that world, and saw what this world was missing for me.*

Alongside holding this wider perspective, acknowledging oppression also means holding a frame that includes the therapist's identity in the picture. The therapist's ability or willingness to implicate themself in their client's experiences, to be challenged and changed by them, can be central to establishing a sense of trust and collaboration. People we spoke with did not necessarily seek out sameness in their therapists, recognizing that having a queer therapist, or a therapist who shared their race or gender, was not a guarantee of a shared perspective. Instead, they sought a sense that a cumulative understanding could be reached, described by one interviewee as the feeling that they and their therapist were "interpreting together".

The feminist philosopher of science Donna Haraway (1988) explores alternatives to notions of objectivity or neutrality as starting points for accumulating knowledge. She finds a resource, rather than a weakness, in our inevitably "partial" vision and "halting voices":

> *The knowing self is partial in all its guises, never finished, whole...it is always constructed and stitched together imperfectly, and therefore able to join with another, to see together without claiming to be another (1988, p. 586).*

A helpful reminder that entering into community with our clients does not require us to flatten our differences, but rather to explore what can be made of them, and to remain aware that we have as many blind spots as our clients.

Our final focus looks to playfulness as a way of entering this shared space, between inner and outer realities, sameness, and difference. We invoke the capacity for playfulness cautiously, mindful of the ways in which queer identities have been positioned in some psychoanalytic theory as developmentally stunted, or as less "real", and of how realities of oppression have been minimized in therapeutic encounters. In Winnicott's writing, however, we find a perspective on playfulness that respects the seriousness of the endeavor.

Rather than a developmental phase that people transition out of, Winnicott sees play as a capacity we seek to strengthen in all our therapeutic work. He locates play at precisely the intersection we are concerned with: "the place where cultural experience is located... in the *potential space* between the individual and the environment" (Winnicott 1967, p. 134). In our reading, being able to make use of this space — of community, of culture, of inner resources and external forces — is what enables us to "expand into creative living" (ibid., p. 138). We propose that this version of "play" holds particular value for those working with queer relationships. To navigate relationships outside of normative trajectories, it becomes necessary to find creative ways to play with language, relationship structures, and identities.

> *The relationship I'm in now is heterosexual — even though it might not look like that to some people — it's heterosexual, it's monogamous, it's kind of conventional in that way. But we can also talk to each other about how our relationship is faggy, and how it is lesbian. We can be playful together with our roles in the relationship, and there is space for the different parts of me.*

Winnicott is at pains to highlight how our environment can inhibit, as well as foster, our ability to play; and while playfulness might be an important feature in queer relationships, it is also one often under threat. Given the anxieties queerness brings up for individuals and society more broadly, play is often curtailed or felt to be too risky. Forces of normality equally infiltrate the minds and relationships of queer people. Pressure to choose a label, or fit into a relationship script, is exerted in the inner and outer world, and the therapeutic space can become another regularizing pressure. We can notice when our own capacity to engage creatively with the potentials our clients bring becomes reined in by certainties, or simplified by affirmations. Or when we find ourselves more comfortable exploring the inner world in a vacuum, losing sight of what is at stake for our clients, what risks this play entails, and what forces, psychic and structural, are marshaled against it.

As Stephen Mitchell (1991) highlights, this playful openness to multiplicity of selves, relationships, and meanings is central to what psychoanalytic approaches have to offer:

> *Psychoanalysis, at its best, makes possible a more variegated experience of self: past and present, fantasy and actuality interpenetrate each other; the phenomenology of the self as independent and separable is illuminated by an awareness of the self's embeddedness within a relational matrix (1991, p. 145).*

Alongside our clients, we can engage with queer and psychoanalytic resources that facilitate this opening up, this unraveling of fixed meanings and narrow selves. Holding on to the transitional space where things can be "neither inside nor outside" (Winnicott 1967, p. 129), me or not me, true nor false, we can foster forms of play that challenge the rules or reimagine the game.

Conclusion

> "Remember: The rules, like streets, can only take you to *known* places. Underneath the grid there is a field – it was always there – where to be lost is never to be wrong, but simply more."
>
> Ocean Vuong, *On Earth We're Briefly Gorgeous*

To embrace the queer potential of relationships is to question the scripts so often imposed on relationships and identities; to question the categories that so many struggle to fit themselves and their intimacies within. As therapists, we can strive to make space in the consulting room for this queering of the relationship in the mind, and help our clients to feel seen in all their expansive, changeable, unfolding complexity.

We can acknowledge the limitations of our own perspectives, and be mindful of the anxieties that arise within us when we feel destabilised by a client's challenge to our theoretical frameworks, or to our own sense of identity. We can recognise the impact of structural violence on queer relationships as well as the potential value of community, of non-biological family, of multiple partners, of hook-ups, broadening our ideas of the intimacies that matter. We can develop a more expansive relation to past and present, recognizing cyclical and overlapping trajectories, valuing connections both established and fleeting. By embracing play as a queer resource, we can accompany our clients in stepping off the narrow, pre-trodden paths that limit meaning and potential, and explore the possibilities that lie in the field beyond.

Acknowledgement

Epigraph quoted from the diaries of Lou Sullivan, *The Louis Graydon Sullivan Papers* (1991–07), courtesy of the Gay, Lesbian, Bisexual, Transgender Historical Society, San Francisco.

References

Bergeret, J. (2002) 'Homosexuality or homoeroticism: 'narcissistic eroticism'' in *The International Journal of Psychoanalysis* 83, 351–62.

Bion, W. (1980) *Bion in New York and Sao Paolo*, Perthshire: Clunie Press.

Britton, R. (2004) 'Subjectivity, Objectivity and Triangular Space' in *Psychoanalytic Quarterly* 73, 47–61.

Butler, J. (1990) *Gender trouble*, New York: Routledge.
Chen, M. Y. (2012) *Animacies: Biopolitics, Racial Mattering, and Queer Affect*, Durham: Duke University Press.
Corbett, K. (2020) 'Gender now' in Hertzmann, L. & Newbegin, J. (eds.) *Sexuality and Gender Now*, Oxon: Routledge, 240–254.
Dean, T. (2017) 'Taking Shelter from Queer' in Giffney, N. & Watson, E. (eds.) *Clinical Encounters in Sexuality: Psychoanalytic Practice & Queer Theory*, Punctum Books, 397–402.
Edelman, L. (2004) *No Future: Queer Theory and the Death Drive*, Durham: Duke University Press.
Green, A. (1973/2018) 'The Neuter Gender' in Perelberg R. (ed.) *Psychic Bisexuality*, London: Routledge.
Halberstam, J. (2011) *The Queer Art of Failure*, London: Duke University Press.
Halperin, D. M. (1995) *Saint Foucault: Towards a gay hagiography*, New York: Oxford University Press.
Haraway, D. (1988) 'Situated knowledges: The science question in feminism and the privilege of partial perspective' in *Feminist Studies* 14(3), 575–599.
Hinshelwood, R. D. (2017) 'On Not Thinking Straight: Comments on a Conceptual Marriage' in Giffney, N. & Watson, E. (eds.) *Clinical Encounters in Sexuality: Psychoanalytic Practice & Queer Theory*, Punctum Books, 197–210.
Keats, J. (1970) *The Letters of John Keats: A Selection* (ed. R. Gittings), Oxford: Oxford Paperbacks.
Khanna, R. (2003) *Dark Continents: Psychoanalysis and Colonialism*, Durham: Duke University Press.
Kuzniar, A. (2017) 'Precarious Sexualities: Queer Challenges to Psychoanalytic and Social Identity Categorization' in Giffney, N. & Watson, E. (eds.) *Clinical Encounters in Sexuality: Psychoanalytic Practice & Queer Theory*, Punctum Books, 51–76.
Lemma, A. (2013) 'The body one has and the body one is: Understanding the transsexual's need to be seen' in *The International Journal of Psychoanalysis* 94(2), 277–292.
Mitchell, S. (1991) 'Contemporary perspectives on self: toward and integration' in *Psychoanalytic Dialogues* 1(2), 121–147.
Quinodoz, D. (1998) 'A fe/male transsexual patient in psychoanalysis' in *The International Journal of Psychoanalysis* 79(Pt 1), 95–111.
Rapoport, E. (2019) 'Bisexual Subjectivity Through the Lenses of Lacanian, Object Relations and Relational Theories' in *From Psychoanalytic Bisexuality to Bisexual Psychoanalysis: Desiring in the Real*, Routledge, 53–66.
Reis, B. (2009). We: Commentary on papers by Trevarthen, Ammaniti &Trentini, and Gallese. *Psychoanalytic Dialogues*, 19: 565–579.
Rubin, G. (1984) 'Thinking Sex: Notes for a Radical Theory of the Politics of Sexuality' in Vance, C. S. (ed.) *Pleasure and Danger: Exploring Female Sexuality* (1989), London: Pandora, 143–178.
Sedgwick, E. K. (1993) *Tendencies*, Durham: Duke University Press.
Sedgwick, E. K. (2003) *Touching Feeling: Affect, Pedagogy, Performativity*, Durham: Duke University Press.
Somerville, S. B. (2000) *Queering the Color Line: Race and the Invention of Homosexuality in American Culture*, Durham: Duke University Press.
Suchet, M. (2020) 'Crossing Over' in Hertzmann, L. & Newbegin, J. (eds.) *Sexuality and Gender Now*, Oxon: Routledge, 213–239.

Vuong, O. (2019) *On Earth We're Briefly Gorgeous* New York : Penguin Press
Weston, K. (1995) 'Forever Is a Long Time: Romancing the Real in Gay Kinship Ideologies' in Yanagisako, S. & Delaney, C. (eds.) *Naturalizing Power: Essays in Feminist Cultural Analysis*, London: Psychology Press, 87–112.
Wiedeman, G. H. (1962) 'Survey of psychoanalytic literature on overt male homosexuality' in *Journal of the American Psychoanalytic Association* 10(2), 386–409.
Winnicott, D. W. (1967/2005) *Playing and Reality*, London: Routledge.
Withers, R. (2015) 'The seventh penis: towards effective psychoanalytic work with pre-surgical transsexuals' in *Journal of Analytical Psychology* 60(3), 390–412.

Chapter 8

The fear of difference and desire to differentiate

Working with two transitioning couples

Linsey Blair and Dorota Mucha

Introduction

In this chapter, we examine the nature of the therapeutic experience of the transitioning couple. Two case presentations will be used to explore the individual's desire to transition from female to male whilst remaining within the couple relationship. We consider each of the couple's shared unconscious phantasies linked to the fear and management of difference and the struggle for differentiation in regard to the transition. In addition, we reflect on the unconscious couple fit and its impact on the therapeutic relationship in the exploration of the transgender experience. Finally, we consider the implications for therapists of working with couples in the process of transition.

A review of the literature on transitioning and the couple relationship

Malpas (2012) notes that historically the decision for one of the partners to transition often resulted in the demise of the couple relationship. However, developments in thinking and practice relating to couple therapy has extended the possibility of the partners having therapy together, in order to explore their individual and shared experiences regarding the transition. Indeed, it is now considered 'good practice' to include partners and families in the therapeutic process, so that the family can be helped to adjust to and hopefully accept the individual's decision to transition. Furthermore, within couple therapy involving the transition of one of the partners, it is assumed that there are two simultaneous transitions taking place, i.e., that of the individual within the partnership and that of the partnership itself. Malpas (2012) also draws attention to the possibility of each of the partners being at different stages in the process, with the trans individual being further along the path towards acceptance than the non-transitioning partner. Therefore, at the beginning of couple therapy, there may be a question in both the couple and the therapist's minds as to whether the partners can

DOI: 10.4324/9781003255703-8

The fear of difference and desire to differentiate 123

manage the transition together. As McCann, 2017, wrote 'A big part of being able to travel the route together seems to depend on whether the non-transitioning partner can manage and work with the impact of their partner's identity change on them' (McCann, 2017, p. 5). To that end, it would appear that couples are more likely to stay together if the partner who wishes to transition has been open about their gender dysphoria from an early stage in the relationship (Nuttbrock, et al, 2009), as the decision to transition does not then come as a complete shock. Moreover, it has also been suggested that the couple relationship itself can be a source of support for the transitioning individual, if the non-transitioning partner has a more open attitude towards gender and sexuality and/or is also a member of the lesbian, gay, bisexual, transgender, queer (LGBTQ+) community (Fuller & Riggs, 2019; McCann, 2017). The implication of these findings is that the more understanding the non-transitioning partner is towards their partner's wish to transition, the more likely it is that the couple will transition together. However, as with many transitioning couples, their families of origin are often unsupportive, something that was certainly the case with the two couples we saw, where both mothers of the transitioning partners threatened to disown them post-transition.

Unsurprisingly, there exists a positive correlation between the emotional support offered by family and romantic partners and the transitioning individual's mental health (Fuller & Riggs, 2019; Farrow, et al, 2019; Israel, 2008). This is particularly important as transphobia within families and more generally within society often leads to rejection, isolation and abuse. Because of this, trans individuals are considered an 'at risk' group (Marshall, et al, 2016; Bailey et al, 2014), with pre-transition rates of suicide being much higher than for those following transition. Also, the longer the transition takes, the greater the risk of suicide, mainly because the individual is essentially trapped between genders and not surprisingly the feelings of incongruity causes deep psychic pain. However, queer academics argue that with good support from therapists, peers and intimate others, the trans journey can be a positive experience. Likewise, it is also argued that there is an overemphasis within the literature on those who regret their surgery (Richards & Barker, 2013; Murjan & Bosman, 2015), particularly given the years of stress experienced by many trans individuals living in a body that feels alien to them.

Saketopoulou (2014), however, highlights the importance of the trans individual being able to mentalise and, in turn, mourn the natal body as part of the process of transitioning. She argues that transgender individuals may attempt to pass over the mourning process relating to the natal body by only allowing attention to be focused on the post-transitioned body, and in the process the patient's body dysphoria may be left unaddressed in the analytic process. Therefore, an absence of curiosity in the trans individual, their partner and the therapist may lead to a very concrete version of therapy relating to the idea of there being a right or a wrong, rather than a more nuanced exploration of anxieties concerning the process of transitioning and its impact on the couple's relationship in its widest possible sense. Consequently, for psychoanalytic therapists working with such couples, we feel that it is important to hold a space of benign curiosity or what Bion (1959) refers to as K.

Lemma (2012) also speaks of the complexity relating to the trans individual's psychic wound linked to their incongruity and the way in which this, through transference and countertransference dynamics, is enacted within the therapeutic relationship. In her MtF case example, she draws particular attention to the internalised experience of not being 'taken in' by the primary object and the way in which this gets played out unconsciously with others. For instance, her patient when dressed as a woman drew rejecting or confused glances from others who were trying but failing to make sense of an incongruent state. The therapist must therefore do what the primary object could not, that is, the therapist must be able to 'house the experience of ambiguity, confusion and uncertainty' and reflect that the experience is survivable (Lemma, 2012, p. 279); something that is believed to be vital to the process of 'working through' the struggle of taking in and being taken in.

In couple therapy, this struggle in being taken in is also evident when one of the partners wishes to transition and the other rejects, attacks or denies their partner's trans desire. In this instance, housing the ambiguity can be technically challenging, especially since the couple may believe that if they were to face into their shared anxieties about the transition, then this would essentially destroy their connection. As a result, the couple may attempt to keep the therapist at bay in order to prevent the transitioning experience from becoming an unstable block in a psychic Jenga game. Indeed, with the couples we saw, it felt that if we pulled too hard at the transgender block, the psychic structure holding the couple together would collapse and as a consequence we were kept at arm's length.

The contribution of psychoanalytic theory to couple therapy

Ruszczynski (1993) speaks of the attachment between two individuals being linked to "the harmony of their unconscious images and patterns of relationships" (p. 8). In other words, the partners unconsciously seek and find similarities in the other's unconscious, which act like hooks for their projections. The attraction to someone who can carry projections of split-off parts of the self, not only constitutes the unconscious couple fit, but also relates to the hope that overtime the partnership can sustain a mutual developmental trajectory, as both individuals work together to manage their internal conflicts and find greater integration. This creative process

The fear of difference and desire to differentiate   125

of healing the self via the relationship can occur if the individuals within the relationship are able to reflect and are curious about themselves, each other, and the relationship as a whole. Morgan (2004) suggests that couples who have come to therapy are struggling with this reflective capacity and so the therapist must hold it for them via a 'couple state of mind'. This internal capacity to reflect is linked in psychoanalytic theory to the internalisation of what is referred to as a third space; something that comes from a successful negotiation of the oedipal situation and a shift from paranoid schizoid thinking to more depressive functioning (Balfour, 2005; Britton, 1989; Nyberg, 2018).

If the couple are unable to inhabit this third space, then the force of their joint unconscious projections into each other may form, what Morgan (2010) refers to as 'projective gridlock'; something that transforms phantasy into rigid beliefs, which in turn severely limit the couple's capacity for development and change. One of the ways in which couples attempt to manage the force of their shared unconscious phantasies is to avoid conflict at all costs, often presenting as of one mind. Essentially, what we are describing here is a merged relationship where the unbearable and hated parts of self are projected outside of the couple relationship, so that the couple itself is idealised, bubble-like and without conflict or difference. Both of our case examples typify this particular couple fit.

Applying psychoanalytic thinking to our work with couples where one or both partners are considering or are actually in the process of transitioning, raises questions concerning technique. Essentially, we consider the nature of the couple fit, and are also interested in what is being projected into the other, or that which is being enacted between the partners. For instance, McCann (2017) considers whether the split within couples where one of the partners is transitioning is not only related to the projection of an internal dilemma within the trans individual, but is also part of a shared unconscious phantasy. He wonders to what extent the non-transitioning partner also has an experience of conflict of not being properly understood or taken in, and therefore, in the couple fit, unconsciously identifies with their partner's struggle for congruence so that between them they can find a home together for their unmet needs. However, during therapy with our two couples, we experienced an absence of thought and a desperate attempt to keep us out, which set up an unhelpful dynamic as we attempted to understand and work with them. Our efforts to think with the couples about their situation, both as a couple and as individuals with separate needs, seemed too threatening for them in the face of such idealised pairings.

An important contextual consideration which may also explain something of the couples' presentations in therapy was that concerning the nature of the therapeutic alliance. In essence, both of the couples we saw had been sent for therapy by their respective gender identity clinics and therefore, although the transition was on the table, it had not been put there by the couple. This therefore poses particular technical challenges for the therapist who may be viewed as an interloper and as someone who might raise questions concerning the gender transition itself. In themselves, these will undoubtedly increase a couple's reluctance to fully engage in the therapeutic process but, as will be seen, there were other factors at play that gave rise to the couples' hesitancy to engage. Nevertheless, it is of note that when seen alone, the transitioning partners were much more open to exploring their situation than in the presence of their partners, something that we will explore further during the case presentations.

Case studies

In thinking about our two couples, we are using the term transitioning to refer to the decision by one of the partners to change and live in a gender different from that which was assigned at birth. We will therefore be referring to the transitioning partners in their chosen gender using the pronoun he/him. It is also worth noting that although transitioning for some individuals may include sex reassignment surgery (SRS) and/or hormone treatment, for others it stops short of these interventions. Hormone treatment for trans men often results in the growth of facial and bodily hair, the deepening of the voice and changes to libido. Surgery can also comprise the removal of breasts (referred to as *top surgery*), and/or phalloplasty (the construction of male genitalia from existing female genitalia), or metoidioplasty (the extension of the female clitoris) (Richards & Barker, 2013).

Both of the couples we saw defined themselves as lesbian at the time of therapy, and in each of the couples, one of the partners was progressing with FtM transition. In scenario one, Blair worked with Ed and his partner Marian and, in scenario two, Mucha worked with Jakob and his partner Lydia.

Case scenario one

In the first of the two couples, Ed (nee Edwina), who was 32 years old when he first came to therapy, elected initially to have top surgery together with hormone treatment, although at the time of the meeting, he was on a waiting list for treatment. Ed had already changed his name and was insistent that his friends, family and work colleagues referred to him by his male name.

On first meeting (LB), Marian was the more outspoken of the two and expressed confusion as to why she and Ed needed therapy. After all, they were in complete agreement with Ed's decision to transition and with his top surgery, especially as he was feeling depressed because of his body dysmorphia. Marian also emphasised the support she was receiving from her family and friends, adding that her mother was actually funding Ed's surgery and that they would be moving into her mother's home following the operation, the intention being that they would become a straight couple and make a new life together.

The fear of difference and desire to differentiate 127

Ed was born in rural England and was the first of two siblings. Although named Edwina, from as far back as he could remember, Ed identified as a boy. As a child, he recalled working on the farm with his father. He described his father as a man who was warm and genial but who struggled to express emotions and tended to withdraw into work in the face of difficulties. Ed's mother had mental health concerns, which became more apparent following the death of one of her parents when Ed was five years old. Following the death, she was prone to violent outbursts towards Ed and his father. Ed's greatest sorrow was that around puberty, he experienced rejection from his father, the outcome he thought of a parental argument in which his mother accused his father of 'masculinising' their only girl. As a result, Ed was no longer allowed to work on the farm and was discouraged from playing sports. He also recalled feeling 'like a clown' in church every Sunday when he was forced to wear dresses. After escaping to university, he began to explore his sexuality and identified as a 'butch' lesbian. Ed was already in individual psychotherapy when he met Marian. With Marian and his therapist's support, Ed became more confident in his identity as a man and began to present as a male in the outside world. Ed remains in touch with his family who, although accepting of his lesbianism, are completely against his decision to transition and his mother has told him that he would not be welcome in their home as a man.

Ed's partner Marian presented as very feminine and full of energy, in marked contrast to Ed's somewhat lethargic presentation. Her father left when she was two years old, occasioned by the death of her younger brother. The parental breakup was acrimonious, and Marian's mother gained sole custody. Marian grew up seeing her father through her mother's eyes and believed him to be selfish, cruel and manipulative. In her late teens, Marian came out as lesbian, and her mother praised this decision. Two years later, Marian's mother also 'came out' as lesbian and is currently in a long-term lesbian relationship. Marian described her mother as her 'best friend'. She denied ever missing her father or feeling that anything was lacking in her life. During the consultation, she noted that Ed's depression was causing low sexual desire and she was therefore hoping that his top surgery would resolve this.

Case scenario two

In the second couple, Jakob (nee Jane), aged 19 years old, wanted full surgery, consisting of removal of the breasts together with metoidioplasty and hormone treatment. His treatment was underway when they came for therapy and, like Ed, Jakob had also changed his name.

Jakob and Lydia were both nineteen years old when, also on the encouragement of Jakob's gender identity clinic, they presented for therapy. Couple work was advised in order to help them 'work through' the transition, especially as Jakob was about to embark on full sex reassignment surgery involving, genital surgery, top surgery and hormone treatment.

In the initial session, the couple seemed joyful and excited. They looked like "high-school sweethearts" and couldn't resist affectionately touching each other throughout the session. They wanted to talk about their mutual excitement in regard to Jakob's transition. However, they expressed concern in relation to their sex life. Jakob's mother had thrown him out of the house and Lydia's mother had taken him in. While the couple were sharing a bed, there had been a marked decline in their sexual intimacy.

Jakob was very masculine in appearance, well-built, tall and with an athletic body. Jakob was the only daughter in a family of four sons, but from an early age had a sense of being in the wrong body and strongly identified with his oldest brother. His mother suffered from a bipolar disorder and following episodes of psychosis was hospitalised for periods of time. She was emotionally unstable and had sudden and frequent outbursts of rage quickly followed by outpourings of love. Jakob did not know his father; he never spoke about him in therapy, and he seemed to lack any curiosity about him. It appears that Jakob's brothers accepted him as gay, but like Ed, his mother was completely against his decision to transition.

Lydia, a curvy and attractive cisgender woman, is an only child of parents who, as a result of her father's affair, divorced when she was four years old. The separation was acrimonious, and Lydia had an idea that her father had tried to return but that her mother had not 'allowed him in'. Lydia has no relationship with her father, but described her mother as her 'best friend'. She was involved in all aspects of Lydia's life, and was variously described as protective, caring and affectionate. Lydia defines herself as gender fluid and her sexuality as fluid.

Already, in terms of background histories, there are marked similarities between the two couples. Both Ed and Jakob have complex relationships with their mothers who struggled to contain their own emotional states of mind and were totally unable to take in or accept their children's gender dysphoria. It seems that Ed and Jakob's mothers also struggled to see or treat them as separate psychic beings and experienced the news of the transition as an attack on them, or more importantly in their minds as an attack on their 'mother-daughter' link. Furthermore, the loss and absence of their respective fathers appears to have complicated the process of individuation by offering no mediation in the painful negotiation between Ed, Jakob and their mothers.

Interestingly, Lydia and Marian (the partners of Ed and Jakob) also had absent fathers and, with no mediating influences, had formed somewhat merged relationships with their mothers. Unlike Ed and Jakob, however, Lydia and Marian's mothers became their best friends and saviours with all the badness lodged firmly in their errant fathers. In many respects, it seemed that both Lydia and Marian had coupled with their mothers, and this may have added to the struggle we had in thinking about these relationships. It is also interesting to note that Marian's mother, having initially identified as heterosexual then aligned her sexual orientation with that of her daughter's, possibly highlighting the importance of sameness over difference. In addition,

The fear of difference and desire to differentiate   129

both Marian and Lydia's mothers were supportive of their daughter's partner's transitions and Marian's mother was actually paying for Ed's surgery, which, for us, raised questions concerning the process of individuation for both Marian and Lydia. Indeed, as therapists, we felt uneasy about the extent of Marian and Lydia's mother's involvement which, given the importance of family support, seemed a surprising countertransference reaction. However, it was as if there was the illusion of an idealized couple fit nested within a completely merged set of relationships between all concerned, which to our minds seemed to take care of the unresolved relations between Ed, Jakob and their mothers, and Marian and Lydia and the loss of their fathers. For us, this highlights a particular challenge in terms of separating out issues that relate to family of origin from those that are specific to the transition itself.

In the face of these tightly bound couplings, we struggled to gain entry or to have any meaningful focus for the work. Essentially, we were experienced by the couples as outsiders who posed a threat to the fragile eco structure of the couple and family relationships which seemed to privilege sameness over difference. Moreover, it has also been noted that low sexual desire, a feature of both couple's presentations, is also believed to be associated with merged relationships. Perrell (2007), for instance, notes that couples who share too much tend to lose curiosity in each other and, as a result, the sex begins to feel mundane, masturbatory and in time non-existent. Blair (2018) also links the development of sexual dysfunctions in relationships to the couple's struggle to allow for difference and an absence of a couple state of mind. Although, as psychosexual therapists, we wondered whether the two couples might welcome a space to think about their sexual relationships, they each took the view that the transition itself would resolve this difficulty, and that if it didn't, then they would seek psychosexual therapy later.

Given that, in many respects, the internal parental couples of all four partners had not provided them with much of an experience of negotiating the triangular nature of the oedipal situation, it is also possible that the introduction and presence of a third within the therapeutic space may have felt threatening. In addition, we struggled to maintain a couple state of mind as the partners joined forces to keep us out. In her work with Jakob and Lydia, (DM) immediately noticed something rather unusual about her countertransference.

The couple felt like one tightly fused organism, constantly talking about their "amazing connection", but the experience in the room was one of an absence of difference and a lack of space for the me to be different. The couple were always in the same mood, always presenting with the same thought, as of one mind, and there was immense pressure on me to reflect the couple's state of mind. Often when writing notes after sessions, I found myself confused as to who had said what and what belonged to Jakob and what pertained to Lydia. The couple idealised and denigrated the work in equal measure. They felt impenetrable and I began to doubt whether the therapy would have any meaning or impact.

Similarly, (LB) also struggled with Ed and Marian, since Marian continued to dominate the sessions whilst Ed remained in her shadow.

> It was apparent during the sessions that Ed looked to Marian to speak for him and often glanced sideways at her when he did speak, perhaps to check that what he was saying was in line with her thinking. When I pointed this dynamic out to the couple (in terms of Marian's 'protectiveness' over Ed), they seemed to agree that because of Ed's depression, linked to his gender dysphoria, Marian had indeed taken on a 'caring' role in relation to him. However, this dynamic made it extremely difficult to see Ed as a separate person with a mind of his own, and inevitably contributed to the struggle that I experienced in properly connecting with him during the couples therapy.

However, the real difference or opening-up came when the therapists saw Ed and Jakob on their own. In these sessions, it was possible for the first time to really think about the transition and its impact on them, and in these moments, there was a loosening of the gridlock. It seemed that in the absence of Marian and Lydia, both men were able to be more open. Ed spoke with sorrow about the trauma of puberty, whilst Jakob mourned the loss of his fertility as a result of the transition. Both therapists felt moved by their openness and were more able to connect with their journey towards the new whilst also mourning the old (Saketopoulou, 2014).

Case scenario 1

In an individual session with Ed (Marian had not attended due to a work commitment), he began to explore aspects of his sexual history and gender dysphoria. He candidly spoke about how it was for him to be raised as a girl when he identified as a boy. With that in mind, we thought together about the horrors of Ed's puberty and the traumatic sexual assault that had occurred, when at the age of fourteen, he met and dated an older boy from his school. Ed spoke of being an early developer and particularly emphasised the size of his breasts, which in his mind seemed to contribute to the assault. We thought about that trauma, as well as the disturbance caused by the denial of his gender dysphoria within his family. In this more open space, we both found ourselves able to reflect and affirm his struggle in the face of the denial and the transphobia that he had experienced. However, it was as if he had gone too far with me and suddenly he wanted reassurance that I would not share any of the discussion we had just had with Marian.

Case scenario 2

Jakob came to the session on his own (as Lydia was feeling unwell). He seemed keen to talk about his recent appointment at the gender identity clinic, where the doctor had told him about the possibility of freezing his eggs before the gender reassignment. Jakob responded by saying that he had never thought about it, but that since the doctor encouraged him to consider it, he had been unable to stop thinking about it, adding that he wanted to be a parent. Jakob admitted that he hadn't discussed this with Lydia, as he worried that she would not understand or that she might get upset. However, I wondered how it was for him to think about this with me. Jakob smiled, and in a soft voice, began to fantasise about his future. He said that he envisioned having a family with children playing around him. I was about to comment on this when his expression suddenly changed, "It's kind of sad you know, I shouldn't have to decide right now how many children I would like, I am only nineteen". I asked Jakob about whether he and Lydia might consider ever having children together. Immediately, he began to close the conversation down, telling me that, "it's my thing now, and I guess I will have to talk to her about it one day, but not now". I felt that Jakob was just beginning to say something quite profound about his relationship in regard to this aspect of his body and the excitement of passing on his genes, but he stopped short of allowing further exploration as he wanted to change the topic.

In both of these individual sessions, it was possible to glimpse the side of Jakob and Ed that housed the more complex feelings relating to the natal body which could only be thought about outside of the projective merger. We certainly felt much freer and seemed to be experienced as less of a threat. This felt very different from working with the partners together where the transferences seemed defensive in nature, and where Ed and Jakob appeared wary of bringing their more nuanced thoughts and feelings to the discussion. However, the importance of being of one mind may best be understood in the context of Jakob and Ed's lifelong struggle to gain acceptance in regard to their gender, and perhaps having found it, they could not risk losing it again. Furthermore, the desperate wish expressed by both men of keeping what they had shared during their individual sessions away from their partners suggested that what they had told us felt like an act of betrayal. We wondered if this might be an unconscious reference to the sense of betrayal they perhaps felt in disappointing their families expectations of them by deciding to transition?

In addition, it seemed to us that Ed and Jacob's transition afforded a projective hook for Marian and Lydia, since they could attend to the internal conflicts in finding identities of their own through the unconditional care they offered to their respective partners. This may have prevented Ed and Jakob bringing the whole of themselves into the partnership for fear of creating conflict, disunity and further abandonment. Nevertheless, working with what Bion (1959) refers to as -K poses particular challenges for therapists in their attempts to speak to the anxiety behind the defence without alienating the couple in the process. That said, perhaps it is not surprising, given the central theme of separation verses merger in our work with these couples, that the separation from us was both dramatic and abrupt and prevented a proper 'working through' of the endings.

Case scenario 1

Three months before Ed was due to have his surgery and about five months into the work, Marian and Ed decided to have a vacation. Things between us at this stage had felt a little different and I was beginning to cathect more easily to the reality of Ed as a man, particularly as he seemed much happier in himself and was desperately looking forward to the surgery. However, although I continued to feel some concern with the couple taking up residence with Marian's mother, this was not open for discussion and I was therefore left holding this particular anxiety on the couple's behalf whilst they took their vacation. Although I was expecting to resume the work on their return, shortly into their holiday, I received an email letting me know that Ed's surgery had been brought forward and that they no longer required further sessions.

Case scenario 2

Three months into the therapy with Jakob and Lydia, they arrived in an angry and upset state. This followed a visit to Jakob's mother where she continually referred to him as Jane. When I attempted to think with them about the meaning of this, it was as if I, like Jakob's mother, was questioning or denying Jakob's trans identity. Despite my attempts to reassure Jakob that this was not the case, he continued to express anger at "people" refusing to accept him as man and without warning he stormed out of the room with Lydia in quick pursuit.

The manner in which both couples left their therapy seemed to encapsulate aspects of the shared unconscious phantasy, i.e., the belief that embracing difference and differentiation would inevitably lead to a breakdown in the relationship, and where psychic separation represented a break in attachment. Therefore, our attempts to create a thinking space for the couples to explore the impact of the transition on them and their relationships was something that felt too threatening. The sense of rejection that we were left holding at the end of the therapy spoke directly to Ed and Jakob's own experiences of rejection at the hands of others. The understandable wish to leave this behind resulted in the partners being careful to avoid any conflict or dissent within their tightly bound couple relationships that offered a refuge from the hostile and threatening external world. Perhaps, in that regard, the transition carried the unconscious hope of closure for the couples and for Marian and Lydia's mothers, by providing the ultimate resolution for all concerned.

Conclusion

Clearly, the process of transitioning for couples is neither straightforward nor without its challenges. However, with careful consideration and negotiation, couples can be helped to navigate a way through. At the heart of the journey towards acceptance and unity is the willingness of the partners to bear both the pain and the hope invested in the transition together. This ability to be open to the experience together ultimately enables a 'working through' and a deepening of the couple connection. Although, for us, the couples we presented struggled to be open in the broadest sense, they nevertheless allowed us to accompany them on at least part of their journey and as the transition became a reality it was time to let us go. It is our hope in writing this chapter that developments in thinking and practice relating to couples, where one or both partners decide to transition, continues to be thought about within our profession. Although, as couple psychotherapists, we have much to learn we also have much to offer and, given the greater incidence of partners deciding to transition, it is likely that we will increasingly find ourselves meeting and working with these couples in our consulting rooms.

References

Bailey, L., Ellis, S.J., & MacNeil, J. (2014). Suicide risk in the UK trans population and the role of gender transition in decreasing suicidal ideation and suicide attempt. *Mental Health Review Journal*, *19*(4): 209–220.

Balfour, A. (2005). The Couple, Their Marriage and Oedipus or Problems come in twos and threes. In F. Grier, (Ed). *Oedipus and the Couple*. London, Karnac Books, pp. 49–71.

Blair, L. (2018). Relations sexuelles intimes et dysfonctionnement: le role de l'espace tiers et do "couple state of mind" (Intimate sex and sexual dysfunction: the role of the couple state of mind). *Le Journal de Psychologues*, *357*: 37–44.

Bion, W.R. (1959). Attacks on linking. In *Second Thoughts*. London, Heinemann, pp. 93–109.

Britton, R. (1989). The missing link: Parental sexuality and the Oedipus complex. In J. Steiner, (Ed). *The Oedipus Complex Today: Clinical Implications*. London, Karnac Books, pp. 83–101.

Farrow, L.P., Bravo, A., & Galupo, M.P. (2019). "Your gender is valid": micro-affirmations in the romantic relationships of transgender individuals. *Journal of LGBT Issues in Counselling*, *13*(1): 45–66.

Fuller, K.A., & Riggs, D. (2019). Intimate relationship strengths and challenges amongst a sample of transgender people living in the United States. *International Journal of Transgenderism*, 1–14.

Israel, G.E. (2008). Transgender persons and their families. *Journal of LGBT Family Studies*, *1*(1): 53–67.

Lemma, A. (2012). The body one has and the body one is: understanding the transexual's need to be seen. *International Journal of Psychoanalysis*, *94*: 277–292.

McCann, D. (2017). The couple and family in transition. *International Review of Psychoanalysis of Couple and Family, no 16-1/2017*: The Family Crisis.

Malpas, J. (2012). Can couples change their gender? In J.J. Bigner & J.L. Wetchler, (Eds). *Handbook of LGBT-Affirmative Couple and Family Therapy*. London, Routledge.

Marshall, E., Claes, L., Bouman, W.P., Witcomb, G.L., & Arcelus, J. (2016). Non-suicidal self-injury and suicidality in trans people: A systematic review of the literature. *International Review of Psychiatry, 28(1)*: 58–69.

Morgan, M. (2004). On being able to be a couple. The importance of a "Creative Couple" in Psychic Life. In F. Grier, (Ed). *Oedipus and The Couple*. London, Karnac Books, pp. 9–30.

Morgan, M. (2010). Unconscious beliefs about being a couple. *Fort Da, 16*: 1.

Murjan, S., & Bosman, W.P. (2015). Transgender - Living in a different gender from that assigned from birth. In C. Richards & M.J. Barker, (Eds). *The Palgrave Handbook of Sexuality and Gender*. London, Palgrave MacMillan.

Nuttbrock, L.A., Bockting, W.O., Hwabng, S., Rosenblum, A., Mason, M., Macri, M., & Bexker, J. (2009). Gender identity affirmation among male to female transgender persons. A life course analysis across types of relationship and cultural/lifestyle factors. *Journal of Sex and Relationship Therapy, 24(2)*: 108–125.

Nyberg, V. (2018): Oedipus killed the couple: Murder on the Thebes Highway. In A. Novakovic & M. Reid, (Eds). *Couple Stories: Application of Psychoanalytic Ideas in Thinking about Couple Interaction*. London, Routledge, pp. 25–46.

Perrell, E. (2009): *Mating in captivity: Unlocking Erotic Intelligence*. New York, HarperCollins

Richards, C., & Barker, M.J. (2013). *Sexuality & Gender: For Mental Health Professionals. A Practical Guide*. London: Sage.

Ruszczynski, S. (1993). Thinking about and working with couples. In S. Ruszczynski, (Ed). *Psychotherapy with Couples. Theory and Practice at the Tavistock Institute of Marital Studies*. London, Karnac Books.

Saketopoulou, A. (2014). Mourning the body as bedrock: developmental considerations in treating transsexual patients analytically. *Journal of the American Psychoanalytic Association, 62(5)*: 773–806.

Chapter 9

They 'went in two by two'

The challenge for couple psychotherapists of working with those in open and polyamorous relationships

Damian McCann

Introduction

In this chapter, I reflect on and explore the nature of relating in open and polyamorous relationships, as an antidote to, or extension of, the more familiar couple relationship at the heart of psychoanalytic couple psychotherapy practice. And, although the development and application of psychoanalytic theory to couple relationships have proved invaluable, unfortunately, its primary focus on dyadic functioning has inevitably limited its interest in and understanding of the relevance of its theory to those in open and polyamorous relationships. Moreover, the inherent belief at the heart of psychoanalytic couple psychotherapy in the importance of monogamy, signifying mature and healthy functioning, has resulted in those who do not adhere to this standard being ignored, seen in a bad light, or believed to be blighted by the challenges of intimacy. Furthermore, traditional psychoanalytic accounts of development, attachment and relatedness, linked to heterosexual perspectives (D'Ercole & Drescher, 2004), have only served to tighten the grip on normative thinking and sealed the outsider status afforded to those in more open and polyamorous relationships.

Theoretical considerations

The primacy of monogamy

When thinking about open and polyamorous relationships, it is noticeable how these particular relationship configurations are often contrasted against the apparent advantages of monogamy and fidelity. Spence (1997), for instance, suggests that monogamy is associated with a deeper sense of intimacy and that both intimacy and sexual desire are found to be positively correlated. Underscoring this point, Jamieson (2004) highlights the belief that sexual fidelity is symbolic of trust and that sexual exclusivity accounts for the 'specialness' in couple relationships. Not surprisingly, these aspects of relating emphasise not just the popular ideals of monogamy, but also touch

DOI: 10.4324/9781003255703-9

on the fundamentals of psychoanalytic theory when applied to couple relationships, which, in my view, emphasise the importance of commitment and exclusivity. The incomprehensibility of open and polyamorous relationships for many continue to reinforce the ideals of monogamy, reflecting notions of maturity and development. For instance, research conducted by Conley and colleagues (2013) strongly suggests that those engaged in non-monogamy are viewed as having poorer and less responsible relationships than their monogamous counterparts. Matsick *et al* (2014), in their research, also found that people seemed more uncomfortable with the idea of strictly sexual relationships than with those involving multiple romantic and/or emotional attachments. And Barker (2013), in their chapter on 'Rewriting the rules of monogamy' captures this thinking when they say that pairing off and getting married are viewed 'as an inevitable, natural, normal and healthy part of development over the lifespan' and that 'relationships outside of the couple are only considered in the context of cheating and infidelity and the damage this can do' (p. 96). How then do those working with couples, where sexual exclusivity is not a reality, engage such couples in ways that avoid reinforcing the ideals of monogamy, and moreover, how might the key theoretical tenets of couple psychoanalytic theory assist those in this endeavour?

The couple state of mind

Ruszczynski (1993) suggests that for the couple therapist, the patient is the couple or, more precisely, the interaction between the partners is the patient, whilst Morgan (2005, 2019) refers to the importance of the therapist holding, what she refers to as 'a couple state of mind'. Taken together, these ideas are at the heart of the therapeutic endeavour and they constitute important organising principles in both the theory and practice of couple psychotherapy. Both concepts essentially promote the centrality of the couple's relationship as being the object of interest and attention, whilst at the same time also cautioning against the dangers of focusing too much on individual partners at the expense of the couple relationship itself. However, it is this aspect of the theory that, in my view, poses particular challenges for those working with open and polyamorous relationships, since it not only raises questions in terms of what actually constitutes the couple, but also in terms of how to think about the needs of individuals within a couple when relating romantically or sexually to others outside of that relationship, something that I will examine in more detail later in the chapter.

The creative couple

A further concept that has influenced the development of thinking about couple relationships within the field is that relating to what Morgan (2005) refers to as *the creative couple*, in which the couple 'can experience their

They 'went in two by two' 137

relationship as an entity, a resource, something they have created and continue to create together' (Morgan, 2019, p. 136). The forerunner to the elaboration of the creative couple state of mind lies in the developmental processes relating to one's early relationship with the mother/caregiver, the negotiation of the triangular nature of the Oedipal situation, as well as dealing with the challenges of adolescence which, when taken together, provide the template for managing separateness and difference alongside intimacy — all of which are felt to be crucial in the development of a creative couple state of mind. In fact, in working one's way through these different stages of psychic development, the individuals concerned are already glimpsing the nature of couple relating with its potential for opening-up what Britton (1998) refers to as a *triangular space*. Importantly, Morgan's belief that 'the movement towards feeling oneself to be part of a couple in which two minds come together to create something (*new*)' (p. 18) provides a helpful illustration of the development of triangular space, whilst challenging both partner's narcissism and omnipotence as they relinquish aspects of independence and autonomy. Yet, within the *creative couple* relationship, there is still the possibility of retaining a measure of psychic separateness without losing connection to one's partner, as both grapple with issues of separateness and attachment, disillusionment and ambivalence (Ruszczynski, 2005). Furthermore, the application of these ideas for open and polyamorous relationships is not something which Morgan foresees as an issue, especially since she believes that there is no limit to the number of such couplings with which one might engage, and instead the emphasis is more on the sense of one's identity being enhanced through these couplings (Morgan, personal communication). Nevertheless, given that these ideas have yet to be properly theorised in regard to open and polyamorous relationships, this chapter provides an important opportunity for further exploration.

Developing the point of separateness and togetherness further, Kernberg (1993) believes that the couple 'acquires an identity of its own in addition to the identity of each of the partners' (p. 63), capturing something of the tension between the individual needs separate from and in relation to couple relationships, which may also have relevance to our understanding of open and polyamorous relationships. Additionally, Ruszczynski (2005) suggests that 'Individual partners in an intimate relationship have to tolerate the fact that *for the purposes* of their relationship, they may sometimes have to give up needs, interests, and aspects of themselves, and tolerate doing so, however ambivalently' (p. 40), raising further questions concerning the meaning that partners in open and polyamorous relationships attach to this particular challenge. Moreover, the requirement for each of the partners to take back ownership of the split-off aspects of self that have through projective identification been put into the other, as evidence of a further developmental shift in relating, will also need consideration when applied to those in non-exclusive relationships. This seems especially important, since Colman (1993) also points to the principle of the couple relationship providing what he refers to as 'good enough' containment for the partners, particularly in regard to containing the 'tension that arises from the need of the individuals to develop outside the relationship as well as within it' (p. 73). In addition, when thinking about dyadic couple relationships, Colman points to the importance of boundaries which offer protection from disruption both inside and outside the relationship, as another essential ingredient for its continuity and development. In other words, the couple's need of a 'shared private space' from which others are excluded, sits in relation to the demands of relating to others that has the potential to continually pull partners in couples away from each other, and which may also pose challenges for those in open and polyamorous relationships. However, at the very heart of this exploration, for both exclusive and non-exclusive couples, is the fundamental question of whether these relationships are developmental or defensive, serving some unconscious motive that works against the potential for intimacy and growth.

Love, desire, sex and attachment

Generally speaking, psychoanalytic thinking when applied to couples holds the belief that sex, love and emotion tend to be directed solely towards one's partner and lived out and contained in one place and, so, when this is not the case, as, for example, with infidelity, this may be viewed as an actualisation of splits within the individual's and couple's shared unconscious organisation. Therefore, 'what had been lived unconsciously between them is now lived out with a third participant who becomes an object, consciously or unconsciously, for both of them, and who receives their projections' (Scharff, 2014, p. 255). Building on this thinking, others have advanced additional perspectives to the question of what can or cannot be contained within the couple relationship. For instance, Kernberg (1991) speaks of unresolved Oedipal conflicts as a major cause of invasion of the couple's sexual boundaries and a vehicle for the expression of dissociated aggression from many sources, whilst also drawing attention to the indissoluble nature of the interaction of libido and aggression, of love and hatred as important factors in determining the nature of the emotional relationship of the sexual couple. Rasmussen and Kilborne (2014), on the other hand, take the view that sexual infidelity occurs when the sexual and/or intimacy needs of one or both partners of a couple are not being satisfied. They also query the assumption that sex and intimacy go hand in hand, by stating that 'sex can and does occur in the absence of intimacy, and intimacy is not always associated with sexual activity' (p. 12). Yet, decoupling sex and intimacy and permitting its existence outside of the committed couple dyad offers the potential for a new and exciting reading of the creative couple state of mind, rather than one that is premised on dysfunction or symptomatic of a failure in the primary couple container.

Benioff (2017) helpfully reminds us that 'desire and sexuality are unruly, capricious, resistant to conscious control, and always threaten to undermine our ideal views of ourselves and our partners' (p. 213). Clulow (2017) calls our attention to an attachment perspective that 'having confidence in someone who can be relied upon to be both available and responsive, creates room for feelings of sexual desire' (p. 198). In other words, partners who feel secure with each other may be able to deepen their sexual relationship because they are not having to contend with the fear of rejection or abandonment that might impact their sexual desire. Eagle (2007), on the other hand, notes that 'there is a good deal of evidence that predictability, familiarity and availability frequently dampen the intensity of sexual interest and excitement' (p. 197), something that perhaps accounts for the demise of so many exclusive couple relationships, whilst also providing at least part of the explanation for why some individuals and couples choose to open their relationship or opt to have more than one romantic partner at any one time.

Clulow (ibid) introduces yet another variable into the mix when he says that 'abstinence, promiscuity, one-night stands, sexual coercion and cyber-sex are behaviours that can be understood in terms of attachment related anxieties' (p. 199), possibly suggesting that secure and insecure attachment patterns of relating may be relevant in distinguishing those in open and polyamorous relationships from those in more exclusive forms of relating. Indeed, there is a proposition that securely attached individuals are found to be more comfortable than insecurely attached individuals with their sexuality and, as a consequence, are more likely to eschew casual sex outside of their relationships (Hazen, Campa & Gur-Yaish, 2006, as outlined by Brown, 2015.) Stretching the point further, Brown (2015) suggests that additional research (Freeney, Noller & Patty, 1993; Ridge & Freeney, 1998) has found that avoidantly attached men tend to have more sexual partners than those who are anxiously attached, and that the avoidantly attached men tend to have more permissive attitudes about sex and report more casual sex outside of their relationships, an attempt, perhaps, to avoid dependence on or being burdened by the needs of others. Brown (ibid) concludes that 'open relationships are more successful when the gay male partners are securely attached or appear to meet each other's emotional needs at a mutually acceptable level through a complementary dyadic pattern' (p. 396).

Reflecting further on these theoretical considerations, I find it interesting that infidelity continues to occupy such a compelling focus for the field in theorizing partners looking outside of their primary relationships. Given the absence of secret non-monogamy as a feature of open and polyamorous relationships, how then might we understand and explain this thinking in regard to those in non-exclusive relationships. Furthermore, although the theory underpinning couple psychoanalytic and attachment theory offers a rich conceptualization and backdrop for practice, I am, nevertheless, concerned about the appropriation of theory in the service of reinforcing beliefs about what may be considered desirable and functional over that in which the reading of the couple's situation, i.e., non-monogamy, may be less welcome or appropriate in regard to their developmental needs. That said, perhaps a more fruitful line of exploration would be that of understanding the beliefs about relating that lie at the heart of open relationships and those who practice polyamory, in addition to understanding how they might feel about approaching a couple psychotherapist for help?

Towards an understanding of open relationships

In a previously published paper (McCann, 2017), I suggested that 'the sense of fluidity of relationships in the non-heterosexual world is, to some extent, shaped by the lack of a sanctioned institutional framework for intimate partnering, in turn creating opportunities for creativity and choice largely denied to couples subscribing to a framework of monogamy' (p. 46). This may explain why, in my practice with lesbian, gay and bisexual couples, there seems to be such openness to thinking about open and polyamorous relationships, in marked contrast to that of my work with straight couples. This is perhaps not so surprising given the recent findings of a YouGov poll (2016) where only 10% of respondents opted for non-monogamy when asked, 'what would be your ideal relationship' and barely 5% indicated that they would be tolerant of their partner's wish to engage in sexual activities with someone else. Yet, the increased tolerance towards open relationships, especially amongst gay men and bisexuals, need not trouble us too much since, in and of itself, it does not seem to be problematic, provided that, according to Spears & Lowen (2010), the couple is able to openly negotiate the rules governing the framework within which the open relationship operates. However, for some couples, there may be a danger of one of the partners pushing to open the relationship and the other attempting to resist, resulting in what is termed 'mono-shaming', an attempt to pressure the resistant partner into submission, or threatening the demise of the couple if the partner does not agree to the opening of the relationship.

Open relationships refer to a form of dyadic couple relationship that is open to partners having sex with others, although not usually forming loving or deep attachments with anyone other than the primary partner. Indeed, within gay male couple relationships, this openness usually takes the form of the men in a primary relationship cruising (either together or separately) for sex with other men. The sexual encounters tend to be brief, although sometimes there may be longer-term sexual friendships. Gay men themselves report varying levels of emotional connection to sexual partners outside their primary relationship, but ultimately, they view their primary relationship as the strongest source of comfort, reliability and security (Pawlicki & Larson, 2011). However, in the same way that sexual infidelity in monogamous relationships constitutes a crisis for the couple, emotional infidelity within an open relationship may be just as devastating, since it suggests that one of the partners has formed a strong emotional connection to a sexual partner outside of the primary relationship, thereby threatening its foundation.

The splitting of sex and emotion that often accompanies the decision to open an existing couple relationship is something that can feel both challenging and alien to many. This is especially so for those holding strong beliefs in the exclusivity of couple relationships and who consciously or unconsciously impart these beliefs onto others. Greenwell (2020) reminds us that queer sexuality that doesn't fit the heterosexual mould of family is still treated with distain. The discomfort and confusion that may accompany a therapist's realisation that the couple with whom they are working is considering opening their relationship, is something that needs careful thought, especially given the dangers of the therapist's implicit bias being communicated to the couple. Yet, Bonello (2009) suggests that sexual variety is often a central motivating factor for most couples who choose non-exclusive relationship arrangements, and for some, it provides freedom from dead, redundant patterns of psychosexual relating as well as an important means of managing discrepancies in sexual desire. Some have even suggested that being in an open relationship actually enhances the sex and intimacy within the committed relationship (Bergstrand & Williams, 2000; Spears & Lowen, 2010). This point is further underlined by Barash & Lipton (2001) who put forward the idea that sexual satisfaction with primary partners is often revived when partners experience each other in a new light and that passionate love may be rekindled when partners venture outside of the primary relationship. However, although the incidence of gay men and bisexuals electing to open their relationships is believed to be high, those turning to therapy suggest particular challenges that may be worthy of further exploration.

Drawing on the work of Constantine and Constanine (1972) and Macklin (1978), in thinking about open and polyamorous relationships, Weitzman *et al* (2009) suggest that couples in non-traditional relationships tend to present for therapy with issues that are not dissimilar to those in more traditional couple relationships. Included in their list of presenting problems are: inadequate communication; differences in the degree of commitment; conflicting expectations; and the search for a balance between autonomy and intimacy, something that has already been discussed (Colman, 1993; Ruszczynski, 1993). Deri (2011), however, suggests that differences in attitude between partners towards sexual intimacy can be enough to create considerable relationship distress, and from my work with gay male couples in open relationships, I have been struck by the depth of the distress and disturbance within the primary relationship that result in these couples presenting for therapy. What seems to be at play in these encounters is a conscious wish for one or both of the partners to address discrepant sexual needs within the primary relationship through the decision to look outside. Moreover, although the majority of the couples I have seen have agreed to a framework and set of expectations for opening their relationship, it is noticeable how, in a number of these cases, the experience of opening their relationship appears to have exerted a destabilizing influence on the couple's primary connection, to the extent that they seek therapy to prevent a separation or divorce. Perhaps new passionate encounters obscure attention to the challenges that most couples face, linked to unconscious processes and feelings that such encounters stir-up in the individuals and couples concerned (see Nathan's chapter in this book for a fuller examination of this phenomenon)

Case example

Matt and Jason, a gay couple of nine years standing, agreed to open their relationship to, as they put it, introduce some excitement into their sex life, which they said had become both dull and routine. The couple had already decided that they would only ever see other men together, a decision that may have been influenced by Jason having cheated on Matt five years previously and Matt having then threatened to leave. It is of note that Jason's father had also cheated on his mother in the past.

In starting psychotherapy, the couple believed that they had worked through the upset caused by Jason's affair, and at the point that they discussed seeing other men together, their intention was to deepen their sexual connection. Nonetheless, in the triangular dynamics of the threesomes, Matt had quickly found himself the outsider, as Jason and the 'third' partnered-up, leaving Matt feeling angry and resentful. Matt then tried to deal with this rejection by suggesting that he and Jason start seeing other men separately, and although Jason was not entirely sure, he did accept that the threesomes were not working so well for them as a couple. Matt, whose father had left when he was two years old, subsequently looked solely to his mother for the fulfillment of his attachment needs. However, when he was nine years old, his mother introduced her own 'third' in the form of a stepfather. Although Matt recounted the event with little emotion, he was clearly deeply distressed by this turn of events, much as he had been when Jason had the affair and again when Jason partnered-up with the outsider in the threesome encounters. Matt's unconscious rage relating to being pushed out led to multiple encounters of his own, and before long, Jason was feeling abandoned and 'betrayed'. Jason soon learned that Matt was forming passionate relationships with two of the guys he was seeing, and sex between Matt and Jason had all but stopped. The couple presented for therapy in crisis, and feelings were running high. The early stages of the work were dominated by the need to provide a container in order to help Matt and Jason begin the painful process of trying to understand what was happening to them and their relationship. During the eleven months of therapy with this couple, I suggested that perhaps Jason was being made to feel some of Matt's unacknowledged pain and outrage. Being on the outside, Jason felt powerless to control Matt's manic attempts to deal with his own psychic pain through the excitement of sex (Nathans 2012). Unfortunately, for the couple, Matt's unconscious retaliation was setting up a rivalrous dynamic in Jason, who was now becoming secretive and punitive towards Matt, by starting his own affairs. Whilst drawing particular attention to the need for the couple to make use of the containment the therapy offered, I did manage to think with them about the shared unconscious pain and disappointment that they were feeling as a result of opening their relationship, especially since it referenced some deep-rooted unconscious associations with their respective internal parental couples. For instance, I understood that Matt and Jason had an identification with their respective fathers, who had both looked outside their primary relationships for something that may have been missing within or, which had felt unresolvable. However, in seeking therapy, it was possible to be curious about the ways in which their past histories interacted with current trends relating to the openness of gay male couple relationships and how what they were doing seemed to be destroying their primary connection. Armed with this knowledge, they seemed to take a step back, and in the reflective space that had opened within the therapy, they were more able to look towards each other rather than to turn away.

Whilst accepting that this composite case illustration raises some difficult questions for those opening their relationships, it is worth noting that there are a number of couples in open relationships that seem to work extremely well (Spears and Lowen, 2010) and, it would also appear that through this means, they secure their primary relationship which might otherwise have faltered. Nevertheless, it is important to acknowledge that un-mourned loss of sexual functioning within the primary relationship, manifest in a conscious or unconscious fantasy that opening the relationship will provide a much-needed solution, may not always go to plan, especially given the need for couples to establish a secure enough base or foundation as a necessary prerequisite for deciding to open their relationship. As with Matt and Jason, the un-mourned loss of their sexual relationship appeared to reference other losses that only became apparent during the course of the therapy, and these served to reinforce their shared sense of abandonment, betrayal and insecurity. Only through identifying and addressing these issues and making the necessary links to the source of the disturbance were the couple able to think about what was happening to them and their relationship. Their decision to keep their relationship open, following the therapy, suggests that there was both a clearer understanding and firmer framework on which to take things forward.

To my mind, the process of therapy with Matt and Jason constitutes a version of the *creative couple* within the meaning of Morgan's (ibid) definition, especially since it demonstrates an ability between the couple to think about the meaning of what it is that is happening to them. This, in turn, enables them to use their relationship as a resource to help them work together in finding a less defensive solution to the problems within their partnership manifested in the opening of their relationship. Further reinforcing this point, Clulow (2017), from an attachment perspective, suggests that an important aim of couple therapy is 'to increase the capacity of the couple relationship to act as a safe haven and secure base for the partners, containing their anxieties and enabling them to weather the storms of life and learn from them' (p. 210). He goes on to describe the therapist's task as that of working with 'the psychological skin around the couple, making their relationship, rather than either of the partners the principle focus of attention and the site for change' (p. 210). I believe that this is exactly what happened in my work with Matt and Jason, who came to see their primary relationship as a safe haven and one that allowed them the freedom to look outside without the fear of abandonment or the demise of their couple connection.

Polyamory

Polyamory (or poly) is commonly defined as a form of consensual or ethical non-monogamy, where individuals and partners maintain multiple, simultaneous relationships of varying degrees of emotional and/or sexual intimacy. According to Deri (2011), 'the term polyamory was coined in 1990 by Morning-Glory Zell, a self-proclaimed polyamorist, and the terms *polyamory*, *polyamorist* and *polyamorous* officially entered the Oxford English Dictionary in 2006'. The increased exposure of polyamory within the society may be viewed as a response to the limitations of monogamy, where exclusive relationships are frequently seen as an unrealistic ideal. Weitzman *et al* (2009) also highlight the importance of clinicians and counselling professionals being prepared to help clients navigate this new relationship terrain, and Anapol (2010) suggests that it is essential that we loosen our attachment to conditioned beliefs about love, sex, intimacy and commitment, especially since polyamory seems to blur the boundaries between sex, friendship and intimacy.

Koyanagi (2018) helpfully identifies four types of polyamorous relationships and usefully explains the differences between them.

*   The *primary partner and others approach* – reflects a relationship between a couple where one or both of the individuals within that relationship have other partners. Although, as a couple, they negotiate the kind of relationship that one or either partner has with the other, in

essence they ensure the protection of their primary relationship alongside all other relationships which are positioned in qualitatively different ways. To my mind, it differs from open relationships, as outlined above, because there is less emphasis on sex, although this may also be a feature of these poly relationships.
- In the *group approach* – an individual may be engaged with multiple people in the same relationship. However, it is important to emphasise that although a person may be having individual relationships, there is also the group dynamic that links the partners to each other and to the group as a whole and, in situations where sexual exclusivity exists within the group, this is known as poly fidelity.
- Within the *egalitarian network approach* – no one relationship is centred as the main relationship in a person's life, and although some of these relationships may replicate that of the primary relationship, the difference here is that the individual in the *egalitarian approach* may have a number of these relationships. Essentially, these are people who have chosen polyamory for themselves and may, for instance, be part of a multi-person household with an entire poly network of lovers all living together or an individual having multiple relationships with partners who do not necessarily wish to meet or live with the other partners.
- The *solo approach* – 'looks like the *egalitarian network approach*, in that each individual person decides how to engage in their relationship with other people and no one central relationship determines the shape of other relationships' (Koyanagi, ibid). However, solo polyamorists never couple-up in a central relationship, such as a primary relationship or a central group, but neither do they couple-up with many different people. Solo polyamorists are in relationships, but as Koyanagi suggests, they maintain the identity of a solo individual and may identify as single even if they are in multiple romantic relationships, or the way they structure their lives is more centred on the individual rather than centring couple-hood or family. Most solo polyamorists choose not to marry or live with anyone and may best be characterised by 'living apart together'.

Case example

It was one year into my work with Eleanor when she revealed that she was in a poly relationship with a married couple named Andrew and Lisa. Eleanor, aged thirty years, had presented with anxiety following the sudden and unexpected death of her mother six months earlier. The beginning stages of the work were dominated by Eleanor's feelings of anxiety and depression, which seemed to be related to the death of her mother, but also linked to her sense of isolation and her lack of success in finding an intimate partnership. Eleanor identifies as bisexual and works as an assistant director for a charitable organization specialising in conservation.

Before Eleanor told me that she was in a poly relationship, I heard that some months ago, she had met a woman called Lisa at a conference and that they had really hit it off. I thought that they had become best friends, but I later understood that Lisa had been keen for Eleanor to meet Andrew, her husband, and that the three of them soon began hanging out together.

In the sessions that followed her disclosure, Eleanor seemed different with me, more alive and more hopeful. However, it took her a while longer to actually let me know what was happening, 'you see I fear the judgment of others'. Yet, we also thought about the stress of Eleanor having to keep this new and exciting relationship secret. She could not at that time see a way of integrating the relationship into her life, a situation that intensified following her decision to move in with Lisa and Andrew. Despite Eleanor telling me that things were going well after moving into the couple's home, she was fraught with insecurities about being the outsider in the 'throuple'. Added to this, she was preoccupied by the fears of what others might think of her if they should ever learn that she was in a poly relationship. Some of Eleanor's anxieties seemed to be related to Lisa and Andrew being a couple and Eleanor's confusion about her position within the group. Furthermore, as the relationship deepened, the partners became more exposed to their differences, i.e., Lisa and Andrew's wish to take care of Eleanor, and Eleanor's need to take care of herself. These differences began to create conflicts in relation to their individual needs and those of the group. On a number of occasions, Eleanor even considered leaving the relationship and seemed desperately conflicted in terms of her wish for closeness and her need for space and separateness. She complained bitterly about the dominance of the couple and of her being second best, but she also accepted that her fear of conflict was not helpful to her in the negotiation of fairness and equity between the three of them, possibly a feature of some poly relationships.

Deri (2011) argues 'that poly is closely aligned with queerness, since polyamorists resist mono-normativity and challenge the dominance of the nuclear family'. Given its radical nature, i.e., a sex-positive community in which 'a variety of forms of sexual sharing between consenting adults are affirmed' (Weitzman *et al* 2009), it seems likely that couple psychotherapists trained to think in terms of dyadic couple relationships may struggle to comprehend their poly clients. This may also explain why so many poly clients fail to disclose their poly lifestyle in therapy, since there may be an absence of mirroring, incongruity between internalized values and the values expressed to others, and confusion concerning one's place within poly networks and rules of engagement. Weitzman *et al* (ibid) suggest that it is important for therapists to distinguish troubled individual, couple or group dynamics from problematic transitions in predominantly healthy poly relationships, for instance, supporting individuals in moving forward with decisions about exploring polyamory in its many forms. Equally, helping those in poly relationships manage fears and insecurities related to letting go of the romantic ideal about being the 'one and only' may be something that is also shared by therapists. Furthermore, attempts to overcome jealousy in poly relationships with *compersion*, i.e., taking delight in a partner's love for another, may be felt by analytically trained therapists as an extreme act of denial.

Developing the thinking further, it seems that the tension outlined by Colman (ibid) concerning the need of individuals in relationships to develop outside the relationship as well as within, may have greater meaning for those in poly relationships, as the partners balance the 'I' and the 'You' with the 'We' and the 'Us'. Moreover, we might assume that the projective system, which has such meaning for couple therapists working primarily with dyadic relationships, can be equally applied to those in poly relationships. Returning to Eleanor's relationship with Lisa and Andrew, it is possible that Eleanor struggled to individuate from a mother who looked to her daughter, following the death of Eleanor's father when she was in her early teens. In the wake of her own mother's death, Eleanor was finally free to pursue her own intimacy needs. Her choice of an established couple, perhaps because it allowed her the possibility of being part of an intimate relationship whilst also being separate from it, might not have been as possible within the tighter confines of a dyadic couple relationship. Similarly, Lisa and Andrew may also unconsciously have chosen Eleanor to mediate something for them related to the sharing of psychic space within the confines of their long-term dyadic relationship. The unconscious relational fit for all three partners might therefore be one of finding a comfortable space within the 'throuple' to accommodate their respective psychological spatial needs. Without the space to think, perhaps with a therapist who helped Eleanor hold the specific tensions of the poly relationship she was in, Eleanor may well have retreated. Instead, she was helped to stay in and face the complexities of her relationship with Lisa and Andrew and their relationship with her — an example of a developmental process. During the work, we also considered whether all three partners might benefit from attending together, but Eleanor was reluctant to consider this, as she believed that the insecurities and anxieties were all hers. Thankfully, in thinking about the projective system, this belief has now shifted, to the extent that she can see more clearly the inner workings of Lisa and Andrew's relationship and the part she plays for them and them for her.

Conclusion

In this chapter, I have attempted to challenge the dominance of dyadic couple relationships in the theory and practice of couple psychotherapy, by considering other relationship configurations, namely, those in open relationships and those who embrace polyamorary. However, this challenge occasions another task, that of considering how theory relating to the functioning of couple relationships come to be thought about and applied to those in non-exclusive relationships. Although I accept that it is not the job of the couple psychotherapist to impose their own preferred models of relating when working with couples, I still think that we need to consider how a therapist holding a belief in the greater functionality of those in exclusive couple relationships might, through the transference and countertransference dynamics of the work, affect the nature of the therapeutic encounter. In addition, there is also the question of the therapist's own openness to working with more than two partners at any one time and, perhaps, the question of how they might think about and manage dual relationships, i.e., the partner in one couple being seen in parallel with a partner from another couple. Ultimately, as for all of us working with difference, it is felt to be helpful for therapists to self-examine and to keep an eye on their approach, and this seems equally important for couple therapists working with those in non-exclusive relationships, even if they rarely encounter these clients in their practice.

References

Anapol, D. (2010). *Polyamory in the 21st Century: Love and Intimacy with Multiple Partners*. Lanham, MD: Rowman & Littlefield.

Barash, D.P., & Lipton, J.E. (2001). *The Myth of Monogamy: Fidelity and Infidelity in Animal and People*. New York: W.H. Freeman.

Barker, M. (2013). *Rewriting the Rules: An Integrative Guide to Love, Sex and Relationships*. Hove, East Sussex: Routledge.

Benioff, L. (2017). Discussion of "How was it for you? Attachment, sexuality and mirroring in couple relationships. In S. Nathans & M. Schaeffer (Eds.), *Couples on the Couch: Psychoanalytic Couple Therapy and the Tavistock Model* (pp. 213–220). New York: Routledge.

Bergstrand, C., & Williams, J.B. (2000). Today's alternative marital styles: The case of swingers. *Electronic Journal of Human Sexuality*, 3(10).

Bonello, K. (2009). Gay monogamy and extra-dyadic sex: a critical review. *Counselling Psychology Review*, 24: 51–65.

Britton, R. (1998). Subjectivity, objectivity and triangular space. In *Belief and Imagination: Explorations in Psychoanalysis* (pp. 41–58). London: Routledge.

Brown, J. (2015). Couple therapy for gay men: exploring sexually open and closed relationships through the lens of hetero-normative masculinity and attachment style. *Journal of Family Therapy*, 37: 386–402.

Clulow, C. (2017). How was it for you? Attachment, sexuality and mirroring in couple relationships. In S. Nathans & M. Schaeffer (Eds.), *Couples on the Couch: Psychoanalytic Couple Therapy and the Tavistock Model* (pp. 193–212). New York: Routledge.

Colman, W. (1993). Marriage as a psychological container. In S. Ruszczynski (Ed.), *Psychotherapy with Couples: Theory and Practice at the Tavistock Institute of Marital Studies* (pp. 70–96). London: Karnac.

Conley, T., Moors, A., Matsick, J., Zeigler, A. (2013). The fewer the merrier? Assessing stigma surrounding consensually non-monogamous romantic relationships. *Analysis of Social Issues and Public Policy*, 13, 1–30.

Constantine, L. & Constantine, J. (1972). Counselling implications of co-marital and multilateral relations. In C. Sager & H. Kaplan (Eds.), *Progress in Group and Family Therapy* (pp. 537–552). New York: Brunner/Mazel.

D'Ercole, A., & Drescher, J. (Eds.) (2004). *Uncoupling Convention: Psychoanalytic Approaches to Same-Sex Couples and Families.* New York: Routledge.

Deri, J. (2011). Polyamory or polyagony? Jealously in open relationships. Doctoral Thesis. Simon Fraser University. (core.ac.uk).

Eagle, M. (2007). Attachment and sexuality. In D. Diamond, S. Blatt & J. Lichtenberg (Eds.), *Attachment and Sexuality.* New York: Analytic Press.

Freeney, J., Noller, P., & Patty, J. (1993). Adolescents' interactions with the opposite sex: Influence in attachment style and gender. *Journal of Adolescence, 16*: 169–186.

Greenwell, G. (2020). The joy of writing about sex. *The Guardian*, 9th May 2020 (pp. 18–19).

Hazen, C., Campa, M. & Gur-Yaish, N. (2006). What is adult attachment? In M. Mikulincer & G.S. Goodman (Eds.), *Dynamics of Romantic Love: Attachment, Caregiving and Sex* (pp. 47–70). New York: Guildford.

Jamieson, L. (2004). Intimacy, negotiated nonmonogamy and the limits of the couple. In J. Duncombe, K. Harrison, G. Allan & D. Marsden (Eds.), *The State of Affairs; Explorations in Infidelity and Commitment.* New Jersey: Lawrence Erlbaum Associates, Publishers.

Kernberg, O.F. (1991). Aggression and love in the relationship of the couple. *Journal of the American Psychoanalytic Association, 39*(1): 45–70.

Kernberg, O.F. (1993). The couple's constructive and destructive superego functions. *Journal of the American Psychoanalytic Association, 41*(3): 653–677.

Koyanagi, J. (2018). The four types of polyamory. YouTube.

Macklin, E.D. (1978). Counselling persons in non-traditional relationships. In C. Simpkinson & L. Platt (Eds.), *Synopsis of Family Therapy Practice* (pp. 134–139). Olney, MD: Family Therapy Practice Network.

Matsick, J.L., Conley, T.D., Ziegler, A., Moors, A.C., & Rubin, J.D. (2014) Love and sex: Polyamorous relationships are perceived more favourably than swinging and open relationships. *Psychology & Sexuality, 5*(4): 339–348.

McCann, D. (2017). When the couple is not enough, or when the couple is too much: Exploring the meaning and management of open relationships. *Couple and Family Psychoanalysis, 7*(1): 45–58.

Morgan, M. (2005). On being able to be a couple: the importance of a "creative couple" in psychic life. In F. Grier (Ed.), *Oedipus and the Couple* (pp. 9–30). London: Karnac Books.

Morgan, M. (2019). *The Couple State of Mind: Psychoanalysis of Couples and the Tavistock Relationships Model.* Abingdon, Oxon: Routledge.

Nathans, S. (2012). Infidelity as manic defence. *Couple and Family Psychoanalysis, 2*(2): 165–180.

Pawlicki, P., & Larson, P. (2011). The dynamics and conceptualisation of non-exclusive relationships in gay male couples. *Sexual & Relationship Therapy, 26*(1): 48–60.

Rasmussen, P.R., & Kilborne, K.J. (2014). Sex in intimate relationships: Variations and challenges. In P.R Peluso (Ed.), *Infidelity: A Practitioner's Guide to Working with Couples in Crisis* (pp. 11–30). New York: Routledge.

Ridge, S.R., & Freeney, J.A. (1998). Relationship history and relationship attitudes in gay males and lesbians: attachment styles and gender differences. *Australian and New Zealand Journal of Psychiatry, 32*: 848–859.

Ruszczynski, S. (1993). *Psychotherapy with couples: Theory and Practice at the Tavistock Institute of Marital Studies*. London: Karnac Books.

Ruszczynski, S. (2005). Reflective space in the intimate couple relationship: the "marital triangle". In F. Grier (Ed.), *Oedipus and the Couple* (pp. 31–47). London: Karnac Books.

Scharff, D.E. (2014). Working with affairs. In D.E. Scharff & J.S. Scharff (Eds.), *Psychoanalytic Couple Therapy: Foundations of Theory and Practice* (pp. 254–268). London: Karnac.

Spears, B., & Lowen, L. (2010). Beyond monogamy: lessons from long-term male couples in non-monogamous relationships. http://thecouplesstudy.com/wp-content/uploads/BeyondMonogamy_1_01.pdf

Spence, H. (1997). Sex and relationships. In W.K. Halford & H.J. Markham (Eds.), *Clinical Handbook of Marriage and Couples Intervention* (pp. 73–101). New York: John Wiley.

Weitzman, G., Davidson, J., Phillips, J.R., Fleckenstein, J.R., & Morotti-Meeker, C. (2009). What psychology professionals should know about polyamory. Baltimore, US: National Coalition for Sexual Freedom. www.ncsfreedom.org

YouGov (2016). d25d2506sfb94s.cloudfront.net

Chapter 10

Psychosexual considerations in working LGBTQ+ couples and individuals

Marian O'Connor

Introduction

Psychoanalysis since Freud has largely ignored sexuality, and Pacey (2018) argues that psychodynamic couple therapy tends 'to separate out mind and body in sex, rather than holding them together and maintaining a tension between them' (2018, p. 3). This chapter will attempt to 'hold together' body and mind by presenting an integrated approach in attending to psychosexual considerations in working with lesbian, gay, bisexual, transgender, queer (LGBTQ+) couples and individuals.

Psychosexual therapy with LGBTQ+-specific considerations

It can be difficult and shameful for anyone to admit to having problems with sex. This was true in the days when sex was regarded as something private, never to be spoken about, and it is true today, when sex has come out of the bedroom and is celebrated in films, TV and social media. Admitting to sexual problems may be particularly difficult for LGBTQ+ clients who may already be carrying the weight of secrecy, shame and trauma left over from their adolescence plus the weight of now having to be 'out and proud' of their sexuality.

Research has shown that most health care workers, including psychotherapists, find it difficult to talk about sexual matters with clients (Byers, 2011). Even when doctors or therapists see a patient with a condition such as advanced prostate cancer (the treatment for which may involve a medical or surgical castration), they will not usually discuss how the treatment might impact the man's sense of self, his sexual relationship, and what the effect might be on his sexual partner. Couple therapists may not fare any better, 'While it is true to say that a sexual difficulty can have a corrosive effect on the entire relationship it is also a notoriously difficult topic to discuss for both patient and therapist' (Seymour, 2014, p. 228).

Talking about sex with LGBTQ+ clients may present additional difficulties. Research 'has consistently confirmed that the majority of therapists

DOI: 10.4324/9781003255703-10

are ill-equipped to work with LGB clients, having had little training on the topic of sexuality, and often expressing a lack of knowledge about such clients' (Evans and Barker, 2010, p. 375).

There are many reasons why psychotherapists might find it hard to talk to their patients about sex. Psychoanalytically trained therapists might argue that they work in the here and now and will not ask in detail about sexual functioning unless their patient brings it up. The counter argument to this is that the mother/child transference relationship prevalent in Kleinian and object relations therapy means patients will not bring it up.

Most psychotherapists are not trained to talk about the specifics of sex and will have no model from their own therapist or supervisor to do so. In addition, what goes on behind the parental bedroom door is a taboo subject in most families, and talking about sex with patients may elicit fear or shame in therapists, 'as if they are peeping through the door of their parent's bedroom. Envy, too, can be evoked; any glimpsed sexual rapture may stir-up oedipal anxieties of being left out and inadequate' (O'Connor, 2019, p. 92). Feelings of shame and inadequacy may be exacerbated in the therapist if clients have a different sexual orientation; concerns about voyeurism may pervade if, for example, a heterosexual therapist asks for specific detail about a gay couple's sex life.

These days, LGBTQ+ couples and individuals who seek psychosexual therapy come not for help in changing or accepting their orientation but to improve their sexual satisfaction. They may present with sexual problems similar to that of heterosexual clients — loss of desire, discordant desire, erection difficulties, lack of orgasm, painful penetration, compulsive use of porn, and it might be comfortable for psychosexual therapists to declare that they treat all clients just the same, regardless of sexual orientation or preference. However, Nichols (2014) cautions therapists not to apply heterosexual standards of normal sexuality to the treatment of sexual minority clients, stressing the importance of keeping an open mind and being flexible in both the method and goals of treatment.

Berry and Lezos (2017) identify important clinical principles for sex therapists working with diverse sexual populations: self reflection, client-affirmation and normalizing.

- *Self reflection* (enabled by personal therapy, supervision, use of transference and countertransference) is a central tenet for psychoanalytically oriented psychotherapists and for psychosexual therapists trained in the integrated model at Tavistock Relationships. When a therapist is aware of a sense of discomfort when listening to clients talking about their LGBTQ+ experiences, they, he or she will question whether the discomfort is coming from personal ignorance, fear of difference, anxieties about voyeurism, or whether the discomfort is coming from the clients' anxiety which is being picked up in the countertransference.

- *Client affirmation and normalizing* may challenge some therapists who will need to question and expand their knowledge if they wish to work with LGBTQ+. Berry and Lezos suggest that therapists need to be open to accepting that psychologically healthy individuals may not want to have sex (asexuality) or may favour non-monogamous relationships; that sexual identity and behaviours can be fluid and that diverse sexual expression is something to be appreciated rather than pathologised. Nichols and Shernoff (2007 p. 381) write, 'Sexuality is powerful, complex, multidetermined and multifunctional: it is part hard-wiring and part early environmental imprinting… sex is by design hostile, dangerous, shame and anxiety evoking, objectifying, and frightening as well as joyful and intimate and sweet.'

Another area under question when working with diverse sexualities is the use of the DSMV classification system (American Psychiatric Association, 2013) to identify particular problems. As course leader of a nationally accredited psychosexual training, I use DSMV, but I agree that words like dysfunction or addiction may be problematic, especially when working with LGBTQ+ who may already suffer from labelling and stigmatisation. Kort (2018, p. xii) writes, 'I no longer see sexual addiction as a useful framework for treatment. In fact, I think it's mostly abusive to gay and bisexual men.' Many therapists now refer to 'sexual problems' rather than dysfunctions and 'problematic, compulsive or impulsive use of porn' rather than 'porn addiction' (which is, by the way, not a DSMV classification). On the other hand, giving a name to a problem can be relieving for clients, especially when they feel they are the only person out there with the issue. For example, using the phrase 'delayed ejaculation' can be helpful to a client who is unable to ejaculate inside his partner and considers himself alone with this problem. Clients often say, with some relief, 'Oh, you've heard of it, then.'

Client affirmation and normalizing are not used uncritically to avoid real disturbance. Both will be tempered by the therapist's self-reflection and experience of the transference/countertransference relationship in the room. For example, a man came to see me because his wife had discovered that he was meeting men for sex. She threatened to leave him and take their son unless he changed. As I sat in the room with him, it became clear that his problem had little to do with whether he was gay, bisexual or straight. His problem was a failure to relate. He spoke about his wife and the men he met for sex in the same, part-object way. They were all means to an end; his wife gave him a home and a son, the men gave him sexual pleasure. I was a part-object too — someone who would stop his wife leaving. He showed no interest or curiosity in me, himself or anyone in his life. Perhaps the extreme forms of BDSM sex he favoured with his male lovers were necessary in order to feel anything at all.

Psychosexual case studies – an integrated model

Psychotherapy alone may not help couples and individuals improve their sexual relationship (Green and Seymour, 2009). The clinical examples below demonstrate an affirmative, integrated approach, using a psychoanalytically informed stance to explore relationship issues and unconscious blocks to a free expression of sexuality; psychoeducation to inform and to counteract sexual myths; behavioural exercises to work directly with the body.

Setting behavioural exercises for homework and asking clients to report back on their experience is a challenge to traditional psychoanalytic work. Pacey (2018) points out that there has been little theoretical thinking about the concept of an integrated psychosexual model and has proposed that working with the body might be likened to Ogden's (1994) concept of interpretive action in psychoanalysis. She suggests using Winnicott as a theoretical base, 'clinical experience indicates that couples do not move smoothly through the sensate focus programme; early bodily experience, often primitive and preverbal, is re-enacted in the intimacy of the exercises.' Winnicott's (1968a, p. 18) concept of the 'experiential conglomerate,' by which all experience is held lifelong in the body, seems to support this observation' (Pacey, 2018 p. 43). The Winnicottian concept of holding can be useful, too, in assessing whether the couple or individual have built up enough trust in the therapist to take on homework exercises, having 'begun to build up a belief in a protective, benign and safe environment' (idem. p. 118).

I will not go into details of a full self focus and sensate focus programme as this can be found elsewhere (Green and Seymour, 2009). Rather I will focus on aspects of particular relevance when working with LBGTQ+ clients. Similarly, I will touch lightly on psychoanalaytic concepts underpinning the therapy.

In order to protect client confidentially, I have used composite case examples.

Ivan – Fear of penetration

Ivan came to therapy aged 27 because he found it difficult to keep his erection in sexual encounters with male partners. He had no medical issues and was able to maintain an erection and achieve orgasm when masturbating. Although he did not admit to himself that he was gay until he left home to go to university, he suffered homophobic verbal abuse in secondary school where he was laughed at for being feminine and a 'homo.'

His sense of being an outsider, that 'something was wrong with him' continued once he came out as gay. At university and later, as a shy, unconfident man attending gay events in London, he found it hard to seek out partners. He assumed that other gay men were confident sexually, did not find anal sex difficult and could sustain an erection for hours. His internalised homophobia meant that it was hard for him to love himself or to believe he could find a gay man who would be loving and kind. 'They all want anal sex on the first date,' he told me.

Work with Ivan involved psychodynamic therapy to examine how his view of relationships was coloured by his parents' unhappy marriage and how his view of himself was affected by his sense of never being good enough for his father. He held unexpressed aggression towards his mother for not protecting him as well as towards his cruel and belittling father. As an adult, he projected this aggression onto potential sexual partners and indeed to the whole of the gay community whom he viewed as uncaring and predatory.

> Arguably the most common problems LGBTQs bring to treatment involve the development of a personal identity that includes sexuality and the resolution of shame and fear round having a socially stigmatized self (Nichols and Shernoff, 2007, p. 383)

Ivan's unassertive character was evident in the transference relationship to me. He was a 'good' client who attended regularly, agreed with everything I said, performed the mindful breathing exercises we did in the sessions and could see how they might be helpful in staying in touch with present sensations rather than being distracted by anxiety. Ivan found it difficult to get in touch with healthy aggression; this came out in a passive form by 'forgetting' to order any book I recommended or 'not having time' to do any exercise I suggested for homework. In the countertransference, I was becoming too forceful, too full of suggestions, and Ivan was refusing to be penetrated by my potency. We spoke about this issue. For Ivan, any form of potency was aggressive or bullying and could be countered only by hiding away, just as his mother closed her eyes to his father's aggression and was unable to protect her son.

As the therapy progressed, Ivan was able to introject me as a 'good enough' (Winnicott, 1958) object to start caring for himself. He bought *The New Male Sexuality* (Zilbergeld, 1999). This was written with a straight readership in mind but has a gentle and reassuring approach towards men's expectations of themselves, very different from that of Ivan's father, and Ivan wasn't yet ready to venture into the world of what he feared might be aggressively loud gay writers. The first two chapters are entitled, 'The Making of Anxious Performers' and 'It's Two Feet Long, Hard as Steel, and Will Knock Your Socks Off: The Fantasy Model of Sex.' These chapters really resonated with Ivan.

Appropriate reading matter for LGBTQ+ clients may involve novels as well as websites or books about sexuality. Ivan, in common with most young people, had grown up reading heteronormist literature and, while great novels can tell truths about the human condition regardless of sexuality, it seemed important to encourage Ivan to read about gay characters who might have experienced some of the struggles he was going through. Most of the gay relationships he was familiar with came from watching online porn, which just served to strengthen his stereotypical assumptions. It had not occurred to him to read any of the widely available gay literature and, once he got over his initial resistance, he read widely. The novel that touched him most was *Release* by Patrick Ness (2018), which is actually a young adult book but Ivan hadn't had the opportunity to read such books as a teenager. He enjoyed, too, *Yay! You're Gay! Now What?* (Khalaf, 2019), which was similarly written for teenagers.

Reading appropriate literature as well as informative books about sexuality can be helpful to therapists as well as to clients. The Megan/Morgan character in *Girl, Woman, Other* (Evaristo, 2019) has helped many have an understanding of what it means to be non-binary.

One of the issues therapists might face in seeing clients of a different sexuality to their own is that they may assume that their clients are experts on all matters to do with their sexual practice. Clearly with Ivan, this was not the case. Despite all the articles and programmes available in the media, there is a huge ignorance about sexual matters in the general population, and this includes therapists, cis-gendered heterosexuals and the LGBTQ+ population. Women often have problems in knowing the difference between their vulva and their vagina. This was reinforced by a recent Channel 4 programme (100 Vaginas, 2019) about a photographer who had photographed 100 vulvas (Dodsworth, 2019). The makers were understandably worried that a programme entitled 100 Vulvas might be mistaken for a programme about a Swedish car. Similarly, when gay clients say they have a problem with anal sex, we can't assume they know how to make this comfortable and, as psychosexual therapists, we might have to assume the role of educators.

For some, both LGBTQ+ and heterosexual, the anus is an erogenous zone. A recent survey (SKYN Condoms Millennial Sex Survey, 2017) of over 3,000 sexually active millennials found that 35% of women and 15% of men engage in anal sex at least some of the time. The anus is full of sensitive nerve endings, so can be very receptive to sexual stimulation, even without penetration. For the insertive partner, the tightness around the penis can be pleasurable and anal sex also stimulates the prostate gland in cis-gendered men, which can enhance their orgasm. Provided that care is taken, with the liberal use of lubricants, slow insertion, trimmed nails or rubber glove, and a condom to prevent sexually transmitted infections (STIs), anal sex can be safe for both men and women.

But what happens in an ongoing sexual relationship where one partner finds difficult or painful what the other partner really enjoys? If a heterosexual man loses his erection and is unable to penetrate a vagina or a woman finds sexual intercourse painful, will the psychosexual therapist suggest the couple find satisfaction in non-penetrative sex, or will a graded exercise programme be considered? Will this suggestion be different when the issue is around anal sex? Perhaps the important thing is to listen to the clients and to find out what they want and what they are willing to try. A survey (Rosenberger et al., 2011) of nearly 25,000 males who had sex with other men found that anal intercourse was practiced by 37% of the men within the previous month, and was most common among men aged 18–24. This statistic can offer relief to men who, like my client Ivan, believe that anal sex is practised 100% of the time by 100% of gay men.

Despite my normalising non-penetrative sex for gay men, Ivan wanted to find out in a safe environment whether anal pleasure would be possible for him. The psychodynamic work we had engaged in helped him believe he had a right to sexual pleasure. He began a series of graded exercises which started off with self focus, being mindful of his own body, his own arousal and noting intrusive thoughts that detracted him from his bodily sensations. He learnt the stop-start technique which involves masturbating to a point just before orgasm, stopping for several minutes and self pleasuring once again. This gave him the confidence to know that he can be aroused, lose his erection and then become aroused again.

Ivan continued to date occasionally and had a few sexual encounters where he was able to say he did not want anal sex and where he did sustain his erection for mutual masturbation. He even met a man with whom he felt sexually confident, and he kept the relationship going even though this man was not the long-term partner he was looking for. In some ways, he was indulging in a teenage sexual exploration that he missed out on first time round. Ivan moved on to homework exercises which focused on anal pleasure. He relaxed in a warm bath while exploring around his anus with his finger. This moved onto masturbation while exploring around his anus and then, using a latex glove and lubricant, he inserted the tip of his finger while keeping a mindful focus on the sensations aroused in his body. He enjoyed the sensation and ordered anal dilators to help him move on to the next stage of exploration.

Marcus and Carlo – Shame and humiliation

Sex therapy can be easier when couples come together for therapy as they are able to look at problems within the relationship which might be getting in the way of them having sex, plus they are able to try out a range of exercises for homework together. Also, most sexual problems appear within a relationship. Many individuals, like Ivan, are able to achieve sexual pleasure and orgasm on their own; problems with desire, erections, pain or orgasms tend to arise when with a sexual partner.

Carlo and Marcus came to psychosexual therapy because they had not had sex for four years. They were a married couple in their thirties and, while both wanted to start a family, they worried that their lack of intimacy and affection would have a detrimental effect on a child. It was also evident from the first session that they argued constantly. Carlo was the main breadwinner and Marcus looked after the home while studying for an arts degree. They each felt the other took them for granted and they rarely showed affection to one another. They had enjoyed anal sex when they first met eight years previously, with Carlo taking the 'top' position. When Marcus developed anal fissures, the couple decided to reverse positions, but Marcus stopped this practice as he said Carlo did not clean himself properly. Carlo felt shamed and humiliated and refused to engage with him sexually in any way.

Marcus and Carlo's relationship was clearly in trouble, and their recriminations and battles demonstrated how couples under stress show similar attachment behaviours to infants under stress — shouting, attacking, causing harm, or sulking, turning away, saying they don't care (Mattinson and Sinclair 1979, 47–51). It took many, many months of couple therapy before we were able to talk in greater depth about the loss associated with their sexual life.

Anal fissures are a common complaint in the general population, but when Marcus sought medical treatment, his doctor told him they were caused by anal sex and that the anus is not intended for penetration. Marcus felt humiliated by the doctor's comments during the consultation. He may then have projected the humiliation onto Carlo by accusing him of not being clean.

There is a scene in the poet Ocean Vuong's semi-autobiographical novel (Vuong, 2019) where he describes the hero being penetrated for the first time. He ends up loosening his bowels and is mortified, but his boyfriend is kind and accepting. Shit may happen and it might be important for therapists to know this and to provide appropriate psychoeducation.

If Carlo and Marcus had been working creatively as a couple, they might have worked through the initial sexual problem by, for example, using a special sheet for sex, a condom, an occasional enema. But neither of them had experienced a creative partnership with a caring parent, and this left them with strong, narcissistic traits whereby they each found it difficult to show real empathy for the other. Marcus felt angry when Carlo showed he had a different mind and body from his own. Carlo gained narcissistic gratification from looking after Marcus but felt rage when Marcus didn't appreciate his efforts. In addition, internalised homophobia resulted in verbal attacks on the other's body and sexuality. They were each reliving an early childhood trauma where they felt there was no one there to care for them and they were repeating solutions they used as infants to protect themselves. The early months of therapy were difficult as they felt easily abandoned or misunderstood by me, and accused me of siding with the other.

As the therapy progressed, a row erupted which resulted in Carlo locking Marcus out of their flat and Marcus throwing a brick through their window. The desperate and physical nature of this row shocked them and, they were able to get in touch with primitive feelings around the terror of abandonment and intrusion which underpinned many of their arguments. It led to an appreciation of each other's vulnerabilities and a greater ability to accept the different mind of the other, although it was still easy for each to get triggered into attack or defensive mode. As the couple became a little calmer and were feeling more held in the therapy, I suggested they start some behavioural work. Marcus had heard about self focus and sensate focus exercises and was scornful of the concept. Sex should be livelier, more spontaneous, he said — a not uncommon complaint from clients.

Self focus and sensate focus exercises (Masters and Johnson, 1970) have been criticised as too genitally centred, male centred and heteronormist. Some of Masters and Johnson's early theories about the sexual response cycle and arousal have been successfully challenged (Basson, 2002), but the principle of re-educating the mind and body to slow down and be mindful of 'here and now' sensations can enhance sensual and sexual pleasure in genital and non-genital sex for heterosexual and non-heterosexual couples. In many ways, the exercises may be likened to Tantric sex practices without the spiritual element, in the same way as mindfulness practice is similar to meditation. 'Tantra offers answers that have the effect of enhancing intimacy and deepening love. Tantra, which removes many tensions from sex by suggesting we relax, surprisingly offers an increased joy and fulfilment' (Richardson, 2008, p. 9).

Carrellas (2007, p. 10) dispels myths about Tantric sex that might also apply to sensate focus. 'Do you think that Tantra and BDSM are about as opposite as you can get?... You can enhance your Tantric practice by borrowing not only conscious sex techniques but also sensation-producing devices from the world of BDSM (bondage/discipline, dominance/submission). Both Tantra and BDSM are erotic arts of consciousness. Both arts add intensity to life and sex... Both involve conscious giving and receiving.'

The first exercise I suggested for Carlo and Marcus was a standing hug, whereby the couple stand fully clothed, facing one another, and move towards each other to have a non-sexual hug for several minutes. The idea is that each partner becomes aware of the otherness of the other, their smell, their warmth, the feel of their back, their chest pressing onto theirs, the rhythm of their breath, the feel of their arms around each other. They are also mindful of their own physical and emotional sensations — do they want to sink in deeper, or pull away, or start touching more sexually? It is a simple exercise but can bring up issues which may be useful to explore before asking the couple to touch each other in more intimate ways.

In this case, Marcus reported in the following session that the hug wasn't comfortable as Carlo had not bothered to clean his teeth and smelt of tuna fish. Carlo reported that Marco held him at a distance with a stiff, rigid hold so it was impossible for him to relax into the hug. We discussed why this simple, passive hug was so difficult for them, how it brought up again for

160 Marian O'Connor

each the terror of intrusion and abandonment and how difficult it was for each of them to trust in the other.

The couple repeated the exercise in the following weeks and were slowly able to enjoy the stillness, warmth and closeness of standing with their arms around one another.

At the same time as starting the standing hug exercises, the couple started self focus exercises, which are a series of graded exercises where each person focuses on their own body. These exercises although apparently simple, like the standing hug, can be challenging for many clients and for LBGTQ+ who may have suffered internal or external taunts about being physically or sexually 'abnormal.' Self focus can bring particular challenges for trans and binary individuals.

Alex and Katie – Working with trans and non-binary clients

Alex and Katie presented for psychosexual therapy because they rarely had sex. They were a very young couple, both 22, who had met as teenagers when Katie and her single mother moved into the same block of flats as Alex. They started a relationship when they were 15 years old. They described themselves as 'soulmates' bound together at that time by their feeling of difference, only children of single mothers, and being lesbian and mixed race in a mostly white community. The relationship had never been very sexual; they were a 'babes in the wood' couple (Mattinson and Sinclair, 1979, p. 54) who clung to one another while projecting all aggression and libidinal energy into the outside world, including their peers at school. Differences were arising between them now, and they decided to seek help to get their sex life on track in the hope this would keep them together as a couple.

The differences were disruptive. Alex, who was female by birth, had, at the age of 18, made a sudden decision to start transitioning. After hormone therapy and a mastectomy and changing from Alice to Alex, Alex now identified as non-binary, pan-sexual and asked to be referred to as 'they.' These seemed huge, loud changes for the anxious, uncertain person sitting in front of me. Katie had changed too. Having been shy and retiring all through school and university, she had recently joined a lesbian 'meetup' group and was enjoying the friendship and attention of other women. She had admitted to Alex that she had shared a passionate kiss with one of them. This was the trigger that brought them to seek help.

As the therapy progressed, it became clear that Katie was expressing for the couple the desire to leave the nest and explore sexually. Alex held the confusion and terror of being abandoned. The couple believed that they could stay together if they got their sex life on track. I was happy to work with them on this as, regardless of the outcome, the individuals in the couple can learn much about themselves and the other, both in the sexual and emotional arena. The process of improving their sex life can be healing for many couples, but for some, it may bring up the realisation that their problems go much deeper than sex.

We started off with self focus exercises. If either of them was ever going to enjoy sex together, it felt important that they could bear to touch and enjoy at least some aspects of their own bodies. It is not uncommon for trans, non-binary and intersex individuals to have complicated relationships with their bodies. I knew that it would be difficult for Alex to focus mindfully on a body they were unsure about. Alex hated the scars from the mastectomy and hated looking at their genitals. As Emily Nagoski points out, self focus for those in Alex's situation isn't about learning to love the body, so much as a way of wishing it well (Nagoski, 2019).

I suggested Alex read *The Nearest Exit May be Behind You* (Bear Bergmann, 2010), which has a kind approach to the body, suggesting that there are more places to be than girl or boy, man or woman, and that deciding to leave one of them does not mean arriving at the other. Could Alex accept that their body might be in a different place, in between or different or even extra to the place they originally came from? Alex surrounded themselves with labels which in Alex's case seemed defensive, designed to push people away — non binary, transmasculine, pansexual. But they refused to be seen naked and or to look at themselves naked even in private.

When treating transgender individuals for sexual issues, Ortmann (2020) stresses the importance of body acceptance and psychoeducation, which might include the creative renaming of parts of the body. I showed Alex and Katie a 3D image of the female clitoris which shows that the clitoris extends down through the labia. Both Katie and Alex were fascinated by this, and Alex decided to rename their own body parts as the penis (the head of the clitoris) and the shaft (the labia). Alex was unhappy about the mastectomy scars but was comfortable with the label 'chest.'

Self focus exercises started off with Alex wearing a t-shirt and shorts, gradually moving on to touching their genital and chest area under clothes and then without clothes. Ortmann (2020, p. 144) suggests that using sexual fantasy can improve comfort and pleasure in both solo and partnered sex, and I invited Alex to do so if it helped during self focus. There had been a huge reluctance to touch the penis or shaft even while wearing shorts, but Alex reported that using fantasy helped overcome this. Katie meanwhile did self focus exercises which included a masturbation programme.

It was time for Katie and Alex to move on from self focus to sensate focus exercises where each partner takes turns to touch one another, on the back of the body and then the front. The first exercises do not include any genital touch, but Alex was initially unhappy about accepting any touch. Their sex life had hitherto consisted of a clothed Alex caressing a naked Katie. Katie was as hesitant about touching Alex as Alex was about being touched. She said Alex's body felt like a foreign territory.

When working with a couple where one partner has transitioned, it is important to be sensitive to the effect of the changes on both partners. In *Queerly Beloved: A Love Story Across Genders* (Anderson-Minshall and Anderson-Minshall, 2014), the authors describe how this might be thought about in a loving relationship:

> *And, as regards the chest, one I didn't recognize, one that wasn't quite done because it needed weeks to recover, I put on a positive face because he was so excited about getting one step closer to a body, and a life that finally felt right (2014, p. 81).*

Because of the anxiety on both sides, the couple started the mutual touching exercises by stroking arms and hands only, then moving onto feet and legs. They kept on tops and shorts in the initial stages, gradually moving on to whole body caresses for which Katie was happy to be naked. Katie said she felt much closer to Alex now that she was able to touch and explore. Alex gradually relaxed into being touched and started to enjoy Katie's caresses, although Alex kept on shorts for all encounters. The couple visited the Sh! sex shop and bought a vibrator for Katie and blindfolds which they both enjoyed wearing.

The couple did not want to continue therapy once they started having a sexual relationship. Alex was delighted to be able to bring Katie to orgasm and to have moved on from an almost aversive feeling towards their own body. Katie felt more sexually confident and had started to be more asser-tive in the relationship, insisting that it was her right to spend some time with her lesbian friends. She tried to encourage Alex to join a trans group, which I supported, but this wasn't taken up. Alex was still too unsure about their own identity to identify with any group, even one which might have given help and support.

Margo and Emma – BDSM and lack of desire

The most common problem for couples seeking psychosexual therapy is that one partner has lost desire. This is true for both LGBTQ+ and heterosexuals.

Margo and Emma were a couple in their fifties who had had an active sex life when they met seven years previously. Margo was into kink and BDSM, and Emma had taken to it with enthusiasm. But in the last few years, Emma had lost all desire for sex. She was occasionally willing to perform the role of dominatrix for Margo's sake, but Margo wanted the desire for kink to be mutual. Margo felt rejected and hurt, and Emma felt pestered and irritated. The couple sought help after Emma bought Margo a single ticket to a fetish club as a birthday present.

I suggested a programme of homework exercises which might help reboot desire and find mutually satisfying sexual contact, but neither wanted this. Emma wanted me to convince Margo that she would never be interested in kink; Margo wanted me to persuade Emma of its attraction. Moreover, neither of them believed it was possible to change their own stance. Emma said that since the menopause, she had lost desire and wasn't prepared to take hormone therapy to help. Margo said that it was vitally important for her enjoyment as a sub that Emma really wanted to dominate.

I spoke to them about Basson's model of responsive desire (Basson, 2000), which suggests that for many people in long-term relationships, the decision to have sex is often driven by desire for intimacy rather than lust. A willingness or receptivity to have sex leads to starting sexual activity, which leads to sexual arousal, which leads to the lust or desire to continue.

The couple agreed to try the exercises, but they had a very slow start. Emma was busy with work and yoga classes after work so had no time. I suggested that she might have to give up some yoga classes, but she refused. I was beginning to suspect that Margo's feelings of rejection and hurt were not just about sex.

I pointed out to Emma that the oxytocin ('the love hormone') released in the touching exercises brought calm and relaxation and that, in addition, it engendered a feeling of closeness. Emma accused Margo and me of pressurising her to do the exercises.

We discussed more in the therapy why Emma felt so pressured or 'pestered.' Emma had not been interested in kink until she met Margo and had originally found great release in being the dominant partner sexually. She had felt oppressed in her family of origin and in previous relationships, but, by taking the role of Dom in the sexual arena, she had felt liberated and eventually allowed herself to trust Margo. At that point, she no longer needed to assert control and dominance in sex.

Nichols (2004) in her paper about rethinking lesbian bed death suggests that women involved with other women spend more time on sex, have more varied sex and were more likely to have orgasm during partner sex than were women involved with men. If they had less sex, it was because they felt less pressure to have sex when they weren't in the mood? I spoke again about the Basson responsive desire model. Would Emma be willing to at least try the exercises to find out whether opening herself up to the possibility of being aroused might put her in the mood?

Emma agreed. The couple worked through the exercises and found a solution that suited them both. Margo would caress Emma for up to an hour, touching breasts and thighs but not the genitals, as Emma did not want this. Then Emma, feeling voluptuous and relaxed, would happily and enthusiastically take on the role of Dom. Working together on this brought changes to their relationship as a whole, which were evident when they were in the room with me. Emma presented as more open and involved and Margo as less anxious and needy.

Conclusion

LGBTQ+ clients may present psychosexual therapists with particular challenges in the changing sexual landscape of contemporary Britain. In order to help clients confront the heteronormist thinking which might be damaging to their sense of self and their sexual functioning, therapists will need to challenge their own heteronormist thinking and training. This will involve self reflection and a willingness to be open to educating themselves about the specific needs of their LGBTQ+ clients.

Working directly with the body is not something that is traditionally associated with psychoanalytic work, but I hope to have shown here how an integrated approach which includes the setting of behavioural exercises can bring up relationship and transference issues which are valuable to psychic as well as sexual growth.

Nichols and Shernoff (2007) suggest that suspending preconceived notions about gender, relationships and unusual lifestyles may enable the traditional therapist to grow in unexpected and satisfying ways. Perhaps suspending preconceived notions about what psychoanalytically informed therapy can achieve will similarly enable therapist and client to grow in unexpected and satisfying ways.

References

American Psychiatric Association (2013). *Diagnostic and Statistical Manual of Mental Disorders, 5th ed. (DSM-5)*. Washington DC: American Psychiatric Publishing.

Anderson-Minshall, D. &Anderson-Minshall, J. (2014). *Queerly Beloved: A Love Story Across Genders*. New York: Bold Strokes Books.

Basson, R. (2000). The Female Sexual Response: A Different Model. *Journal of Sex & Marital Therapy, 26:1*, 51–65.

Basson, R. (2002). Women's Sexual Desire: Disordered or Misunderstood? *Journal of Sex and Marital Therapy, 28:Suppl 1*, 17–28.

Bergman, B. (2010). *The Nearest Exit May Be Behind You*. Vancouver: Arsenal Pulp Press.

Berry, D. & Lezos, A. (2017). Inclusive Sex Therapy Practices: A Qualitative Study of the Techniques Sex Therapists Use When Working with Diverse Sexual Populations. *Sexual and Relationship Therapy, 32:1*, 2–21.

Byers, S. (2011). Beyond the Birds and the Bees and Was It Good for You?: Thirty Years of Research on Sexual Communication. *Canadian Psychology, 52:1* 20–28.

Carrellas, B. (2007). *Urban Tantra*. Berkeley: Celestial Arts.

Dodsworth, L.(2019). *Womanhood: The Bare Reality*. London: Pinter and Martin.

Evans, M., & Barker, M. (2010). How Do You See Me? Coming Out in Counselling. *British Journal of Guidance and Counselling, 38*, 375–391.

Evaristo, B. (2019). *Girl, Woman, Other*. UK: Hamish Hamilton.

Green, L. & Seymour, J. (2009). 'Loss of Desire, a Psycho-sexual Case Study', 141–164. In C. Clulow (Ed.) *Sex, Attachment and Couple Psychotherapy*. London: Karnac.

Khalaf, R. (2019). *Yay! You're Gay! Now What?: A Gay Boy's Guide to Life*. UK: Lincoln Children's Books.

Kort, J. (2018). *LGBTQ Clients in Therapy: Clinical Issues and Treatment Strategies*. New York: W.W. Norton.

Masters, W. H. & Johnson, V. E. (1970). *Human Sexual Inadequacy*. Boston: Little, Brown.

Mattinson, J. & Sinclair, I. (1979). *Mate and Stalemate: Working with Marital Problems in a Social Services Department*. London: Institute of Marital Studies.

Ness, P. (2018). *Release*. UK: Walker Books.

Nagoski, E. (2019). *Come as You are Workbook*. Kindle location 155. London: Scribe.

Nichols, M. (2004). Lesbian Sexuality/Female Sexuality: Rethinking 'Lesbian Bed Death.' *Sexual and Relationship Therapy*, 19, 363–371.

Nichols, M. & Shernoff, M. (2007). 'Therapy with Sexual Minorities: Queering Practice', 379–415. In S. R. Leiblum (Ed.) *Principles and Practice of Sex Therapy*. New York:The Guildford Press

Nichols, M. (2014). 'Therapy with LGBTQ Clients: Working with Sex and Gender Variance from a Queer Theory Model', 309–333. In Y. M. Binik & K. S. K. Hall (Eds.) *Principles and Practice of Sex Therapy*. New York: The Guilford Press.

O'Connor, M. (2019). 'Let's talk about Sex', 90–103. In *Engaging Couples: New Directions in Therapeutic Work with Families*. Abingdon: Routledge.

Ogden, T. H. (1994). The Concept of Interpretive Action. *Psychoanalytic Quarterly*, *63:2*, 219–245.

Ortmann, D. (2020). 'The Pleasure of Power: Sex Therapy in the BDSM Community. Principles and Practice of Sex Therapy', 423–252. In K. Hall & Y. Binik (Eds.) *Principles and Practice of Sex Therapy*. Guilford Press.

Pacey, S. (2018). An investigation into psychodynamic couple psychotherapists' theories of 'sensate focus' in clinical practice. Doctoral Thesis. https://repository.uel.ac.uk/item/86v6x (Accessed July 2020).

Richardson, D. (2008). *The Hear of Tantric Sex: A Unique Guide to Love and Sexual Fulfillment*. Hants, UK: O Books.

Rosenberger, J., Reece, M., Schick, V., Herbenick, D., Novak, D., Van Der Pol, B., Fortenberry, J. D. (2011). Male-Partnered Sexual Event among Gay and Bisexually Identified Men in the United States. *Journal of Sexual Medicine*, *8:11*, 3040–3050.

Seymour, J. (2014). 'Assessing the Sexual Relationship'. In D. Scharff & J. Savege Scharff (Eds.) *Psychoanalytic Couple Therapy: Foundations of Theory and Practice*. Abindgon, Oxon: Routledge.

SKYN Condoms Millennial Sex Survey (2017). https://www.prnewswire.com/news-releases/2017-skyn-condoms-millennial-sex-survey-reveals-nearly-50-of-respondents-sext-at-least-once-a-week-300401985.html (Accessed July 2020).

Winnicott, D. W. (1958). The capacity to be alone. *International Journal of Psychoanalysis*, *39:5*, 416–420.

Winnicott, D. W. (1968a). 'Communication Between Infant and Mother, and Mother and Infant, Compared and Contrasted', 15–25. In W. G. Joffe (Ed.) *What is Psychoanalysis?* London: Institute of Psychoanalysis.

Vuong, O. (2019). *On Earth We're Briefly Gorgeous*. London: Jonathon Cape.

Zilbergeld, B. (1999). *The New Male Sexuality*. New York: Bantam Doubleday Dell.

100 Vaginas (2019). https://www.channel4.com/programmes/100-vaginas.

Chapter 11

The process of ageing for same-sex couples

David Richards

Introduction

The experience of growing up as a lesbian, gay or bisexual (LGB) person within traditional western societies means that one is very likely to have encountered discriminatory and hostile attitudes from others. This experience is probably more pronounced for those growing up in the first half of the 20th century, when such attitudes were generally more pervasive than they are today. Recent changes in legislation and civil opportunities seem to have positively impacted attitudes, although developments such as civil partnerships and gay marriage do not automatically erode well-established discrimination or intolerance linked to difference and the associated feelings of fear and hatred towards the "otherness" of LGB individuals and couples. Indeed, such social attitudes may sometimes become even more acute when confronted with, and provoked by, the greater visibility of the LGB man or woman. Furthermore, the impact of growing up within such an environment may well lead to the internalisation of negative beliefs and attitudes and an identification with the aggressor/oppressor. Faced with this psychological position, one assumes that it will not only have significance for the individuals concerned but also affect the development of relationships and partner choice. Moreover, for older LGB people, the impact of societal ageism, in addition to homophobia, may well be significant; thus, the combined negativities historically and currently towards both the elderly and those who are gay can place older LGB people in a position of double discrimination.

Older LGB individuals and couples in focus

Psychoanalytic approaches to understanding and working clinically with couples have become a central component of therapeutic work (Morgan, 2018; Ruszczynski, 1993), and within this broader frame, work on understanding the experience of older couples has also emerged (Amos & Balfour, 2007). The development of specific thinking about gay and lesbian couples is at last receiving attention, as this book makes evident. In particular, the

DOI: 10.4324/9781003255703-11

application of our understanding of object relations and Oedipal dynamics and development in regard to same-sex couples has been valuably reflected on (Hertzmann, 2015, 2020). However, specific thinking about older same-sex couples is much less developed, and this chapter aims, therefore, to provide greater awareness in order to include this particular couple in our thinking. Valuable reflections on older gay men (Ratigan, 1996) and on older lesbians (Young, 1996) have already been articulated, and although focusing primarily on individuals, texts which also include reference to the couple or relational contexts of later gay life can be found in Isay (1996) and Richards (2011). Nevertheless, it is vitally important when reflecting on the older couple as a unit that we do not neglect the same-sex couple and, equally, when reflecting on the same-sex couple identity that it does not exclude the older couple. After all, there is a tendency within the so-called "gay community" to remain primarily focused on the younger population at the expense of older LGB individuals and couples. It may be a combined truism that within both broader society and gay society, the old are much less visible and generally less valued than the young.

My reflections in this chapter will generally refer to "older" or "later life" as a broad but meaningful unit of time, whilst also being specific about the age of any individual or couple directly referred to. However, it is important to note that actually a wide range of developmental stages are implicitly referenced here, although these stages may vary significantly in terms of personal emphasis, and both psychological and physical pre-occupations. I should add that my clinical experience has not in fact included extensive work with older same-sex couples, which I find surprising, given that I have worked significantly in specialist contexts for both LGBT and older people throughout my career, as well as concurrently working in private practice. This may indicate that older same-sex couples have not been able or, indeed, encouraged to find their way to therapeutic services. However, within the last twenty years, social and support services for older LGBT people have been developing in the UK (e.g., through the organisations Age UK and Opening Doors London), following in the footsteps, as is so often the case in this arena, of developments in the USA (e.g., the organisation Sage, established in 1978). One hopes that in the future, older same-sex couples may begin identifying therapy as a valuable resource for themselves, just as younger same-sex couples have done for many years. For the purpose of this chapter, I have used my more extensive experience with individual older gay patients, some of whom have been partners in couples during the time that I was working with them. In addition, I have interviewed a number of older gay/lesbian individuals and couples who are part of my broader social circle as a way of gathering further experience, attitudes and reflections for inclusion. I have amalgamated material in some cases, combining accounts from both patients and those interviewed, as a way of presenting ideas and experience in an effective and fluid way, and equally ensuring sufficient confidentiality.

168 David Richards

Case example

One of my own earlier clinical encounters was with a gay man of ninety years old, who lived with his partner of sixty years in increasing ill-health and severely limited physical mobility, and who conveyed powerful and disturbing attitudes of internalised ageism and homophobia. I have written about this work in two previous papers (Richards, 2001, 2011), which I think speaks to the significance of this encounter for me as a younger gay man who was in his early forties at the time that I worked with him. In terms of relational dynamics, this couple had on the one hand established a close and caring partnership, and, on the other, at the time of our meeting, the patient was actually being cared for by his partner. However, in my work with the patient, he did at times display persecutory guilt related to his sexual activity as a younger man, which he referred to as promiscuity — echoing one of the most familiar heterosexist critiques of gay men. He also held a belief, as an older man, that he had betrayed the love and fidelity of his partner through his past sexual behaviour. This was linked to his stated hatred of ageing and he described to me how he had mocked the old when he was a much younger man, seeing them as frail and hopeless figures. As I learned more of his history, I came to understand that his internal world and its horror of the old was significantly influenced by his mother and their tortured and uncaring relationship. His mother had become psychologically frailer as he grew up, and had never really been able to offer him sufficient loving attention. One could say that he thus suffered doubly from his identification with his mother's infirmity, alongside internalised homophobic attitudes and emotions, and as he approached the end of his life, he was full of self-hatred for past sexual behaviour and current aged infirmity. Another way of putting this is in terms of a struggle between liveliness (past sexual activity) and deadliness (age and illness/fragility). What was lacking was a more benign sense of holding onto his past sexual life as a positive internal experience, whilst equally appreciating his advanced years as a significant achievement that offered him a peaceful and fulfilling last stage of life with a loving and supportive partner. In traditional psychoanalytic terms, we can see here a vivid expression of Erikson's notion of the ultimate struggle for old age being between ego integrity and despair (Erikson, 1965).

Embedded in this case scenario are certain broader themes outlined in my introductory remarks, which can focus our awareness on the historical environmental backdrop to growing up and ageing as an LGB person, which naturally affects relational and interpersonal development and the potential for healthy intimacy. The clinical scenario also evokes within the transference/countertransference dynamic between patient and therapist another aspect of same-sex partnerships, namely that of generational difference, the partnering of older and younger gay men. While a familiar relational type, this is not of course unique to gay and lesbian partnerships — perhaps most neatly framed conceptually in the Jungian archetypes of Puer and Senex (Giaccardi, 2020; Lingiardi, 2002) — the young man and the older/more senior man, reflective of the ancient Greek cultural practice and ideal. I will return to this theme later in the chapter, but what is most pertinent to note here is the impact this older patient's narrative had on me as a younger practitioner. For instance, I found myself struggling with fears of my own, evoked by the clinical material as I became drawn into his tortured psychic world. My wish to help and support him towards a more peaceful and accepting attitude towards his own self and history were but one aspect of my experience with him, since, at the same time, I tried to hold myself back from being invaded by his ambivalence and deeply conflicted sense of self. Apart from any other more specific considerations, it is well documented that younger therapists are likely to be confronted with their own future ageing and mortality when working with older patients (Martindale, 1989, 1998). In this case, sometimes I felt in touch with a powerfully malign developmental "gay" trajectory of life, which I needed to resist in order to maintain my own psychic health and liveliness, and the hopes for my own future.

Patterns of same-sex couple relating

Fundamentally, one significant idea in discussing the "gay couple" of any age is the inevitable association of the notion of coupledom with hetero-sexuality and heteronormativity. This particular version of coupledom may have little meaning for many gay people, and may indeed be seen as an expression of social oppression rather than equality. This attitude may be particularly prevalent for older LGB people who have grown up in a more segregated, less integrated society where gay sexuality was less visible, and because of legal considerations remained hidden. One gay man in his seventies told me that, however much the world has changed from when he was a younger adult, he "will forever bear the scars" from growing up in times of social, legal and religious "hatred and persecutions." He added to these painful reflections his awareness that society tends to privilege younger gay men, choosing not to imagine or perceive that gay men also grow old. This denial may serve to reinforce the sense of the timeless or ageless in regard to certain aspects of gay identity, as well as accounting for the matter of age differences within some gay partnerships, a difference that may hold less significance than it tends to for older and younger partners in heterosexual relationships (Giaccardi, op.cit.). Although this may in part be a product of ageism, the absence of mature lesbian and gay role models and narra-tives will undoubtedly have a major impact on the younger LGB identity, and also potentially serve to reinforce an aversion to ageing. The absence of figures to identify with was inevitably even more pronounced in earlier times, and for gay men in particular in the decades prior to the 1967 Sexual

Offences Act (which partially de-criminalised homosexual acts), they were forced to conduct their relationships in the shadows, occupying the position of social and legal outcasts. The legacy of this state of affairs for older gays and lesbians cannot be emphasised enough, as the conscious and unconscious imprint continues to live on in their relationship to self and to others. One aspect of this is the internal developmental process for the LGB man or woman, and as with my ninety-year-old patient, there may be significant challenges to one's growth and psychic health as a result of growing up in a world marked by homophobia and heteronormativity. Such challenges include the possibility of life experiences being delayed or even derailed, as the gay psyche suffers and potentially internalises abuse from society's homophobia, complicating further the impact of ageing. Fundamentally, physical ageing is unavoidable and confronts us all with some degree of discrepancy between our internal world (where we may never age) and the external and physical reality, an experience that is often much more complex for LGB people.

One of the factors likely to be more common in older LGB adults is that of having been married to someone of the opposite sex as a younger person, possibly also with a family (Isay, 1996; Neal, 2014). In recent times, having children has become increasingly common for both male and female same-sex couples, although historically an LGB man or woman would be likely to have their own children only in the context of a "heterosexual" marriage or relationship. There are many reasons as to why such a marriage might happen, and certainly in the past, as indicated above, the social pressures towards a traditional marriage could be immense. But personal psychic pressures, as well as social ones, can push a gay man or lesbian woman towards marrying someone of the opposite sex as a means of avoiding powerful internal conflicts and of seeking to deny the truth about themselves, as well as hiding from self and others in the apparent safety of the marriage. These circumstances are likely to place severe limits on the personal psychosexual development of the individual, meaning that sexual contact with the same sex, if present at all, has to be a secretive and a hidden part of one's life. Equally, a partnership with someone of the same sex may only be a possibility later in life, if indeed it happens at all.

Other gay men and lesbians in their seventies and eighties have described the difficulty of being open in all circumstances about their sexual orientation or the nature of an intimate relationship, even when settled in a same-sex partnership of some years. They have identified that after many years of secrecy as younger adults, it becomes natural for them to maintain a degree of opaqueness about their sexual selves, certainly in wider social circumstances. Such a position is not difficult to understand, and is reflective of various aspects of social history outlined above: the legacy of personal, social and legal restrictions, resulting in a lack of visibility and, in some cases, the need to remain hidden.

However, as in the example of my ninety-year-old patient, same-sex partnerships may also be established much earlier in adulthood and last for many years. Several older couples, or individuals who are part of couples, have described to me the joys and challenges of their experience in such long established relationships, experiences which are no different in essence to those of heterosexual couples. At the same time, there has sometimes been a degree of opaqueness as described above, enacted perhaps in a benign way, but still expressive of a need not to be explicit about the reality of being a gay couple. As one couple put it, while their sexual identity did not need to be hidden, equally it did not need to be stated. This, I would suggest, is different to a typical younger same-sex couple in today's society, who, as a gay couple, are much more likely to be open and explicit about their identity. Indeed, reflective of current trends, they may use different language/terminology altogether, "Queer" for example, to describe their relationship. Context may also be of significance here, since living in a large urban centre such as London or a similarly diverse community may increase security, and at the same time offer other resources (artistic, for example) and social opportunities which can serve to bring LGB people together. Paradoxically, a large city can provide both a safe and stimulating context for meeting other LGB people, whilst also making it easier to hide if one chooses to. Outside such large centres, discrimination may be more common, reflective of being in the minority, and the potential for less "enlightened" attitudes within heteronormative communities.

Dependency within and outside of a partnership, particularly as health and mobility decrease, can be very challenging and confront couples with painful aspects of ageing. Likewise, adjusting to the potential need for care, either in the home or within an institution, can be extremely difficult. For instance, many of the issues referred to above concerning openness, disclosure and security may for same-sex couples be foregrounded once again, even if sufficiently resolved at an earlier stage when the couple remained in good health. This is generally the most sensitive issue raised within discussions I have had with couples over the age of seventy: that is, the linked fears of becoming dependent of necessity within a generic (i.e., non-gay) setting, or having to be cared for intimately by a carer who is not sensitive to their sexual identity. I have spoken to older LGB men and women in residential and nursing homes who have retreated to the closet, despite having been "out" prior to this, mainly because they feel exposed and fear discrimination. If cared for at home, the arrival of a professional physical carer may be experienced as an intrusion, and the enclosed world of the care home can seem to be the recreation of the hostile heteronormative world of earlier years. More specifically, it is also the case that hostile cultural and religious attitudes to LGB identities may be active, as many carers come from communities where same-sex attraction is not considered acceptable. Although we may expect standards of care and awareness of "diversity" to be developing appropriately within the care system, the reality for many LGB elders in residential or nursing homes may remain a very challenging experience (Heaphy et al, 2003; Knocker, 2006).

Intergenerational relationships

Another aspect of older gay and lesbian relationships is the intergenerational couple: older LGB individuals partnering with significantly younger individuals. Such relationships, as with any couple dynamic, have a range of meanings for both partners. My reflections here come partly from discussions with older and younger men in such relationships. Arguably, one of the most interesting but also elusive aspects of such a partnership is the relation between the sexual attraction towards the older partner and other aspects of desire and relational interest. One common feature is the notion of "the wise old man," in some cases experienced from boyhood through characters in books and films, and which can be understood as expressive of an attraction to a sense of wisdom and maturity in the other, the older man perceived as possessing qualities that the younger man does not have. This sense of a mutually satisfying partnership for each of the men is directly evocative of the Greek male union referred to earlier in the chapter, which itself is taken up and developed within current Jungian analytic thinking (Giaccardi, op.cit.; Lingiardi, op.cit.).

One specific perspective linked to this is the archetypal notion of a father/son bond which has a potentially valuable meaning for both partners; the older being able to offer his history, experience and knowledge, and the younger being able to receive these in the shape of a psychological inheritance. The evocation of father and son also serves to remind us of a re-visiting of traditional Oedipal theory for the gay boy and his father, as examined by Isay (1989) — the understanding here being that the father rejects the intimacy, physical and emotional, that the gay son desires. The son may subsequently obtain this through a partnership with an older man. The often conflictful and/or distant relations between gay sons and their actual fathers can make a union of older and younger highly meaningful for both partners, and, from my experience, can have a hugely reparative effect following painful paternal rejection or hostility from childhood.

Another important aspect, whether or not consciously identified by either partner, is the attraction towards someone who embodies significant difference, a sense of adding to oneself rather than more simply reflecting oneself; or in slightly different words offering an opposite, or other, rather than a figure that is directly identified with. This is an interesting riposte perhaps to the traditional Freudian notion of same-sex attraction being essentially narcissistic (Freud, 1905). The bodies of course are identical anatomically/genitally, but I think the sense of difference referenced here is meaningful in relational terms. One could argue that this searching for and attraction towards the "other" is resolved in a very concrete way in such relationships; however, that seems to me no reason to deny its power and meaning. Equally, however, there is a difference that is literally embodied. Older partners have talked to me of their powerful awareness of their body being much less flexible and possibly less healthy than their younger partner's physique. This may also affect their sexual relationship if there is a discrepancy between each partner's level of desire, and indeed potency. The status of the older man or woman is actually an ambiguous one, authoritative and holding the power of experience, yet at the same time potentially more vulnerable. This may lead to feelings of anxiety, especially as times passes, and if or when that older body becomes more disabled by age.

Cinematic explorations are also notable in terms of the intergenerational couple. For example, in *The Killing of Sister George* (1968), we witness a lesbian older/younger couple fighting in increasingly infantile ways and indeed the younger woman is even nicknamed "Childy" by the older partner. More recently, *Gerontophilia* (2014) portrays a young man with a girlfriend who finds a job in a nursing home as a way of meeting older men to whom he feels a strong erotic attraction. While the narrative arguably becomes somewhat melodramatic, the scenes which show the sexual relationship between the young man and one of the older male residents display a thoughtful sensitivity towards such a sexual attraction and union. At the same time, the film's trailer refers to the central character's particular sexual inclination as a fetish, evocative of the concept of gerontophilia as a paraphilia and originally identified as such by Krafft-Ebing in 1886 (2018). This should alert us to the dangers of viewing younger men or women seeking older partners as inherently pathological. A parallel relational experience is portrayed in another recent film *Call Me by Your Name* (2017), in which we see a rite of passage or coming of age poignantly presented through a summer romance between a seventeen-year-old and a twenty-something year-old man. As a sign of significant cultural interest in age-differentiated same-sex relationships, various other films can be referenced: for example, *Carol* (2015) in which a mother/daughter dynamic prevails; *Notes on a Scandal* (2007), in which a predatory older woman pursues a friendship with a younger colleague; and *A Single Man* (2010), in which a middle-aged man grieves the loss of his younger lover following a fatal car accident. Collectively, these narratives serve to remind us of society's interest in different kinds of age-related same-sex relationships, including both critical and sympathetic portrayals. As such, they are not all identified as love relations, since some concentrate more on power dynamics rather than the straightforward romantic ideal or sexual desire.

Visible or invisible?

Returning to the older couple, but staying within the world of art and creativity, we find the artists Gilbert and George, an openly gay couple now in their later seventies, and whose work places themselves centre-stage. They are always identically dressed (same suits in different colours) and would seem to promote themselves very much as an undifferentiated pair, a unit. Their appearance, as well as their elusive and playful style in press interviews, could thus be seen as an ambiguous comment on identity, sexuality and relationship. They are, as it were, simultaneously "out" and highly visible, whilst also remaining hidden or hard to discover as individuals. This prompts awareness of a feature of earlier life for some older gay men and lesbians, in which mourning is felt for the degree of the hidden or secret life which characterised the social context in the UK before the 1967 Sexual Offences Act (which finally implemented the recommendations of the Wolfenden report of 1957). Both men and women have spoken to me, in the context of the forbidden and illegal act of forming same-sex relationships, of the "frisson" and appeal of transgressing these prohibitions. It is worth highlighting the fact that for men, it was actually illegal before the 1967 Act to have sex even in private with another man, although lesbian sexual activity was never made illegal.

Ageing and sex

One complex component of ageing within a couple, for both LGB and heterosexual men and women, is that of sex. The experience and negotiation of sexual contact and intimacy are a major element in our ageing and in the developmental shifts of a long-term partnership. The way in which sex is experienced and managed within any couple will of course be in the context of that relationship's sexual history. It is common, although not to be presumed, that sexual desire will decrease in later life. For some couples, this can be experienced as a great loss, although for others, it can be more of a relief. For male same-sex couples, sex has often been negotiated in terms of whether monogamy or any degree of an "open" sexual relationship is wanted by one or both partners. A common prompt for younger and middle-aged gay couples to seek therapy is that of trying to address the degree of openness within their relationship, especially when only one partner really wants an open arrangement, or both want it in theory but find it harder to achieve and manage in practice.

Another significant aspect of experience for many gay men, and often lesbians too, is that of HIV and AIDS, a major and tragic development in the UK from the 1980s onwards, resulting in huge personal losses for many men of partners, friends and members of wider social circles. For those who were young and middle-aged adults at that time, these memories and losses may well be activated in older age and impact both their psychological and physiological attitudes towards sex. The possible survivor's guilt may be hard to overcome, especially if one's partner died some years ago and the other is living with HIV.

Lived experience

I will now present, with their permission, two short vignettes of couples I have talked with about their lives and experience of ageing, as a way of gathering up some of the themes already discussed and of contextualising them within the particular couple relationships.

The female couple, together for over thirty years and of a similar age, is identified significantly by a mutual involvement in political activism in young adulthood. Both partners recognise that this experience included not only a wish for collective lesbian feminist action but also a wish to be "defiant." They agreed with my suggestion that perhaps their political engagement, while clearly of great personal meaning, may also have served a protective function. However, in their sixties, the couple has a much less defined sense of their place in society and may even feel unwanted. This includes their shared sense of being considered a threat to heteronormative society by both men and other women, and this is understood as an expression of misogyny and patriarchal discrimination. The experience they described to me emphasises the role of women in western society, in terms of feminism and equality, the menopause with its psychological and physiological consequences, and the limited roles available to older women in the eyes of society.

The women talked of still being referred to as "the girls" within their families. As older women, they also had the experience of being confronted by strangers' apparent curiosity about them, for instance, in being stared at and questioned as to whether they are sisters, "which is ageist and unwittingly homophobic." They were able to assert themselves against this to some degree by challenging such a question or identifying themselves as a couple, and we agreed that this assertion referenced their younger political activism. This also speaks to a theme central in their experience of ageing as a lesbian couple; that of being seen or even feeling of a lower social status. As they say, "It's never been desirable to be a lesbian…because we're not seen as needing men, lesbians are viewed with suspicion and hatred." They commented on the current political emphasis of the transgender movement being very different from that of the lesbian activism of their youth. Both partners also expressed a degree of ambivalence towards the advent of same-sex marriage: wondering if one can be equal without "aping heterosexuality." This, I think, resonates with the position that a number of gay men and women hold, although lesbians, because of the history of feminism and oppression, may feel particularly strongly about embracing heteronormativity. As this couple articulated, lesbian women have a complex and ambiguous place within the larger female community, and their experience, as summarised here, speaks eloquently of some of the issues that remain hugely challenging for women growing older together in same-sex couple relationships.

I will now briefly present a male couple, both partners in their late eighties, and in a relationship for over fifty years. Health and mobility are beginning to deteriorate for one of the partners, and that partner has had the experience of a carer visiting the home and displaying some "bemusement" at finding a gay couple and needing time to adjust to that experience. Prior to this, the life that the couple described was that of living in a kind of artistic and "gay-friendly" world identified earlier in the chapter. As younger men, one of the partners described growing up in what he called "a heterosexual model" of relationships within an upper middle-class milieu, although this did not prevent him from developing a relatively open sexual identity as he grew up; while the other partner described a more liberated sexual identity from adolescence. The couple demonstrated a relatively benign sense of ageing together, effectively dented only by the emergence of ill-health and the threat that this posed to their relationship in terms of health and care.

In both of these scenarios, there is the implicit reference to economic inequalities, which are so often a harder reality for women. These inequalities also inevitably impact health needs as well as the cost of care and, as such, they form a major part of the experience of ageing.

Therapist considerations

I will now consider some of the challenges therapists face in working with older same-sex couples. As addressed elsewhere in this book, the issue of whether gay patients need a gay therapist is something that warrants further attention. While I think that personal choice is important, my clinical work with heterosexual couples would suggest that having a different sexual orientation need not be a prohibitive factor in doing good work, whether the identity of the therapist is known to the couple or not. However, younger same-sex couples that I have seen, have generally preferred a gay therapist. As stated previously, it remains noteworthy that older same-sex couples have rarely been seen in my practice. That said, my own feelings in regard to my ninety-year-old patient highlight some important considerations, not least the need for the therapist to be thoughtful about all relational elements both literal and transferential, including any age difference and its meaning for the couple. As ever, it is imperative for the therapist to pay attention to his or her countertransference, and this is certain to include feelings about one's own ageing, one's achievements personal and professional, and ultimately one's mortality. For the ageing patient/couple, there will be losses to mourn: of previous personal and professional roles, previous relationships, decreasing levels of sexual activity, issues of personal care, the potential loss of one's partner and the increasing awareness of one's death.

Conclusion

As ever in our practice, the process of working with older same-sex couples, although not always easy, is nevertheless meaningful and rewarding. I have come to value greatly the learning, both personal and professional, in my years of working therapeutically with older adults and in my involvement with gender and sexual minority individuals and couples. However, for older gay and lesbian patients, possibly within a long-established couple relationship, therapy may not necessarily be an obvious option; although, for those who do embrace it, the benefits may be enormous, as they work through multiple aspects of their lives and loves through time. Given that both ageing and sexual orientation are protected categories under the Equalities Act (2010), it is important for therapists to remain open and to be careful in not discriminating on grounds of ageing or sexuality.

"For Paul, as we age together"

References

Amos, A. & Balfour, A. (2007) Couples psychotherapy: separateness or separation? An account of work with a couple entering later life. In: Davenhill, R. (Ed) *Looking into Later Life: A Psychoanalytic Approach to Depression and Dementia in Old Age*. London: Karnac.

Erikson, E. (1965) *Childhood and Society*. London: Hogarth Press.

Freud, S. (1905) *Three Essays on the Theory of Sexuality* (Standard Edition vol. 7). London: Hogarth Press.

Giaccardi, G. (2020) Mending the symbolic when a place for same-sex desire is not found. In: Hertzmann, L. & Newbigin, J. (Eds) *Sexuality and Gender Now: Moving Beyond Heteronormativity*. London: Routledge.

Heaphy, B., Yip, A., & Thompson, D. (2003) *Lesbian, Gay and Bisexual Lives over 50: A Report on the Project 'The Social and Policy Implications of Non-heterosexual Ageing'*. Nottingham: York House Publications.

Hertzmann, L. (2015) Objecting to the object: encountering the internal parental couple relationship for lesbian and gay couples. In: Lemma, A. & Lynch, P.E. (Eds) *Sexualities: Contemporary Psychoanalytic Perspectives*. London: Routledge.

Hertzmann, L. (2020) Losing the Oedipal mother and loss of sexual desire. In: Hertzmann, L. & Newbigin, J. (Eds) *Sexuality and Gender Now: Moving Beyond Heteronormativity*. London: Routledge.

Isay, R.A. (1989) *Being Homosexual: Gay Men and Their Development*. New York: Farrar, Straus & Giroux.

Isay, R.A. (1996) *Becoming Gay: The Journey to Self-Acceptance*. New York: Vintage Books.

Knocker, S. (2006) *The Whole of Me: Meeting the Needs of Older Lesbians, Gay Men and Bisexuals Living in Care Homes and Extra Care Housing*. London: Age Concern.

Krafft-Ebing, R.V. (2018) *Psychopathia Sexualis*. London: Wentworth Press.

Lingiardi, V. (2002) *Men in Love: Male Homosexualities from Ganymede to Batman*. Chicago: Open Court.

Martindale, B. (1989) Becoming Dependent Again: The Fears of Some Elderly Persons and Their Younger Therapists. In: *Psychoanalytic Psychotherapy* 4: 67–75.

Martindale, B. (1998) On Dying, Death and Eternal Life. In: *Psychoanalytic Psychotherapy* 12: 259–270.

Morgan, M. (2018) *A Couple State of Mind: Psychoanalysis of Couples and the Tavistock Relationships Model*. London: Routledge.

Neal, C. (2014) *The Marrying Kind? Lives of gay and bi men who married women* www.candescentpress. co.uk.

Ratigan, B. (1996) Working with older gay men. In: Davies, D. & Neal, C. (Eds) *Pink Therapy: A Guide for Counsellors and Therapists Working with Lesbian, Gay and Bisexual Clients*. Buckingham: OUP.

Richards, D. (2001) The Remains of the Day: Counselling Older Clients. In: *CPJ (Counselling and Psychotherapy Journal)* 12: 10–14.

Richards, D. (2011) Working with Older LGBT People. In: *Therapy Today* 22: 10–14.

Ruszczynski, S. (1993) *Psychotherapy with Couples: Theory and Practice at the Tavistock Institute of Marital Studies*. London: Karnac.

Young, V. (1996) Working with older lesbians. In: Davies, D. & Neal, C. (Eds) *Pink Therapy: A Guide for Counsellors and Therapists Working with Lesbian, Gay and Bisexual Clients*. Buckingham: OUP.

Chapter 12

Responding to the challenge that same-sex parents pose for psychoanalytic couple and family psychotherapists

Confronting implicit bias!

Damian McCann and Colleen Sandor

Introduction

Although there have been obvious developments within society regarding same-sex couples and same-sex parenting, i.e., lesbian and gay marriage, assisted reproductive technologies involving egg donation, donor insemination, embryo donation and surrogacy which, together with fostering and adoption, increase the possibilities for same-sex couples becoming parents, there remains an enduring belief that the traditional nuclear family is generally considered the best environment in which to raise children. Moreover, efforts to dispel this belief, for instance, through years of research involving same-sex parents and their children, Golombok (2015) reminds us that it is the quality of family relationships and the wider social environment that has more influence on children's psychological development, than the number, gender, sexual orientation or biological relatedness of their parents, or indeed the method of conception. With this argument firmly before us, in this chapter, we will examine developments within psychoanalytic thinking and practice that attend to the particular challenges posed by same-sex parents for psychoanalytic couple and family psychotherapists. At the heart of this exploration lies implicit bias and the management of this by psychotherapists.

History repeating itself

The year, 2019, presaged the 50th anniversary of the Stonewall Inn riots that ushered in the era of gay pride. Month-long celebrations marked this important moment, and the LGBTQ community revelled in the many rights and freedoms it had gained since Stonewall. In light of the 50th anniversary, two remarkable events occurred. First, the NYPD Commissioner apologized for the Stonewall raids, declaring that their actions were wrong and that the laws that prompted the raids were discriminatory and oppressive. Several weeks later, the President of American Psychoanalytic Association

(APsaA), Lee Jaffe, apologized for the role psychoanalysis had played in oppressing the lesbian, gay, bisexual, transgender, queer (LGBTQ) community. In a statement he said, "Regrettably, much of our past understanding of homosexuality as an illness can be attributed to the American psychoanalytic establishment. While our efforts in advocating for sexual and gender diversity since are worthy of pride, it is long past time to recognize and apologize for our role in the discrimination and trauma caused by our profession and say, 'we are sorry.'" These two public apologies were an attempt to make right the harm caused by long-held policies and beliefs used to stigmatise and oppress members of the LGBTQ community, and they were nothing short of monumental as they addressed the oppression each institution had contributed. Similar developments also took place in both Britain and Europe.

Though the apologies are important, we must not be lulled into thinking that the LGBTQ community is no longer subject to oppressive policies and discriminatory politics. Rather than a static point, they are an opening, an opportunity to shed further light on the oppressive attitudes and biases that still exist within the larger community. Though oftentimes subtle, biases towards this minority group are powerful and often have damaging and lasting effects.

Implicit bias

One phenomenon we must examine in our work with LGBTQ patients is that of unconscious or implicit bias. Unconscious bias is characterized as stereotypes we all hold outside of our conscious awareness that originate from our need to make sense of the world by categorizing it. Unconscious bias is more prevalent than explicit bias or conscious prejudice and is often at odds with our values and morals. Unconscious bias begins to emerge in middle childhood and continue throughout our development, leaving us with well-established stereotypes, attitudes and beliefs before we are even aware of them (Navarro, 2019). In an address to the IPA (International Psychoanalytic Association) regarding gender, Irene Matthis (Junkers, 2002) cautioned that analysts need to be "aware of the ever-present unconscious bias in thinking about issues of sex and gender arising not only within the patient but also within the analyst." This caution should apply to our biases around same-sex relationships as well as same-sex parenting. LGBTQ individuals, couples and families face many challenges both within the community and in the consulting room, and our understanding of their issues and our own will go far in helping establish strong working alliances with our patients.

Many studies on implicit bias toward the LGBTQ community in criminal justice, educational and health care settings have been conducted. In one such study, Burke, Dovidio and Przedworski (2015) examined implicit and explicit bias toward LGBTQ patients by medical students. In their study, they noted that explicit attitudes are prone to being influenced by social desirability bias and influenced by the advancements that LGBTQ individuals have gained in recent years. So, it would appear to be socially desirable to hold positive views of LGBTQ individuals. However, implicit bias, as noted above, is ingrained and most likely not recognized by the person holding it (Dovidio and Fiske, 2012). Results of Burke's study indicated that 46% of heterosexual first-year medical students held explicit biases while 82% held some degree of implicit bias. Therefore, while many students had positive views of their LGBTQ patients, the majority of them held beliefs that would likely negatively affect how they would approach them or manage their care.

There is also a growing body of literature demonstrating that mental health professionals have their own implicit biases toward the LGBTQ community. As well intentioned as we are, we may hold beliefs that would cause us to neglect important areas of concerns for our patients or engage in microaggressions, thereby eroding the therapeutic relationship and our ability to help the patient gain an understanding of their dilemmas. One such bias that we may hold is that of heterosexism. In the article "Deconstructing Heterosexism: Becoming an LGB Affirmative Heterosexual Couple and Family Therapist," McGeorge and Carlson (2011) explore the way heterosexism can affect the lives of our LGBTQ clients and how it may negatively influence the therapy process. They urge therapists to examine three areas of implicit bias that may affect our work with LGBTQ patients in individual, couple and family therapy. The first area is that of heteronormative assumptions, which results in holding the heterosexual relationship as the ideal, with all of its traditional norms and roles. The second is institutional heterosexism, which can be used as a form of social control to maintain heterosexual dominance. Though we have seen the lessening of some of these controls with the granting of marriage rights for example, there has been an upswing in heterosexual control coming in the form of maintaining religious rights to refuse services to those from the LGBTQ community. Finally, the third area of implicit bias is heterosexual privilege. These are the unearned rights and privileges granted to individuals simply because they are of the dominant sexual orientation. McGeroge and Carlson stress the importance of the heterosexual therapist understanding the impact of heterosexism on the LGBTQ client and couple, as well as their own heterosexism, which may contribute to their own unconscious bias affecting their patients. It would be of equal importance for the LGBTQ therapist to examine their own heterosexism and how it may be influencing their approach to treatment.

Consequently, there are several areas that the couple and family analyst must be aware of in working with the LGBTQ population; their own unconscious bias as well as that of the internal state of the client. In their article "Moving Counselling Forward on LGB and Transgender Issues: Speaking Queerly on Discourses and Microaggressions," Smith, Shin and

Officer (2012) raise the idea that the dominance of heterosexist language in our society leads to microaggressions and microinvalidations toward sexual minorities. In one instance, they site how important it is to confront language that assumes a heteronormative hierarchy. Such an example can be applied to the term "LGBTQ affirming therapist." While on the surface this seems like a harmless and even noble phrase, the authors note how it fortifies heteronormativity, placing one group of people who hold the power in the position over the group that "needs" affirmation. They explain that queer theorists would seek to deconstruct the heteronormative paradigm rather than seek affirmation and acceptance by it. What this trend demonstrates is the need for further exploration of language and how it affects individuals in the LGBTQ community, especially the language that appears positive on its face. We must continually engage in the process of gaining a deeper understanding of our attitudes and behaviours toward sexual and gender minority patients in order to confront our biases and the attitudes that may block efficacious treatment.

Finally, to demonstrate the importance of examining how language and attitudes affect the LGBTQ population, we must consider the idea of homophobia and internalized homophobia. Smith, Shin and Officer (2012) discuss homophobia in the context of current thinking. The term phobia, they say, refers to a certain clinical condition with specific symptoms, placing the term within the medical model, potentially pathologizing the individual. This maintains the dominant discourse and may harm the therapeutic relationship. Internalized homophobia places the onus on the individual to manage a difficult internal state and minimizes the idea that there are external factors that foster both prejudice and discrimination, causing the individual distress. We must be aware of both the internal and external struggles individuals of the LGBTQ community face as well as the internal and external pressures we, the analyst, may feel based on our unconscious biases and participation in a heterosexist and heteronormative world. Can psychoanalytically minded therapists be agents in deconstructing current paradigms, both externally and internally, thereby freeing up our thinking and helping our patients access couple and family configurations that best serve their needs or, are we in danger of unwittingly fostering the current paradigms, cementing the status quo and furthering the oppression of this group?

Implicit bias and same-sex parenting

When working with LGBTQ couples, an important challenge to these ideas occurs when couples are making the transition to parenthood. Heterosexism, heteronormativity and unconscious bias can greatly affect the couple, the couple as parents, and the manner in which the couple transitions to parenthood as the individuals adjust to all of the stresses and demands of parenting within the context of a heteronormative society. Couples, and individuals, in the LGBTQ community come to parenthood through many avenues: having been in a heterosexual relationship; as a committed choice between two same-sex partners; through adoption; through insemination with a known donor who may or may not have some degree of participation in the child's life; and insemination with an anonymous donor who the child may likely never know. Considering all of these scenarios, and understanding the specific challenges LGBTQ parents face in a heteronormative world, internally and externally, will help us gain an understanding of the specific challenges posed to the therapist treating this population. For instance, Patterson and Farr (2017) raise the question of how lesbian or gay couples select last names for their child and the meaning of this for the couple and the child given that it will not be based on patronymic convention. Furthermore, how do we think of parenting roles? Do we hold them along tightly held gender lines or are we free to think of them as more flexible and fluid? Is the role of father, in the traditional sense, a reaffirmation of heteronormative values and roles or does a traditional father role fit for some LGBTQ families, implying choice? How can we deconstruct this role and that of mother in an effort to bring more access and freedom to the relationships lived out on a daily basis? Do the roles of mother and father need to fall along gender lines or can each member of the same-sex couple be free to adopt whatever function fits for them, constructing new roles and ways to explore and live them out that best fits the family, maximizing the idea of a creative couple. What if the couple unconsciously holds the heteronormative paradigm even though it may not fit for them and is reaffirmed by microaggressions and microinvalidations from society and the therapist? We must explore what we hold internally and what we communicate, unwittingly to the couple and each individual. As well, we must help our patients explore the beliefs and values they hold within themselves with regard to the couple and the role of parenting and what this may communicate to the child.

The impact of implicit and explicit bias on same-sex parenting research

Golombok (2015) reminds us that it was once argued that children who grew up with lesbian mothers would be inadequately parented because it was believed that lesbian mothers were less nurturing than heterosexual mothers, that they would be ostracized by their peers and, most troubling of all to the courts, that "the children would show atypical gender development such that boys would be less masculine in their identity and behaviour, and girls less feminine, relative to boys and girls from heterosexual homes" (p. 34). This thinking, to a large extent, provided the impetus for researchers conducting studies into the lives, experiences and outcomes of children raised by same-sex parents. Begun in the late 1970s, primarily to support lesbian mothers fighting for custody of their children following the mother's disclosure of her lesbianism within marriage, these early studies sought to reassure the courts that the wellbeing and development of these children would not be harmed if the judge allowed the children to remain with their mothers. Although a number of early studies (Kirkpatrick, Smith and Roy, 1981; Golombok, Spencer and Rutter, 1983) did much to reassure the courts, concerns continued to persist. Because school-age children provided the focus of this research, questions were raised about the development of older age adolescents. To answer these concerns, longitudinal studies, i.e., Tasker and Golombok (1997), attempted to follow a group of children originally recruited to their lesbian mother study into their teens and again in their twenties. When compared with the control group, i.e., children raised by divorced mothers, they found that the children and young adults from the lesbian mother households had just as good relationships with their mothers and even better relationships with their mother's partner than did children growing up in a heterosexual family with their mother's new male partner.

The shift in focus towards researching children raised from birth in planned lesbian households produced further positive results, showing, for example, that children born through donor insemination showed no difference in terms of psychological adjustment or gender development from children born through donor insemination in two-parent heterosexual families. Yet, according to Golombok, despite these positive findings, further questions were raised of the research alleging sample bias. For instance, it was suggested that those families in which children were experiencing problems would be less motivated to take part in the research. Mobilising their efforts to counter these concerns, researchers in the UK (Avon Study) and the US (Gartrell Study) set about conducting large-scale, longitudinal, epidemiological studies. Consistent with previous findings, these representative samples showed that children in lesbian mother households did not differ in terms of psychological adjustment or gender development from children growing up in heterosexual female households.

Despite the many attempts by researchers to reassure those with concerns about the wellbeing of children growing up in lesbian mother households, it seems that the very same questions are now being asked about the children of gay fathers. These questions not only reflect the dominance of heteronormative thinking, i.e., that families that deviate from the norm of the traditional two-parent heterosexual family are believed to pose particular risks to the psychological wellbeing of the children (Golombok, 2015), but also questions about gay men's suitability for parenthood. Thankfully, we have moved away from the notion that same-sex children of gay fathers are likely to be molested sexually by their fathers, their father's lovers and gay friends, but Bigner (1996) draws our attention to the fact that gay fathers must reconcile the two polar extremes of what it means to be both gay and a father. Gay father studies, such as those conducted by Farr, Forsell and

Patterson (2010) and Golombok *et al* (2014) — of adoptive children raised by gay fathers — convincingly report positive parent child relationships as well as positive outcomes in regard to children's adjustment and wellbeing. It is telling, however, that data on children of parents identifying as bisexual remains woefully under-represented in the research to date, suggesting perhaps another kind of implicit bias at work within the field.

Taken as a whole, the body of same-sex parenting research demonstrates that children growing up with lesbian and gay parents are no different from children growing up with heterosexual parents in terms of psychological adjustment or gender development (Patterson, 2004). It would seem, therefore, that the gender and sexual orientation of the parent is much less important for children's psychological wellbeing than the quality of the family relationships themselves. Golombok (2015), pushing the point further, suggests that neither parent's sexual orientation or their gender make a difference to children's own gender identity, gender role behaviour or indeed their sexual orientation and, if anything, it seems that children growing up with same-sex parents are more open-minded and appear to be more confident in expressing their sexual orientation whatever it may be.

Managing implicit bias in same-sex parenting

Despite the positive outcomes contained in decades of research, same-sex parents continue to encounter a host of challenges specific to their gender and sexuality. For instance, Bos, van Balen and van den Boom (2007) suggest that lesbian mothers have concerns about rearing their children in a homophobic society and feel more pressure in justifying the quality of their parenting than their heterosexual counterparts, a particular aspect of the negative outside world scrutinizing the worth of same-sex parents. Attention has also been drawn to the absence of support from families of origin (Oswald, 2002), as well as the paucity of positive role models for same-sex couples, although the increased visibility of same-sex parenting within the wider community must surely be lessening this particular concern. Additional considerations concerning the internalized impact of implicit bias for lesbians and gay men themselves will be examined through a number of clinical examples.

In regard to same-sex parenting, particular emphasis seems to have been placed on the conscious decision to have children, a consequence perhaps of the complexities and choices same-sex couples face in actually deciding to have a child. Yet, unsurprisingly, a number of lesbian and gay male couples present for therapy precisely because of unconscious motivations and arrangements regarding the decision to have a child and the actual care of that child coming to exert a destabilising impact on the couple relationship itself and hence their presentation in therapy. D'Ercole (2008) stresses the importance in clinical work with same-sex couples of attending to internalised experiences relating to feelings of difference. This is because, as has already been discussed, negative social attitudes are believed to produce internal conflicts within the individual, manifest in feelings of guilt, alienation, confusion and hostility, etc. that may then become activated and enacted within the couple relationship. It is therefore suggested that these internalized homophobic feelings and attitudes need careful "working through" in order to help the partners in same-sex couple relationships achieve integration.

Bea, a lesbian mother and her female partner, Jess, sought therapy two years after the birth of their son, Jack. The reason they sought help was that Elliott, the gay donor father and friend of Bea's sister, had apparently "betrayed" the couple by his failure to have any contact with Jack. The women were incandescent, complaining bitterly about how Elliott had let them down, although they were hopeful that he might be willing to join them in the therapy. When the couple were seen with Elliott, Bea accused him of abandoning her and their son. Elliott was equally indignant, pointing out that he had never agreed to be an active father in Jack's life and questioned Bea's memory of events. The therapist queried the importance of Elliott being actively involved in Jack's life, especially as the two women constituted a parental pair, although it was clear that they did not feel complete without the presence of a father for Jack. Crespi (1995) notes that some women in lesbian relationships struggle to embrace motherhood because they are unable to mourn sufficiently the heterosexual object and identification. Thinking further with Bea about her anxieties, she spoke of the importance of children having both a mother and father in their lives, possibly the consequence of her own parents divorcing when she was seven years old. Whilst directly referencing the impact of Bea's internal parental couple on her, the therapist also felt the need to examine Bea's insistence on the presence of a father for Jack, especially as Jack had other important male influences in his life, and felt that it was a cloaked reference to her own internalized heteronormative assumption that same-sex parents are not in themselves enough for a child, simply because they fail to offer that child a cross-gendered pairing that is felt to be so important for their wellbeing and development. Yet, in situations of donor insemination, the procreative act does not mirror that of the majority of heterosexual couples nor does it map neatly onto a straight couple's transition to parenthood since, in truth, it is more akin to separated and post-divorce couples living in separate abodes and negotiating contact arrangements across the divide. For Bea and Jess, the therapy was focused on helping them embrace the value of what they were offering Jack and to create a space for Elliott to be part of his son's life if he so wanted. Interestingly, as the mothers stepped back, Elliott began to show more of an interest in Jack and, at the point that the therapy ended, Elliott was in the process of establishing a routine of seeing him on a weekly basis.

Adam and Martin are a gay male couple in their late twenties who were advised by their social worker to seek an initial consultation from a couple-based specialist adoption service. Although, at one level, we see a couple that are consciously onboard with the idea of having a child, at another level, they were completely unprepared for the havoc it would unleash in both their external and internal worlds. At the time of the referral, the couple had been caring for Max, a ten-month-old boy who had been placed with them with a view to adopt. Adam and Martin are a couple who met online and who described a strong bond between them with many shared interests and a good network of friends. Influenced by the increasing number of gay men within their circle having children, the couple decided to adopt. Goldberg (2010) suggests that the decision concerning the route to parenthood is often related to the importance of having a biogenetic relationship to one's child, i.e., passing on one's genes or physically resembling one's child. She suggests that where this is not of consideration, then couples are more likely to adopt, although she also highlights the fact that gay men become parents amidst institutional discourses that privilege heteronormativity and thus present challenges to their parenting pursuits. Additionally, same-sex couples themselves may grapple with these normative assumptions, and this is exactly what Adam and Martin reported to their therapist. For instance, following the decision to adopt, Max had come too soon and Adam was forced to relinquish his much-loved job in order to care for Max, a decision based solely on Martin's earning potential and which Adam was struggling to accept. Adam immediately felt cast in the role of "housewife," as he put it, an identity he completely eschewed, whilst in Adam's mind, Martin became the man of the house.

At the point that the couple sought therapy, Adam was acutely in touch with a longing to be free of the constraints and responsibilities of childcare and Martin was busily trying to avert a crisis in their relationship by reconfiguring his work schedule to care for Max. However, although admirable in itself, this attempted solution failed to address Adam's internal discomfort in terms of his masculinity feeling compromised by assuming the primary caregiving role for Max, and, at the same time, it averted Adam's rivalry with Martin for a more equitable arrangement concerning Max's care. The clue to Adam's deep discomfort at being a gay dad was evident in the various references to him feeling judged by others, especially when he and Martin were out together with Max. For instance, Adam expressed deep resentment in regard to the scrutiny he and Martin felt under, for instance, in passing through border control when the guard seemed to question the fact that they could be Max's parents, an obvious example of a micro-aggression that has the effect of invalidating the couple and their right to parent. To some extent, this resonates with Bigner's (1996) thinking about boundary controls for the children of gay fathers, who attempt to control the disclosure of their father's sexual orientation, for example, by refusing to be seen in public with their father and his lover, or in controlling one's behaviour with peers by refusing to bring them to the family home. Hence, we see the importance of patrolling the border between what is private and what is public, in order to afford some modicum of protection from the negative gaze of the outside world.

Yet, it is clear that the discomfort Adam experienced in the outside world referenced his deep internal discomfort with being a gay dad, something he was able to admit during the course of therapy. He had already said that he couldn't bear the judgmental eyes on him and admitted that when out together as a couple with Max, he felt anxious about Max playing-up, since it would draw attention to him being a gay dad. He went on to explain that it was a very different feeling being out with Max on his own where he could pass as a straight dad, an identity for which he could feel proud and comfortable. This helped the therapist see more clearly Adam's internal conflict concerning the integration of his masculine self with his gay identity. For both men Max had come too soon, but the therapist came to see that this was an unconscious reference to Adam and Martin's prolonged struggle to settle things between them and of finding a more comfortable home within their couple relationship in which to welcome Max. Perhaps the decision to adopt was a shared unconscious attempt to force a resolution rather than allowing a careful "working through" of the couple's complex issues relating to being gay and of being gay fathers. By speaking directly to these issues, regarding the internal and external conflicts associated with their separate and shared gay identities, it was noticeable how the men began to reclaim their couple relationship from the grip of external forces that were felt to be threatening their connection.

A final case scenario raises some additional considerations. For instance, how do we think about the position of the non-biological parent in same-sex parental couple arrangements involving a known gay donor? It seems that these parental arrangements raise fundamental questions concerning the meaning and construction of family particularly given that there are three potential couples: the biological paring, the gay donor dad and his partner, and the biological lesbian mother and her partner, all of which need consideration within same-sex parenting networks. Bowen (2008) suggests that interesting family dynamics arise in regard to those who are able to claim their status as parent based both on their legal understanding of parenthood and their interaction with the dominant culture. In other words, such arrangements as those outlined above, create particular dynamics for the partners, the children, and the family as a whole.

James seeks therapy because of issues relating to his longstanding partner, Neil. James explains to the therapist that he has a seven-year-old daughter named Ellen, born through donor insemination using his sperm to impregnate Amy, one of the legal partners in his firm. He described Amy as a formidable character coming from a well-heeled family and who was determined to ensure the best for her daughter. Although James and Neil had regular contact with Ellen during the week, Amy put pressure on the men to join her and her partner Helen, with Ellen on weekend retreats to her country home. James experienced difficulty refusing the invitation, since he loved spending time with Ellen but could see that the arrangement did not suit Neil so well. Although committed to Ellen, Neil felt less secure of his place within the wider parental arrangements and was concerned about Ellen monopolising their couple relationship. James, who struggled to say no, felt between a rock and a hard place, as he tried to keep Amy, Ellen and Kevin happy. He also noticed that during the weekend visits, Kevin and Helen seemed to be pairing off, suggesting a particular reading of the complex workings of the couple and family relationships within the system as a whole. Essentially, the focus of the work was in helping James establish more appropriate boundaries for his relationship with Neil, separate from his co-parenting relationship with Amy, and one that included Ellen but which also allowed a protected space for James and Neil.

This case scenario draws particular attention to the varying and complex needs of same-sex partners, as the parties navigate the transition to parenthood with its myriad expectations and fantasies about how it will be and the types of challenges these parental couples might face. Glazer (2004) believes that "societal definitions of family are changing, in part due to advances in reproductive technologies, increased availability of adoptions and advances in gay and lesbian civil rights" (p. 104). She also believes that "contemporary psychoanalysis ... finds itself moving away from a belief in the causal links between gender, object choice and maternal strivings" (p. 104). This suggests that perhaps in this new era, it is not only same-sex parents who are facing the challenges of parenting their children, in an uncertain and, to some extent, unfriendly and hostile external environment, but that psychoanalytically informed practitioners are also being forced to renegotiate these new relational networks in regard to their theory and practice.

Conclusion

This chapter has examined developments in thinking about same-sex parents and couples. It uses implicit bias as a central and organising principle in understanding the ways in which, despite advances within society and within psychoanalysis, these families of difference continue to suffer from heteronormative thinking and practice. Not surprisingly, as the numbers increase, psychoanalytic couple and family psychotherapists are increasingly encountering and working with these parents and children in their consulting rooms. The extent to which they feel open and equipped to challenge the dominance of the cross-gendered pairing as the highest context marker for the parenting of children, remains to be seen, especially as same-sex parents may feel freer to construct parenting differently and not necessarily within prescribed gendered roles.

References

Bigner, J.J. (1996), Working with gay fathers: Developmental, post-divorce parenting and therapeutic issues. In J. Laird & R.-J., Green (eds.) *Lesbians and Gays in Couples and Families: A Handbook for Therapists*, 370–403. San Francisco: Jossey Bass.

Bos, H., van Balen, F., and van den Boom, D.C. (2007), Child adjustment and parenting in planned lesbian-parent families. *American Journal of Orthopsychiatry, 77, 1*: 38–48.

Bowen, D. (2008), The parent trap: Differential family power in same-sex families. *William and Mary Journal of Women and Law, 15*, 1–49.

Burke, S.E., Dovidio, J.F., and Przedworski, J.M. (2015), Do contact and empathy mitigate bias against gay and lesbian people among first-year medical students? A report from the medical CHANGE study. *Academy of Medicine, 90*: 645–651.

Crespi, L. (1995), Some thoughts on the role of mourning in the development of a positive lesbian identity. In T. Domenici & R.C. Lesser (eds.) *Disorienting Sexualities*, 19–32. New York: Routledge.

Dovidio, J.F. and Fiske, S.T. (2012), Under the radar: How unexamined biases in decision-making processes on clinical interactions can contribute to health care disparities. *American Journal of Public Health, 102*: 945–952.

D'Ercole, A. (2008), Homosexuality and psychoanalysis III: Clinical perspectives. *Journal of Gay & Lesbian Mental Health, 12, 4*: 368–371.

Farr, R., Forsell, S.L., and Patterson, C. (2010), Gay lesbian and heterosexual adoptive parents: Couple and relationship issues. *Journal of GLBT Family Studies, 6, 2*, 199–213.

Glazer, D.F. (2004), Teasing apart gender, object choice, and motherhood in lesbian relationships. In A. D'ercole & J. Drescher (eds.) *Uncoupling Convention: Psychoanalytic Approaches to Same-Sex Couples and Families*. Chapter 6, 103–113. New York: Routledge.

Goldberg, A. (2010), *Lesbian and Gay Parents and Their Children: Research on the Family Life Cycle*. Washington, DC: American Psychological Association.

Golombok, S. (2015), *Modern Families: Parents and Children in New Family Form*. Cambridge, UK: Cambridge University Press.

Golombok, S., Mellish, L., Jennings, S., Casey, P., Tasker, F., and Lamb, M.E. (2014), Adoptive gay father families: Parent-child relationships and children's psychological adjustment. *Child Development, 85, 2*, 456–468.

Golombok, S., Spencer, A., and Rutter, M. (1983), Children in lesbian single-parent households: Psychosexual and psychiatric appraisal. *Journal of Child Psychology and Psychiatry, 24, 4*, 551–572.

Junkers, G. (2002). Gender and psychoanalytic method. *International Journal of Psychoanalysis, 83, 4*: 922–925.

Kirkpatrick, M., Smith, C., and Roy, R. (1981), Lesbian mothers and their children: A comparative study. *American Journal of Orthopsychiatry, 51, 3*, 545–551.

McGeorge, C. and Carlson, T.S. (2011), Deconstructing heterosexism: Becoming an LGB affirmative heterosexual couple and family therapist. *Journal of Marital and Family Therapy, 37, 1*, 14–26.

Navarro, J.R. (2019, November 15). Unconscious bias. Retrieved from https://diversity.ucsf.edu/resources/unconscious-bias.

Oswald, R.F. (2002), Resilience within the family networks of lesbian and gay men: Intentionality and redefinition. *Journal of Marriage and the Family, 64, 2*, 374–383.

Patterson, C.J. (2004), Lesbian and gay parents and their children: Summary of research findings. *Lesbian and Gay Parenting: A resource for psychologists*. American Psychological Association, 5–22.

Patterson, C.J., and Farr, R.H. (2017), What shall we call ourselves? Last names among lesbian, gay and heterosexual couples and their adopted children. *Journal of LGBT Family Studies, 13, 2*, 97–113.

Smith, L.C, Shin, R.Q., and Officer, L.M. (2012), Moving counseling forward on LGB and transgender issues: Speaking queerly on discourses and microaggressions. *The Counseling Psychologist, 40, 3*, 385–408.

Tasker, F., and Golombok, S. (1997), *Growing Up in a Lesbian Family*. New York: Guildford Press.

Chapter 13

The LGBTQ couple choice of therapist he/she/they, straight or gay

Creativity vs defense

Colleen Sandor

Many therapists who identify as lesbian, gay, bisexual, transgender or queer (LGBTQ) and who regularly see LGBTQ couples, do so because their clients seek them out and choose to work with an LGBTQ therapist. In addition, many LGBTQ clients choose to work with therapists of the same assumed gender. These decisions are important to the couple and are often influenced by the experience over many years of their identity being disavowed or oppressed. However, whilst we understand the conscious desire to see a same gender or LGBTQ couple's analyst, nevertheless, these decisions must also be understood in regard to the couple's unconscious fantasies and dynamics. In this chapter, I will explore how growing up in a heteronormative society, with its views of marriage, relationship roles and norms, shapes the LGBTQ individual long before they form a same-sex partnership, and the ways in which this exposure affects the couple relationship itself. I will also explore what may be in the mind of the couple as they begin to work with an LGBTQ therapist and whether the choice of therapist represents a defensive function or whether it constitutes an important ingredient in the development and progress of the work itself.

Overview

While the literature on psychoanalytic treatment with couples has been more inclusive of LGBTQ couples in the last few decades, there remain many issues to explore with regard to this population. Most articles fail to mention work with these couples, assuming that treatment of heterosexual couples translate neatly to treatment with LGBTQ couples. And while many of the theories, techniques, issues and skills pursuant to couples' work does indeed translate, there are, nevertheless, many unique facets of the work with LGBTQ couples that go unaddressed. The failure to include LGBTQ couples in the mainstream analytic couples' therapy literature renders them invisible, at best, and disavowed at worst. So, while the analytic couple's community gives voice to supporting LGBTQ couples, and I truly believe that it does, the lack of writing about them underscores a literature still steeped in the tenets of heteronormativity. Lewes (2005) goes even further by suggesting that analytic work has a long history of homophobia. And while more recently there have been efforts to correct this, for example, in American Psychoanalytic Association's (APsaA's) apology to the LGBTQ community, it is my belief that homophobia still exists in a more disguised form or is subsumed within a gay-friendly attitude.

Generally speaking, analytic couple's work has advanced our understanding of couple dynamics a great deal, allowing us to examine the early object relations of each individual as it plays out between the pair both intrapsychically and interpersonally. It also facilitates our understanding of the couple's projective system, their shared unconscious beliefs and fantasies, and their individual and shared transferences to the therapist. Analytic work can also help us move couples away from their rigidly fixed interactions and roles to a more creative and generative way of relating, thus promoting movement and growth. As Nathans (2017) states, "Thus for the couples therapist, object relation theory offers a way of holding in mind the object relations field of each partner, the interpersonal dynamics between the partners, and most crucially, the ways in which both the intrapsychic worlds exert mutual influence on one another" (pg. 4). Object relations theory can help us understand the dynamics that all couples, LGBTQ or straight, share, such as communication difficulties, intimacy struggles, and stress during transitions. It can also help us explore those issues that are unique to the gay and lesbian couple and that affect the functioning of their relationship, for example, internalized hate, internal bias, rejection by family members, and coming out issues.

While the analytic lens offers us a view into the dynamics that are crucial to understanding the LGBTQ couples' difficulties and strengths, it can and does fall short if it only focuses on the internal world of the couple and ignores external realities. It is especially important to take account of the societal and institutional structures that LGBTQ couples face in their early development as individuals as well as their current life together. Many individuals will come to the partnership with a history of secrecy, fear and oppression concerning their identity and sexuality. The extent of this will be determined, among other things, by family attitudes, religious upbringing and regional differences in attitudes toward homosexuality. The societal pressures and realities LGBTQ individuals and couples encounter is also a crucial component to consider in the work. As Abse (2016) says:

> *Psychoanalytic work with couples involves an encounter, not just with the individual intrapsychic world of our patients, but with the lived reality of their relationship with each other, to their children, to the wider family, and indeed to their working lives. Effective psychoanalytic work with couples involves walking the line; this line has on one side the intimate world of the couple where unconscious phantasy is played out and, on the other,*

the challenges of external realities, such as redundancy, housing issues, money worries, problematic in-laws, and, of course, real life children. We walk the line because our work is where these external and internal realities intersect and we try to understand the interplay between them. Unlike in intensive individual work, we must not retreat to the intrapsychic world where the relationship between the analyst and the patient can become the whole world and where external reality can become a distant, interfering noise (pg. 151).

For the LGBTQ couple, if the external reality becomes a distant and interfering noise, we lose the opportunity of understanding a significant aspect of the couple's development and subsequent struggle, disavowing the potential attacks that may threaten the very livelihood of the couple. One particular area of focus must be on how the external reality of homophobia and heteronormativity as well as the couple's internal life intersects; we must try to understand how these pressures shape and affect the couple. The therapist of the LGBTQ couple walks the line between the intimate world of the couple and the external realities that influence their intrapsychic life and relational functioning.

One of the many external realities LGBTQ individuals and couples live with is that of having been raised in a predominantly heteronormative society. According to Van der Toom, Pliskin and Morgenroth (2020), "Heteronormative ideology refers to the belief that there are two separate and opposing genders with associated natural roles that match their assigned sex, and that heterosexuality is a given" (pg. 160). Regardless of the gains in LGBTQ rights in the past 30–40 years, the message remains that heterosexuality is the norm and that LGBTQ life is an outlier. By the time the individual begins to explore and define their identity and sexuality, they have been immersed in a heteronormative world and have internalized expectations and roles according to their gender and assumed heterosexuality. Van der Toom, Pliskin and Morgenroth go on to say that heteronormativity is pervasive, ubiquitous, unrelenting and insidious. It is a persistent pressure that the nascent LGBTQ individual faces and which eventually causes all sorts of difficulties, including self-hatred. Heteronormativity is in the fabric of our upbringing, like the air we breathe. If one's development is consistent with these norms, then there will be little internal strife; however, the developing LGBTQ individual may experience a great deal of discomfort when they realize they do not fit within this mold. They are left with a number of hard choices, i.e., to meet these expectations and reject the self, to reject the self publicly and act out privately, or to accept the self and face the potential of rejection from family and society.

One of the consequences experienced by the LGBTQ individual growing up in a heteronormative world is that of internalized homophobia. The insidious nature of heteronormativity that Van der Toom, Pliskin and

Morgenroth speak of results in a state of self-disdain and hatred that can be equally insidious and pervasive. Dreyer (2007) notes that heteronormativity enhances homophobia. According to him, heterosexism includes pervasive heterosexuality and homophobia. While this causes difficulty for the individual, it will also affect the couple dynamics a great deal. Hertzmann (2011) says that, "there can be a mirroring of the societal indictment of homosexuality reflected in the couple's relationship." (pg. 347). She says that the homophobia can damage the couple and lead to a state of paralysis in the relationship and in the work. This will affect the couple's ability to form a creative and generative partnership. As a result, the individuals and the couple may adhere to strict normative roles to defend against the fear of rising homophobic feelings.

The ubiquity of heteronormativity shapes each individual in the couple, and each comes to the partnership with certain beliefs, norms and roles based on heterosexist and heteronormative ideals, as well as some level of internal bias or homophobia with regard to their own sexuality. Instead of allowing the couple to form a generative, unique, creative couple, these preconceived roles and norms may bind the couple into fixed relating and a certain hostility toward the relationship, toward themselves, and towards each other. While some couples may be aware of these beliefs, many will be unaware of the extent to which they hold these implicit biases about the functioning of their couple relationship. As well, one partner in the couple may hold a certain heteronormative ideal while the other does not, creating conflict and a rigidity around roles and norms within the dyad. This rigidity and inflexibility may hamper the ability of the couple to attain a "creative couple" state of mind. According to Morgan (2019), "the couple can use their couple state of mind to think creatively together" (pg. xxiv). This allows the couple to tolerate their differences and create something new between them. However, if the LGBTQ couple is in a rigidly defined structure based on heteronormative roles, this may preclude them from exercising a creative couple state of mind about the relationship, inhibiting growth and flexibility in the partnership. A more creative attitude can foster the partners' freedom to take on multiple roles in their relationship with no prescribed norms. According to Siegel and Walker (1996), "Becoming homosexual requires a good deal of unlearning of values, standards, and beliefs, and creativity is the currency for that survival" (pg. 43). One may have to give up a great deal for one's freedom.

When it comes to couples therapy, the LGBTQ couple may seek out a gay or lesbian therapist or a therapist of their same assumed gender. This choice may be for defensive purposes or in an effort to enhance the creativity of the couple, or both. I will discuss this more fully below. Once the choice of therapist begins to take shape in the mind of the couple, the transference begins immediately, often much earlier than the first contact. The couple will come to the first session with many assumptions, hopes and fears already in place.

The shared unconscious fantasy that drives the specific choice of analyst must come to light during the therapy, as it helps towards understanding certain aspects of the unconscious functioning of the couple and the shared fantasies that they hold about us. For example, does the couple assume the therapist to be straight or gay, do they assume the therapist is understanding or alternatively that the therapist represents the homophobic other. In addition, the couple's therapist must be aware of their own heteronormative biases and, if LGBTQ, their own homophobia and self-hatred. While we will need to be aware of the usual countertransference issues of working with couples, those that may be unique to our work with LGBTQ couples must be examined and used to inform our interventions.

Gender of the couple analyst

While many analytic therapists would argue that gender does not make a difference in the treatment or the transference, others would contend that it does, especially at the beginning of a treatment. Bhati (2014), for instance, suggests that in therapeutic work, one of the most widely recommended demographic matches has been that of the client and therapist's gender. It has also been a major theme in counseling research. And while this may be an important factor at the beginning of treatment, or in the choice of the therapist, it will change over time as the therapeutic relationship develops. Gelso (2002) contends that at the beginning of treatment, realism plays a large role. That is to say, evaluating a therapist on their objective qualities (e.g., gender) rather than the inherent transference projection, can significantly affect the therapeutic relationship. The objective quality of the therapist plays a larger role at the beginning of therapy and fades as the treatment progresses and the transference projections become more prominent. Concerning gender in the transference, Raphling and Chused (1988) write, *"Without question the external reality of the analyst's gender will bias the development of the transference…The analyst's gender is an organizer of transference, though it may concurrently serve as a resistance. Patients use reality as a disguise for their forbidden unconscious fantasies, with the external world as a source of resistance…Unless the analyst's actual sex and his other realistic attributes are subjected to analytic scrutiny as a nidus of hidden resistance…the transference image may be overshadowed"* (pg. 99–100).

While Raphling and Chused underscore the idea that the choice of the gender of the therapist may be a resistance that needs to be analyzed, we should remain open to the idea that for the LGBTQ couple, the choice of a same gender therapist may actually be less about resistance and more about external affirmation and identification. Choosing a same gender therapist may be the only way a couple will consider even coming to the work, thereby representing a very concrete choice. But as the transference emerges, the issue of the gender of the therapist must be explored for its deeper unconscious meaning.

Writing about couples, Morgan (1992) notes that the gender of the therapist can affect the transference development in a myriad of ways. She says that "...the patient's choice of analyst reflects his or her pre-existing fantasies, not necessarily the actual effects of the analyst's sex on the therapeutic process" (pg. 146). We must be open to exploring the myriad of ways the gender of the therapist can affect the treatment of the couple.

As opposed to resistance, the gender of the therapist may actually serve as a holding and containing function for the couple, especially in the early stages of the treatment. Susan and Britta were a lesbian couple who came to therapy to deal with issues regarding intimacy in their relationship. Each had taken a passive role around their intimacy, expecting the other to be the one to initiate sex, and felt at a loss about how to rekindle their sex life. They were at a certain standstill around sex, hoping to increase the frequency but both not wanting to be the initiator, given its associations with being the aggressor. Britta had a history of sexual abuse from male perpetrators beginning in her early teens, while Susan had a father who left when she was 6 years old, leaving the family in difficult financial circumstances. Both Britta and Susan said they chose me as their therapist because they wanted to work with a female. They said that they would not even consider coming to couples work if they had to work with a male. It was clear from early in the work that one of the couple's shared unconscious fantasies was that I would be a safe harbor because I was a female, and I would neither leave them nor aggressively penetrate or hurt them as males in their lives had done before. They felt held and contained as a couple by this shared view of me. As the work progressed, however, the initial assumption about me as a female gave way to a more complex examination of the transference in light of my gender. When I began to make more aggressive interpretations about their passivity and reluctance to approach each other sexually, each, in her own way, felt betrayed by me, thinking that as a female therapist I should be more nurturing, warm and compassionate, not aggressive and "pushy." I had betrayed their heteronormative idea of a conventional female, the very roles that were making their relationship difficult as they donned a passive stance toward one another and split off their aggression and sexuality from the relationship, leaving them in a sort of stasis. Gradually, we examined the couple's unconscious fantasies and shared beliefs about their gender roles and their desire to be rid of aggression, as they thought it might destroy the couple. As a consequence, they were in time more able to be intimate, using the aggression in a productive way, to meet their sexual needs. So, while my gender served as an entry point to the treatment in hopes of a shared vision of female roles, that fantasy was actually being used as a defense against aggression and insight in the couple. This understanding moved us to a point of exploration about assumed roles that the couple was able to make use of. Once this was brought to light, the couple moved out of their paralysis and functioned more flexibly and creatively in their roles with one another.

In her article, Morgan (1992) describes the Tavistock Relationships early model of couple's treatment where a male/female therapist dyad was assigned to work with couples. She states that, *"The issue of gender for couples is relevant at many levels. It relates closely to the development of the self in relation to key figures in infancy, childhood, and adolescence, and to object choice in intimate adult relationships. On a more prosaic level, it relates to how couples manage their day to day lives and how free they feel to make choices in this area, or how bound they are to follow prescribed internalized gender messages about how men and women 'should be'"* (pg. 141). The male/female therapist dyad serves as a model in working with couples but implies a heteronormative ideal. In working with LGBTQ couples, we might wonder how the transference would emerge with a female/female dyad working with a lesbian couple or a male/male dyad working with a gay couple. These same gender therapist dyads would provide the LGBTQ couple with a working model of functioning productively in a same-sex partnership. While financial concerns usually preclude co-couple therapist dyads in treatment, we would assume the complexity of the transference issues would emerge and the shared unconscious fantasies about the same-sex couple would give us a view into the internal world of the couple in treatment.

Sexuality of the analyst

Either coupled with gender choice or separate from it, the LGBTQ couple may seek a therapist who is gay or lesbian themselves. On the other hand, the couple may seek a heterosexual therapist, although each of these choices may be used both defensively or as a means to enhance the couples work. Regardless, the choice of a therapist based on sexuality warrants further exploration and understanding in the context of the couple dynamics.

As noted earlier, each individual will come to the partnership with varying degrees of internal bias and homophobia which will affect the couple dynamic. And in choosing a gay or lesbian therapist, the couple may have a shared fantasy that the analyst will serve as a reparative object. The couple may seek affirmation and validation by an LGBTQ analyst as a way to legitimatize themselves and their relationship, repairing what has been damaged by the heteronormative ideal each has been raised with. However, this choice may also be defensive; as Guthrie (2006) says, "a gay patient may seek a gay therapist in order to avoid exploring painful material, such as internalized homophobia...the self-loathing gay people may feel for themselves" (pg. 64). Many years ago, I had a lesbian patient in a couple who struggled with the idea that she was a lesbian and whether or not this was ok for her, an acceptable way to live, even though she had been with her partner for two years. She wanted to be happy in her relationship but had a great deal of guilt and shame due to her strict religious upbringing. Because I work in a small community, this patient knew my wife, a factor that was instrumental in her idealizing our couple relationship. When I explored this with her, she expressed the view that I lived a very heteronormative life complete with traditional values and roles. According to her, we looked like Ozzie and Harriet except that there were two women on the top of our wedding cake rather than a man and a woman. She used this image of me as a way to legitimize gay relationships but also to excoriate herself for having trouble accepting herself and the relationship she was in. Over time, she was able to settle more comfortably into her own sexuality and thereby the relationship, and the couple was able to define the roles and norms that were uniquely generative for them. It was stable and creative, and far from an Ozzie and Harriet life in terms of the roles each assumed within the partnership.

As gay and lesbian therapists, we may feel pulled in many ways by the LGBTQ couple. As Hertzmann (2011) reminds us, there is often a "pull by the couple to use specific interactions as proof that their sexuality is wrong or abnormal, and also to attack both their sense of self and the relationship" (pg. 351). While true of the couple interactions, there may also be an internal pull for the therapist to criticize the partnership based on the therapist's own homophobia and internal bias, thereby becoming the homophobic other, persecuting the couple like others in their lives have persecuted the individuals. As well, there may be a pull for the therapist to collude with the couple around a heteronormative ideal, perhaps as a way of sanctioning their relationship and fending off feelings of pain and shame relating to the couple's homophobia. We must neither condemn the couple nor outwardly affirm a heteronormative choice (e.g., marriage) as we attempt to remain as neutral as possible and allow the couple to define themselves as creatively as possible, leading to a more flexible and generative life together.

Another area for the gay or lesbian couple therapist to be aware of when working with LGBTQ couples is the difference in the individuals in regard to their sexual identity development and the degree to which they have internalized a heteronormative ideal. If there is a disparity for the individuals in terms of development, the couple may unconsciously choose an LGBTQ therapist, as a way to validate the sexuality of the partner who is still struggling. For example, if one individual is out and the other is not, he or she may feel enormous pressure from their partner to come out and live more freely. The LGBTQ therapist may also feel a pull to endorse this view, thereby increasing the pressure on the closeted individual. The difference in development and what it means for the couple must be understood in terms of the couple dynamic. For example, the closeted individual may hold the shame for the couple while the out individual may hold the freedom. Siegel and Walker (1996) discuss the idea that often partners are at different stages in their identity development and resolution about their orientation. For instance, the partner who is "out" may feel held back while the one who isn't may feel pressured to be somewhere they are not yet ready to be. Each may look to the LGBTQ therapist for an endorsement of where they are.

The therapist must be aware of their own identity development and how this may unconsciously be communicated to the couple. A therapist with more unresolved issues may side with the "closeted" patient while the one with a more activist stance may feel more sympathetic to the patient who is "out," thereby closing the space for exploration of the difference and what it means unconsciously for the particular couple.

Self-disclosure is a hotly contested topic in analytic work that is well beyond the scope of this chapter. However, it holds particular meaning in undertaking work with gay and lesbian couples. One of the most salient issues for the LGBTQ therapist is whether to disclose their sexuality. Has the couple knowingly chosen an LGBTQ therapist or have they, as Phillips (1998) suggests, made a silent assumption about the therapist's heterosexuality? If the couple have made an assumption about the LGBTQ therapist's sexuality, either straight or gay, does the therapist self-disclose? While some LGBTQ therapists choose to disclose at the point of the first phone call, others do not. Still others may choose to disclose their sexuality at some point in the treatment for a variety of clinical reasons. There are a number of issues with self-disclosure, of the sort I am describing, and it may either shut the work down or open it in productive ways for the couple. Guthrie (2006) points to the importance of exploring the issue of self-disclosure with LGBTQ clients. He says it is never a neutral issue and will affect the treatment profoundly. For that reason, therapists must always consider this an important point of exploration with LGBTQ couples. Guthrie goes on to say this issue is no different from other characteristics of the therapist and yet in some ways it is uniquely different. For example, while a therapist may grow up in a shared religious community or culture and enjoy some degree of comfort or ease, an LGBTQ therapist most likely has grown up in a heteronormative family and community where they have to hide their emerging sexual identity. So, if the therapist is assumed to be straight, the straight therapist will not face a decision point about disclosure while the LGBTQ therapist is confronted with whether they come out in the therapeutic relationship or remain hidden, as they had to do in their early life.

Many LGBTQ clients grow up having to hide themselves and lie about their identity. Their development is often characterized by shame and guilt. If the therapist chooses not to reveal their LGBTQ identity to the couple, allowing them to assume that they are heterosexual, this may reinforce the shame and guilt the individuals and couple feel about their own identity (Guthrie, 2006). On the other hand, by self-disclosing, the therapist can serve as a role model for the couple. However, if the therapist reveals their sexual orientation prematurely, they most certainly will close down the space for exploring the fantasies and dynamic meaning of the therapist's sexuality for the couple. LGBTQ therapists will need to decide in each treatment with a LGBTQ couple whether to reveal their sexuality or not. It is worth noting that one may be asked directly or be the subject of an indirect inquiry from the couple. While a direct inquiry pressures the therapist for an answer, an indirect inquiry, such as the client hinting at the therapist's sexuality, will give the therapist a chance to decide to take up the issue of her sexuality or not. Not doing so may speak to the feelings the therapist holds toward their own sexuality. It also may be a collusion with the patient not to discuss difficult issues relating to sexuality, cementing the idea of shame and guilt (Guthrie, 2006). Every moment in each case will demand that the therapist explore what is best for the couple and the treatment with regard to self-disclosing their sexuality.

Finally, while the couple may choose an LGBTQ therapist, they may turn their shared homophobia toward the therapist as a way to disavow the work and the gains the couple may make in terms of self-affirmation and acceptance. Consciously having sought an LGBTQ therapist in the hope that the therapist may affirm their identity and communicate a belief in their couple relationship, the couple may hold an unconscious belief that a gay therapist might be, as they are, "unworthy members of the same club" (Siegel & Walker, 1996, pg. 37). The couple may use this to attack and defeat the therapeutic work, as a way to cement their own self-hatred and homophobia and continue to find themselves locked in a system that perpetuates this hatred.

One lesbian couple, Tara and Jane, sought me out for couple's therapy assuming, but not certain, that I was a lesbian. When the question arose, I did not answer directly but allowed the question of my sexuality to hang in the air. We explored the importance of the question for them, especially with regard to their coming out process, and both Tara and Jane said that knowing would help them see me as a role model. They had both grown up in religious conservative households in rural towns where neither, as far as they knew, had ever met a lesbian. As we delved into this issue, their assumption was that I would be able to understand them better if I were a lesbian. And while I did, being a lesbian, understand some aspects of their coming out process, I had to fight to keep the space open by not assuming I knew or shared their experience. I took nothing for granted and pushed deeper into the affect around their coming out to their families, which resulted in a significant loss of support. At times, the couple had difficulty moving into the painful material around the shame they felt about their sexuality in light of their religious upbringing, and they would use their assumption about my sexuality as a defense against going deeper into their pain. In this instance, the shared assumption of the couple concerning my sexuality served as a defense against going more deeply into the work relating to their identity development and the subsequent process of coming out.

Conversely, while some couples may choose an LGBTQ therapist, some may seek a heterosexual therapist. One of the reasons for this choice is to legitimize the couple in the eyes of the heteronormative world. If there is a high degree of internalized homophobia in the couple and in the individuals, the couple may hold a secret hope that the therapist can "cure" them of their gayness, homophobia or internal bias. Siegel and Walker (1996) suggest that the choice of a straight therapist can signify an "unconscious fantasy that a straight therapist as representative of dominant US culture, will provide a blessing that will dissipate gay self-hatred" (pg. 31). Thus, straight therapist as a representation for the heteronormative ideal may be used as someone who could absolve the couple of their sins and misdeeds. In this instance, the heterosexual therapist represents a reparative object.

Contrary to an object of repair, the heterosexual therapist may be chosen in an effort to solidify the couple's self-hatred. Hertzmann (2011) states that:

Internalized homophobia, functioning as an unconscious introject, acts as host for aggressive aspects of the superego potentially resulting in a very punitive attitude towards the homosexuality of the self and of others. In lesbian and gay couple relationships where internalized homophobia exists unconsciously in one or both partners, and therefore in their shared unconscious world, it can act as a host for the couple's superego (pg. 350).

In the couple work, the clients may unconsciously choose a heterosexual therapist in an effort to project this hatred into them and then see the therapist as a persecutory object, for instance, representing the straight world and its hatred toward gays and lesbians. If this gets enacted in the therapy, it could give credence to their homophobic beliefs about themselves and about their couple relationship. Consequently, the couple's analyst will need to resist the urge to affirm the patient as an ally and instead examine the function of the couple superego with regard to the relationship and to the therapist. This can lead to very tedious and painful work but important work nonetheless in bringing to light the shared persecutory object, one that has inhabited the world of the LGBTQ patients through their development and the formation of their partnership.

A final consideration is that of the heterosexual therapist being open to exploring the ways in which heteronormativity has affected the LGBTQ couples, and themselves. The straight therapist's sexuality and identity development will not have been challenged in the ways that the LGBTQ individual has. The internal bias one holds, as a result, must be a source of examination in the work. As Siegel and Walker (1996) say, "I think it's sometimes difficult for a non-gay therapist to distinguish the uniqueness of the way in which a person negotiates a homophobic culture" (pg. 33). This is also true for how an LGBTQ individual has to negotiate the heteronormative culture, both in becoming a couple and in sustaining the relationship. The many silent pressures of a heteronormative society must be explored within the couple dynamic, and the heterosexual therapist must be alive to the issues the couples are bringing as a result of socialization.

Conclusion

In this chapter, I have attempted to highlight the myriad ways in which the choice of the therapist can act, unconsciously, as a defense and/or as an affirmation for the LGBTQ couple. Specifically, the couple may seek out a therapist of the same sex or with a shared sexuality as a means to protect against societal heteronormativity and homophobia, or as a way to confirm their self-hatred. It is important to note that the choice of an LGBTQ therapist, and for that matter a straight therapist, can act as either a defense or affirmation, depending on the unconscious fantasies and unresolved issues the couple hold. While I have highlighted a number of issues, this was, in no way, an exhaustive examination of the topic. In fact, given that each couple is different, each individual's gay identity development is different and each couple's therapist is different, there really is no exhaustive examination of this topic. We must hold to the idea that every couple's therapy is unique and will be characterized by the shared fantasies of the couple, the shared and individual transferences, and the countertransference of the therapist. Each piece of work will have its own fingerprint.

However, it is important to note that while LGBTQ couples may look and act like heterosexual couples in terms of the issues they bring to the work, they also come with unique relational and intrapsychic aspects relating to the particularities of their developmental challenges and stresses in familial and societal relationships having been raised in a predominantly heteronormative society. Heteronormative socialization will also have an impact on both LGBTQ and heterosexual therapists and affect what they bring to the work, and what may be communicated unconsciously to the couple. Both LGBTQ and heterosexual therapists must be open to continued examination of themselves with regard to their own internal bias and assumptions. This may challenge us in ways that are uncomfortable, and we may wish to return to established norms and ideas as a way to guard against this discomfort. Pellegrini and Saketopoulou (2019) caution that when working with non-binary gender patients, we refrain from stabilizing ourselves by grasping for what is familiar. I would say this is the case with LGBTQ couples as well. We must, as these two analysts say, remain "vibrantly curious." If we do, I believe the work will stay alive in ways that will benefit our LGBTQ couples and extend our own analytic understanding.

References

Abse, S. (2016). Renewal and social justice. *Couple and Family Psychoanalysis*, 6(2):149–152.

Bhati, K. (2014). Effect of client-therapist gender match on the therapeutic relationship: An exploratory analysis. *Psychological Reports: Relationships and Communications*, 115(2):565–583.

Dreyer, Y. (2007). Hegemony and the internalisation of homophobia caused by heteronormativity. *HTS Theological Studies*, 63(1):1–18.
Gelso, C. J. (2002). Real relationships: the "something more" of psychotherapy. *Journal of Contemporary Psychotherapy*, 32(1):35–40.
Guthrie, C. (2006). Disclosing the therapist's sexual orientation: The meaning of disclosure in working with gay, lesbian, and bisexual patients. *Journal of Gay and Lesbian Psychotherapy*, 10(1):63–76.
Hertzmann, L. (2011). Lesbian and gay couple relationships: When internalized homophobia gets in the way of couple creativity. *Psychoanalytic Psychotherapy*, 25(4):346–360.
Lewes, K. (2005). Homosexuality, homophobia, and gay-friendly psychoanalysis. *Fort Da*, 11(1):13–34.
Morgan, M. (1992). Therapist gender and psychoanalytic couple psychotherapy. *Sexual and Marital Therapy*, 7(2):141–156.
Morgan, M. (2019). *A Couple State of Mind: Psychoanalysis of Couples and the Tavistock Relationships Model*. London: Routledge.
Nathans, S. (2017). Introduction: Core concepts of the Tavistock couple psychotherapy model. In S. Nathans and M. Schaefer (Eds.), *Couples on the Couch: Psychoanalytic Couple Therapy and the Tavistock Model* (pp. 1–29). London: Routledge.
Pellegrini, A. & Saketopoulou, A. (2019). On taking sides: they/them pronouns, gender and the psychoanalyst. (https://www.psychoanalysis.today/en-GB/PT-Articles/Pellegrini167541/On-taking-sides-they-them-pronouns,-gender-and-the.aspx. (Accessed 10 November 2020).
Phillips, S. H. (1998). A new analytic dyad: Homosexual analyst, heterosexual patient. *Journal of the American Psychoanalytic Association*, 46(4):1195–1219.
Raphling, D., & Chused, J. F. (1988). Transference across gender lines. *Journal of the American Psychoanalytic Association*, 36:77–104.
Siegel, S., & Walker, G. (1996). Conversations between a gay and a straight therapist. In J. Laird and R. J. Green (Eds.), *Lesbians and Gays in Couples and Families: Central Issues* (pp. 28–68). San Francisco: Jossey-Bass.
Van der Toom, J., Pliskin, R., & Morgenroth, T. (2020). Not quite over the rainbow: The unrelenting insidious nature of heteronormative ideology. *Current Opinion in Behavioral Sciences*, 34:160–165.

Chapter 14

Understanding and responding to intimate partner violence and abuse in same-sex couple relationships

Damian McCann

Introduction

Given that the incidence of intimate partner abuse in same-sex couple relationships is believed to be comparable to or even higher than that seen in heterosexual couple relationships (Turell, 2000; Messinger, 2011; Kelly & Lewis, 2012; Barrett & St Pierre, 2013; as cited by Rolle et al., 2018), it seems surprising that there has been so little interest in understanding and working with such couples. In a recent representative US study, almost a third of the sexual minority male respondents and up to a half of the sexual minority female respondents in intimate couple relationships indicated that they had been the victims of physical and/or psychological abuse (Breiding, Chen & Walters, 2013). Although, unsurprisingly, heterosexism, homophobia, internalised homophobia and minority stress are all implicated in the prevalence of violence and abuse in same-sex couple relationships, I will in this chapter extend the thinking by advancing some additional concepts central to couple psychoanalytic theory, which I believe offer a more comprehensive perspective on abuse within same-sex couple relationships. In addition, utilizing McCann's (2011) research on the meaning and impact of violence and abuse within the couple relationships of gay men, it will also be possible to provide greater insight into the workings of abusive same-sex couple relationships, whilst also considering how best to respond to such presentations in therapy.

The nature of violence and abuse in same-sex couple relationships

McCann (2011) suggested that research on intimate partner violence and abuse in same-sex couple relationships was a relatively new area of interest. Sadly, as a result of the silence surrounding this form of abuse within the field, the situation remains largely unchanged. Furthermore, it seems somewhat ironic that feminist thinking and practice, which did so much

DOI: 10.4324/9781003255703-14

to transform domestic violence from a private trouble into a public issue during the 1970s (Harne & Radford, 2008), should in part be contributing to this silence. The reason for this is that feminists believe that violence within intimate couple relationships is firmly rooted in patriarchy — involving men's power and control over women. Unfortunately, whilst not only reinforcing the dominance of heterosexism as a focus of interest in regard to domestic violence and abuse, this thinking also tends to militate against the recognition of men as victims and women as perpetrators of violence, both of which remain an obvious feature of abuse within same-sex couple relationships. In addition, the silence is further reinforced by the lesbian and gay community itself, fearing that to expose abuse within its ranks would further stigmatise an already oppressed and socially marginalised group (Kaschak, 2001; Ristock, 2002). Not surprisingly, therefore, those whose experiences fall outside the public story of violence and abuse, are often prevented from even recognising or naming their abuse (Ristock, 2002; Barnes, 2008; Donovan et al., 2006). Moreover, the additional victimization and homophobia experienced by many lesbian, gay and bisexual individuals in their attempts to report the abuse to police and other professionals has led to yet more silence.

Despite the reluctance of individuals within abusive same-sex couple relationships to come forward, existing research sheds some light on the internal workings of these relationships, as well as providing an understanding of the nature of the abuse and its impact on the partners. Messinger (2011), for instance, believes that the myriad forms of abuse, familiar through research conducted with heterosexual couples (i.e., emotional, physical injury, social isolation, property destruction, loss, disruption to work, education and career development, etc.) are even more likely to occur within the couple relationships of lesbians, gay men and bisexuals. This is because of the unique features experienced by same-sex couples, such as minority stress, which is thought to increase the risk of conflict and abuse, as well as providing a major obstacle for those in abusive relationships from seeking help. Attention has also been drawn to the confused power dynamics that seem to operate within same-sex abusive relationships, giving rise to the danger, particularly for gay male couples, of the abuse being defined as mutual and its severity and impact being diminished (McClennan, 2005). Similarly, as with violence and abuse in heterosexual couple relationships, there is also concern relating to the over-emphasis on the physical aspects of violence at the expense of other forms of abuse, including emotional and psychological (Finneran & Stephenson, 2013).

Renzetti (1992), however, believes that what really matters is determining the context in which the violence occurs, the motivations underlying the use of violence in a specific situation and the consequences of that abuse. Despite this, Island & Letellier (1991) adopt a more pragmatic position, asserting that gay men's domestic abuse is not a relational act, but rather a deliberate, violent and criminal act perpetrated by one man towards another. Yet, a participant in Barnes' (2008) study returns us to the suggestion that lesbian couple relationships have more complex power relations and that by simply dividing partners into victims and perpetrators, one misses the complexities of the relational dynamics. Taken together, these different voices highlight tensions between, on the one hand, the victim and perpetrator divide and, on the other, the relational aspects of violence that are believed to contribute to the abuse within both straight and same-sex couple relationships. However, in addition, psychoanalytic couple psychotherapists would be anxious to ensure the extension of this thinking to incorporate some understanding and appreciation of the role of unconscious processes that may also be at work in giving rise to the conflict and to the abuse.

From the work that has so far been undertaken, a number of theories have been advanced to explain same-sex partner violence and abuse, i.e., the *social psychological model*, which includes attention to personality characteristics, the *feminist socio-political analysis*, which examines the contexts of sexism, racism and homophobia that encourage and support acts of violence, and the *social learning theory*, based on modelling and reinforcement. From her research, Renzetti (1992) identifies seven factors which she believes are strongly correlated with the occurrence of lesbian partner abuse and which appear to also hold in regard to gay male partner abuse. These incorporate a mixture of individual and societal-based explanations and include: power imbalances; dependency and jealousy; intergenerational transmission of violence; substance misuse; internalized homophobia and personality disorder. Extending this further, a framework of intersectionality expands a gender-based analysis of violence to one that considers the connection of relationship violence to all systems of oppression, and which takes a both/and stance (Russo, 2001). To some extent, this is consistent with Renzetti's belief that it is important to examine how people are differently located and the ways in which, race, class, sexism and heterosexism affect the causes and consequences of violence (Renzetti, 1998).

It is generally recognised by those researching same-sex partner abuse, that the societal contexts in which these relationships are formed and maintained, contribute at some level to the violence and abuse experienced by lesbians and gay men. To embrace the argument, one has to comprehend the pernicious effects of heterosexism and homophobia. Ristock (2002) suggests that these social contexts create isolation and invisibility, a point that was earlier endorsed by Eaton (1994) who saw the enforced invisibility of lesbianism as a factor that must be considered when accounting for abuse. Indeed, it seems that, for instance, a lesbian's fear of 'coming out' may be used by her partner to control both her behaviour and her relationships with other lesbians in the community (Donovan *et al.*, 2006). And, although some couples may attempt to manage the hostile external world by uniting against heteronormative forces, this kind of merging and isolation is also believed to create its own pressures that in time may give rise to conflict and abuse. Therefore, the combination of external and internalised sources of prejudice, which Meyer (2003) refers to as *'minority stress'*, expose all lesbians and gay men to feelings of shame, unworthiness, depression, etc. Furthermore, it is suggested that when a partner's internalised homophobia is triggered, this too can lead to inexplicable arguments involving frustration or self-hatred, which is then directed towards one's partner (Green & Mitchell, 2008). Extrapolating further on their clinical work with such couples, Green & Mitchell suggest that minority stress can also cause sexual desire or performance difficulties as well as depression, which may then manifest in withdrawal or ambivalent behaviour within the relationship that, in turn, may lead to further stress and conflict. It is also worth noting that because of internalised homophobia, some lesbians and gay men may actually feel that they are acceptable targets of abuse.

In sum, it would appear that to properly understand the causes of violence and abuse within the couple relationships of lesbians and gay men, it is necessary to adopt a multidimensional perspective incorporating socio-cultural variables with individual psychological factors. This is explained by the range of influences that appear to be at work in creating the necessary conditions for the emergence of violence and abuse within these relationships. For instance, power imbalances, gender role socialisation, personality difficulties, alcohol and substance misuse, the intergenerational transmission of violence and abuse, stress relating to internalized homophobia and the impact of secure and insecure attachments, all seem to play their part in the advent of violence and abuse in the couple relationships of lesbians and gay men.

Towards a relational approach

Given the dominance within the field of the victim and perpetrator divide, much has been made of clinicians recommending separate services for lesbian, gay and bisexual partners in preference to couple therapy (Bourne *et al.*, 2007). This is because, seeing partners together is believed to imply mutual responsibility (a form of victim blaming) and, additionally, there is the risk of increasing the violence through the intensification of emotions during the therapy itself. Merrill & Wolfe (2000) also found that couple therapy was not helpful in intimate partner violence with same-sex couples, because it made it more difficult for victims to end the relationship, and they also believe that because of the fear of reprisals, the value of conducting assessments with both partners present is potentially hazardous.

Farmer & Callan (2012), however, highlight the limitations of working separately with abusive partners in couple relationships, believing that it provides only a partial understanding of the couple's problematic dynamics, not to mention the difficulty of seeing the interpersonal dynamic first-hand.

Others, including Dykstra *et al.* (2013) and Vall *et al.* (2018) emphasise the benefits of working with partners together, precisely because it provides a more accurate assessment of the dynamics of the relationship and the associated risks. In fact, there are many accounts of practitioners within the US, Canada and in the UK, working safely and effectively with couples, helping them tackle abuse within their relationships and addressing the important underlying factors that perpetuate the violence, whilst also ensuring the continuation of the couple relationship (Antunes-Alves & De Stefano, 2014; Goldner *et al.*, 1990; Vetere & Cooper, 2001). Moreover, it is also suggested that couples therapy has a positive impact in decreasing recidivism and, in some instances, is the better treatment option over more standard approaches (Karakurt *et al.*, 2016).

A key consideration and one that is fundamental to the development of new approaches within the field, and which honours the nature and complexity of violence and abuse within intimate relationships, is the recognition that not all violence is the same. Kelly and Johnson (2008), for example, draw important distinctions between violence and abuse within couple relationships that contain elements of coercion and control from that which is defined as situational couple violence. The prevailing view that domestic abuse is primarily conducted by men against women and driven by men's power and desire to control their partners, which is also applicable to gay men and their partners (Island & Letellier, 1991), denotes a particular type of violence that Kelly and Johnson refer to as coercive controlling violence. This involves one partner abusively controlling the other through isolation, threats of harm or actual physical violence. The violence is often frequent, severe and takes a variety of forms. Interestingly, according to Kelly and Johnson, coercive controlling violence is usually only present in 11% of cases.

Case example

Andrew is partnered with Max and both are white and British. Max is eight years older than Andrew and they met when Andrew was twenty-four years old. Theirs was a relationship that lasted just over two years, and although they lived together, nine months into the relationship, Andrew left for a time following a violent incident when Max punched him in the face, but he later returned when Max apologised and promised that it would never happen again. The pattern of violence within the relationship, which included physical, emotional, financial and sexual abuse, was heavily suggestive of Kelly and Johnson's definition of coercive controlling violence, in that, Max attempted to control Andrew by whatever means. Andrew believed Max to be alcohol dependent and indicated that he was particularly violent when drunk. Andrew finally left the relationship when Max threw him down the stairs and Andrew feared for his life.

In terms of the experience of violence and abuse, Andrew described a relationship that was very much conducted on Max's terms. For instance, Max would decide what they would do and where they would go, something Andrew felt he had to accept. In addition to the emotional and financial abuse, *"there was always the physical stuff, there was always the punching, and sexually too it was very much his kind of gratification rather than mine"*. Jealousy was also a feature of Max's abusive behaviour, in that, he accused Andrew of having sex with other men, something which Andrew says *"I would never have dared to do"*. Nevertheless, Andrew believed that it was his fault *"because I had given him cause to get jealous and to get upset"*. Contrary to the presentation, Andrew had a strong commitment to making the relationship work *"you know I loved him"*. The admission that Andrew was in an abusive relationship came, Andrew believes, in response to the fact that *"it was something I couldn't hide"*. Nevertheless, Andrew worked hard at convincing others that he was dealing with the violence and that Max was addressing his drinking. Yet, an increase in the intensity of the violence by Max towards Andrew ultimately convinced him that he had to leave, although it took many months before Andrew finally gained enough strength to walk away.

In contrast to coercive controlling violence, situational couple violence involves both partners reacting to particular strains within the relationship, where the flare-ups do not necessarily escalate or involve serious or life-threatening injuries and, where fear and control are not the primary mechanisms driving and directing the relationship. As Antunes-Alves and De Stefano (2014) point out, "in many couples, violence is not a means to control but, rather, as research shows, an ineffective strategy for trying to deal with personal and interpersonal issues" (p. 65).

Case example

Rachel, white British, and Cara, of Irish decent, are a couple who have been together for just over a year. From the outset, there were tensions within the relationship related to Cara's bisexuality. Rachel knew when they met that Cara identified as bisexual, and that before meeting Rachel, Cara had a number of relationships with both men and women. Although Rachel did not anticipate Cara's bisexuality being a problem, she was often tense when Cara was in the company of men and lately she has been feeling insecure and angry with Cara's interest in a work colleague and accuses her of leading him on. Although Cara attempts to reassure Rachel that her and Will are just work colleagues, it is clear that Cara enjoys his company and most days they have lunch together. Rachel has now become preoccupied and anxious, and the rows between them are becoming more frequent and more intense. Recently, after discovering that Rachel was going through her texts, Cara physically lashed out and hit Rachel in the face, although Rachel says that she was only looking for a phone number which she knew was in Cara's contacts. It also seems that Rachel is drinking more than usual, and during one of their intimate evening meals, Rachel threw a plate at Cara which struck her on the shoulder. The incident followed another row in which Cara accused Rachel of becoming obsessed with Will, and Cara raised the idea of her and Rachel having some time apart. During this argument, Cara also suggested to Rachel that her struggle with Will was really an excuse for her own unhappiness in a job that she hates and the ongoing struggle with a mother who has never really accepted her daughter's lesbianism. It seems that until Rachel met Cara, she had only ever dated men, but given the increasing awareness that she was more interested in women, Rachel eventually met Cara online. Despite Rachel's distress and fury with Cara, Rachel believes that they should seek couple therapy.

Generally speaking, the presence of coercion or control within a couple relationship, as with Andrew and Max, would be viewed as a strong counter-indication for couple's therapy. Some would even argue that it is highly unlikely that someone like Max would ever be open to attending couple's therapy; nevertheless, it remains imperative that assessors ensure that coercion and control are not present when embarking on conjoint work. Furthermore, if the presence of coercion and control only become apparent during the course of treatment, then the therapy must be terminated. One of the ways in which clinicians approach the assessment and the determination of risk, as a basis for agreeing couple therapy, is to initially see each of the partners alone, followed by a further session with the couple together. Others, however, before commencing the couple's therapy, may prefer to undertake the assessment with both partners present or to offer an extended assessment (perhaps with the option of seeing both partners separately as well as together) mainly to ensure that the nature of the violence and abuse is properly understood and that the couple is committed to living together safely (Vetere & Cooper, 2001; Goldner *et al.*, 1990).

In essence, the conditions for offering therapy to couples troubled by violence and abuse are as follows: the violence must be low to moderate; both partners should voluntarily agree to participate in conjoint work; and they must have a shared commitment to remaining together and to working on their difficulties together (Stith *et al.*, 2005). Further refinement of these criteria extend to the importance of both partners sharing similar views about the nature and extent of the violence, as this offers some protection against attempts by one or both partners minimising the abuse or diminishing the responsibility for it. Furthermore, the application of a mentalization-based approach in working with domestically violent couples seems an entirely appropriate and helpful way of managing the problematic dynamics that operate within these relationships. For instance, Fonagy and Target (1995) observe that violence is the product of a person's lack of a capacity for reflection or mentalization. Therefore, mentalization-based techniques are designed to create an increased capacity to manage affective states, precisely in order to allow for a deeper exploration of the underlying issues that often result in the abusive dynamics. Pickering (2011) observes that couples often present for therapy precisely because their couple relationship has failed to contain them. It is particularly important, therefore, to explore the experiences that each individual has had of containment. Ruszczynski (2007) links the absence of containment with a predisposition in some people to act out their violent feelings. He argues that when feelings have not been taken in and properly understood by another, emotional experiences are left unprocessed, and the "psychic toxicity" that remains, limits the capacity for reflection or mentalization.

Towards an understanding of the abusive dynamics in same-sex couple relationships

According to Ruszczynski (2007), "Both Freud and Klein understood psychological development as grounded in the interweaving of love and hate, life and death instincts, involving both body and mind" (p. 23). Essentially, this line of thinking pulls us back to the importance of one's early development and the way in which the "aggressive element of hate is contained, and comes under the influence of the capacity for concern for the other and therefore of love" (Ruszczynski, p. 23). However, when aggressive elements of hate are not contained, or indeed where there is actual hatred or rejection by a parent, then the individual is left holding something unbearable, unprocessed and unmanageable.

Andrew felt that he deserved the abuse he received because of being gay. It seems that he had been verbally and physically bullied and abused at school because of being gay and, as a consequence, came to believe that he deserved unhappiness and that he also deserved the violence and abuse he suffered at the hands of Max. For him, this was related to the shame and guilt he felt growing up as gay, feelings which actually emanated from the physical abuse he suffered at the hands of a father who rejected him, *"you see I wasn't the son that he wanted me to be"*. Andrew then finds himself partnering with Max who, according to Andrew, *"loathed himself for being gay and my being there reminded him of what he couldn't feel himself"*. Max had grown up with parents who defended against vulnerability and softness by adopting a tough unforgiving front. The need for Max to internalise a tough macho image seemed to be in direct conflict with his gayness, an identity that he completely rejected. Andrew talked of Max trying to *"pass"* as heterosexual, hence his decision to only ever drink in straight bars. In fact, it seems that Max turned against all that was gay, a clear manifestation of his internalised homophobia. It therefore seems surprising, in terms of the couple fit, that Andrew, who identifies as effeminate and gay and who suffered abuse all his life, should find himself attracted to a partner such as Max who himself violently eschews all that is effeminate in men and yet partners with an effeminate gay man. It is for this reason that psychoanalytic couple psychotherapists look to the unconscious processes that are operating between the partners to properly understand their complex and problematic dynamic.

One of the ways in which we may begin to make sense of Andrew and Max's particular couple fit is through the mechanism of projective identification, where "part of the unconscious need in partner choice is to find someone who can take in one's more difficult and vulnerable feelings, and who, having some of these feelings themselves, can identify with them" (Humphries & McCann, 2015, p. 162). Developing the point further, Catherall (1992) argues that "Couples who engage in repetitive projective identification cycles are often composed of two individuals with valences for similar issues — such as problems with self-esteem, anger, dependency, or separation/individuation" (p. 355). However, projective identification relies on a split within the couple where the shared anxiety is managed by one of the partners, Max, projecting unwelcome aspects of his vulnerability into Andrew who, in turn, projects unwelcomed aspects of his unexpressed anger and rage into Max. Unsurprisingly, shortly after the couple meet, Andrew becomes Max's *"little project"*, where Max attempts to turn Andrew into *"a real man"*, manifested in the decisions about what Andrew should and shouldn't wear and how he should and shouldn't behave. And, although Andrew admitted to feeling controlled, at the same time, he also felt that he had no option but to go along with Max's wishes, although it is entirely possible that a part of Andrew wanted to change, especially given the abuse he had already experienced hitherto because of being gay.

Stoller (1975) speaks of the aetiological importance of experiences in which the individual is humiliated with regard to their sexuality or gender, resulting in a storing-up of hatred and a desire for revenge upon the object. In that light, perhaps we catch sight of the real conflict that blighted Andrew and Max's relationship, where Andrew wished to fight back against his abusers but was too frightened to do so and, in time, unconsciously recruits Max, who has no trouble whatsoever in attacking and killing-off that which threatens him. At one and the same time, we also glimpse the conditions that give rise to the development of the sadomasochistic couple fit, which ultimately leaves both partners at the mercy of their unresolved individual developmental challenges. After all, both men find themselves locked into a seriously dangerous and escalating couple dynamic, reinforced by Andrew's admission that *"the sex was wild"* and that he actually liked *"the dangerous edge, the excitement of the risk and the attraction to the wild"* and Max's equally disturbing take on their relationship encapsulated in the statement *"I love you and you have the scars to prove it"*. These states of mind carefully track Stoller's (1975) ideas of perversion, embodying "the erotic form of hatred" where aspects of hostility, revenge, triumph and dehumanisation of the object prevail (Stoller, 1976).

Ruszczynski (2007), underscoring this point, suggests that where the aggressive element of hate is not contained and fails to come "under the influence of the capacity for concern for the other and therefore of love" (p. 23), then relationships, "sexual and non-sexual, are recruited in the service of malignant aggression, and sexuality in particular may be hijacked and become expressed as sadomasochistic, perverse and destructive" (p. 24).

Further development of this thinking suggests that the intensity of sadistic and masochistic couple relating "are ways of engaging intensely with another to militate against the dangers of separateness, loss, loneliness, hurt and destructiveness" (Ruszczynski, 2007, p. 30). However, a distinction has been drawn between that which is referred to as *self-preservative aggression* and that defined as *the sadistic act*, although in reality the two are not mutually exclusive since they operate as part of a spectrum. In *self-preservative aggression*, it is the elimination of the threat that is essential, manifest in Max's fundamental conflict in the statement *"I love you and you have the scars to prove it"*, which references his need to kill-off his own sexuality through his self-preservative attacks on Andrew. In that regard, the object's emotional reaction and the meaning of the behaviour to the object are both irrelevant, since the main objective of the violent act is that of restoring psychic equilibrium. "This is essentially a violent and cruel state of mind and at its most extreme is murderous" (Ruszczynski, 2007, p. 30). *The sadistic act*, on the other hand, preserves the object in the service of tormenting and controlling the feared other, and in this arrangement the object's emotional reaction is crucial to the unconscious contract. The specific aim of such violence is to cause the object physical and mental suffering, which in Max's case was primarily used as a method of projecting his own suffering into Andrew, who would then be made to feel all that Max could not feel for himself. Although, for a time, Andrew met Max's projections with his own masochistic valance, after receiving support from those close to him and drawing strength from his individual therapy, he was finally able to break free of Max's grip. However, as predicted in such couple scenarios when the dependent and victimised other leaves, Max is finally exposed to the full force of his own internal world and faced with this he attempts to take his own life.

A somewhat different set of circumstances appear to be operating within Rachel and Cara's relationship. Although there are indeed violent exchanges between the two women, these are clearly bidirectional in nature, and in thinking with them at assessment, there was no evidence to support the idea of there being any coercion or control and, to my mind, the couple met the criteria for Kelly and Johnson's definition of situational couple violence. During the assessment, the couple were also able to think and reflect on their struggle in managing the strains of Cara's bisexuality and Rachel's insecurity relating to her transition from heterosexuality towards fully embracing her lesbian identity. Taken together, both women begin to see that the unfolding dynamic between them was contributing to something akin to an advance and retreat dynamic, embodying aspects of Bowlby's *attachment theory* and Glasser's *core complex*.

Bartholomew *et al.* (2001) suggest that particular forms of insecure attachment appear to put individuals at risk of becoming involved in and having difficulty leaving problematic and abusive relationships. It is suggested that individuals who are securely attached will experience consistent and responsive caregiving which, over time, promotes high self-esteem and an inability to establish and maintain close intimate bonds with others without losing a sense of self. On the other hand, individuals exposed to inconsistent and insensitive caregiving will, through internal working models of relating, be predisposed to certain forms of insecurity within an intimate couple relationship that may account for violence and abuse. After all, Bowlby proposed that the strength of attachment bonds is unrelated to the quality of the attachment relationship, meaning that some abused individuals may actually feel strongly attached to their abusive partners. Alternatively, the strength of the attachment bond leaves certain individuals, such as Rachel, anxiously attached in ways that are likely to result in rage and violent outbursts if the partner attempts to distance, or to leave. Such a violent reaction could be viewed as a dysfunctional use of protest, and rather than closing the gap, it is likely to increase it.

Bartholomew and colleagues identify three attachment patterns, as part of the couple fit, that may ultimately result in domestic violence. In the first, we find two preoccupied partners locked in a highly volatile and conflicted relationship and which may be mutually abusive. In the second, fearful and disorganised individuals, partner with preoccupied men (*or women*) who then use coercive and controlling techniques to ensure their partners never abandon them. In the third, a preoccupied partner, such as Rachel, finds herself partnering with a fearful and avoidant other, such as Cara. In this arrangement, although the abuse may be mutual, it is largely driven by the desperate need for contact and security. In this instance, we observe Rachel, through her frustrated attachment needs, lashing out at Cara, who, in turn, responds with distance and avoidance. Clearly the mention of Cara needing a break appears to have triggered heightened insecurity and panic in Rachel, who then finds herself redoubling her efforts to ensure that Cara doesn't leave.

In an attempt to deepen our understanding of Rachel and Cara's dynamic, I will make use of Glasser's (1979) *Core Complex*. Wood (2007) believes that the core complex emerges in response to frustration in early relationships linked to experiences of separation. She suggests that "the response to this frustration is to pursue a search for blissful union with the object, which appears to promise the eradication of deprivation and need for the total containment of destructive feelings" (173–4). However, this urge for union can also arouse fears of annihilation, i.e., a fear of being completely taken over by the other and the loss of oneself. In that regard, Anya's bisexuality, as an active component of her core identity and a known element of the couple relationship, appears to be under attack by Rachel's disapproval of Cara's friendship/relationship with Will. Yet, before meeting Cara, Rachel herself had relationships with men and, so, Cara might well have stirred-up feelings in Rachel that go well beyond abandonment anxieties, which constitutes another feature of the core complex envelope. In that regard, both women appear to be caught up in what Rey (1994) refers to as a claustrophobic and agoraphobic dilemma, which leaves both partners at the mercy of feelings of insecurity and mounting tension, which then give rise to violent outbursts within the couple relationship.

A further aspect of Rachel and Cara's conflict is that involving *stage discrepancy* and which Ristock (2002) draws particular attention to in her research relating to lesbian partner abuse. Ristock found that 61% of the lesbian respondents in her study, women who had entered their first relationship with an older and more 'out' lesbian found themselves being abused by the more experienced partner, a finding that was also endorsed by Donovan *et al.* (2006). The thinking behind this finding is that the older and more experienced partner occupies a position of power within the relationship and, under certain conditions uses that power to her advantage. It is of note that this was Rachel's first lesbian relationship with a woman who confidently identified as bisexual and who had a number of relationships with both men and women prior to meeting Rachel. Unsurprisingly, Rachel looked to Cara for security within the relationship, whilst Cara clearly needed something less defined. However, by entering couple therapy, Rachel and Cara were helped to confront their shared unconscious phantasies, namely, that their relationship could avoid the conflicts that existed within their respective individual developmental challenges, linked to Cara integrating her bisexuality within her primary couple relationship and Rachel looking beyond the couple relationship for what may have been missing more generally in her life. Through the couple therapy, Rachel and Cara were both able to make use of the containment that the therapy offered and were also helped to open difficult and painful aspects of themselves and their relationship. This, in turn, allowed both partners to find a deeper connection in regard to their differing needs of the relationship, i.e., where Rachel assumed that Cara would offer an exclusive attachment and where Cara failed to negotiate the active expression of her bisexuality within the confines of her relationship with Rachel. Allowing the couple the opportunity of exploring the conflict associated with these beliefs helped to rescue the partners from the grip of the claustra/agoraphobic dynamic that had taken root, and which had come to define their relationship.

Conclusion

In this chapter, I have shown that abuse within same-sex couple relationships is a phenomenon that requires further attention, primarily in order to address the specific needs of these couples. I have also highlighted the nature, extent and dynamics that operate within these relationships and the specific conditions under which abusive same-sex couples can be safely offered a couple-based intervention. However, in my view, it is necessary to extend the theoretical lens to incorporate aspects of attachment, psychoanalytic and sociological thinking, to ensure a thorough examination of both internal and external forces that may account for and which give rise to the violence and abuse within these relationships. Abusive same-sex couples deserve the same level of interest and investment as their heterosexual counterparts, otherwise we are in danger of maintaining the prejudice that relegates such couples to the margins of society and which perpetuates the silence and neglect that surrounds them.

References

Antunes-Alves, S., & De Stefano, J. (2014). Intimate partner violence: Making the case for joint couple treatment. *The Family Journal*, *22*: 62–68.

Barnes, R. (2008). "I still sort of flounder in a sea of non-language": the constraints of language and labels in women's accounts of woman-to-woman partner abuse. In K. Throsby & F. Alexander (Eds.) *Gender and Interpersonal Violence, Language, Action and Representation*. Basingstoke: Palgrave Macmillan.

Barrett, B.J., & St Pierre, M. (2013). Intimate partner violence reported by lesbians, gay, and bisexual identified individuals living in Canada: An exploration of within group variations. *Journal of Gay and Lesbian Social Services*, *25*: 1–23.

Bartholomew, K., Henderson, A.J.Z., & Dutton, D.G. (2001). Insecure attachment and abusive intimate relationships. In C. Clulow (Ed.) *Attachment and Couple Work: Applying the Secure Base Concept in Research and Practice* (pp. 44–61). London, UK: Routledge.

Bourne, H.F., de la Bretonne, D., Kulkin, H.S., Laurendine, J., & Williams, J. (2007). A review of research on violence in same gender couples: A resource for clinicians. *Journal of Homosexuality*, *53*: 71–87.

Breiding, M.J., Chen, J., & Walters, M.J. (2013). *The National Intimate Partner and Sexual Violence Survey (NISVS): 2010 Findings of Victimization by Sexual Orientation*. Atlanta, GA: National Centre for Injury Prevention and Control.

Catherall, D.R. (1992). Working with projective identification in couples. *Family Process*, *31* (4): 355–367.

Donovan, C., Hester, M., Holmes, J., & McCarry, M. (2006). Comparing domestic abuse in same-sex and heterosexual relationships. *ESRC Report*: *University of Sunderland & University of Bristol*.

Dykstra, R., Eckhardt, C.I., Murphy, C.M., Sprunger, J., Whitaker, D.J., & Woodard, K. (2013). The effectiveness of intervention programs for perpetrators and victims of intimate partner violence. *Partner Abuse*, *4*: 196–231.

Eaton, M. (1994). Abuse by any other name: Feminism, difference and intra-lesbian violence. In M.A. Fineman & R. Mykitiuk (Eds.) *The Public Nature of Private Violence: The Discovery of Domestic Abuse* (pp. 195–224). New York: Routledge.

Farmer, E., & Callan, S. (2012). *Beyond Violence: Breaking Cycles of Domestic Abuse*. Centre for Social Justice.

Finneran, C., & Stephenson, R. (2014). Intimate partner violence, minority stress and sexual risk-taking among US men who have sex with men. *Journal of Homosexuality*, *61*: 288–306.

Fonagy, P., Target, M. (1995). Understanding the violent patient: The use of the body and the role of the father. *International Journal of Psychoanalysis*, *76*: 487–501.

Glasser, M. (1979). Some aspects of the role of aggression in the perversions. In I. Rosen (Ed.) *Sexual Deviation* (2nd Edn.). Oxford, New York, Toronto: Oxford University Press.

Goldner, V., Penn, P., Sheinberg, M.S.W., & Walker, G. (1990). Love & violence: Gender paradoxes in volatile attachments. *Family Process*, *29*: 343–364.

Green, R.J., & Mitchell, V. (2008). Gay and lesbian couples in therapy: Minority stress, relational ambiguity and family of choice. In A.S. Gurman (Ed.) *Clinical Handbook of Couple Therapy* (pp. 662–680). New York: Guildford Press.

Harne, L., & Radford, J. (2008). *Tackling Domestic Violence: Theories, Policies and Practice*. Berkshire, England: McGraw Hill.

Humphries, J., & McCann, D. (2015). Couple psychoanalytic psychotherapy with violent couples: Understanding and working with domestic violence. *Couple and Family Psychoanalysis, 5* (*2*): 149–167.

Island, D., & Letellier, P. (1991). *Men Who Beat the Men Who Love Them: Battered Gay Men and Domestic Violence*. New York: Harrington Park Press.

Karakurt, G., Whiting, K., Esch, C., Bolen, S.D., & Cakabrese, J.R. (2016). Couples therapy for intimate partner violence: A systemic review and meta-analysis. *Journal of Marital and Family Therapy*, *42* (*4*): 567–583.

Kaschak, E. (2001). *Intimate Betrayal: Domestic Violence in Lesbian Relationships*. Binghamton, NY: Haworth Press.

Kelly, J.B., & Johnson, M.P. (2008). Differentiation among types of intimate partner violence: Research update and implications for intervention. *Family Court Review*, *46* (*3*): 476–499.

Kelly, M.L., & Lewis, R.J. (2012). Minority stress, substance use and intimate partner violence among sexual minority women. *Aggression and Violent Behaviour*, *17*: 115–119.

McCann, D. (2011). *What does violence tell us about gay male couple relationships? (Unpublished Doctoral Thesis)*.

Mc Clennen, J.C. (2005). Domestic violence between same-gender partners: Recent findings and future research. *Journal of Interpersonal Violence, vol, 20, 2, pp,* 149–154.

Merrill, G.S., & Wolfe, V.A. (2000). Battered gay men: An exploration of abuse, help-seeking and why they stay. *Journal of Homosexuality*, *39* (*2*): 1–30.

Messinger, A.M. (2011). Invisible victims: Same-sex IPV in the national violence against women survey. *Journal of Interpersonal Violence*, *26*: 2228–2243.

Meyer, I.H. (2003). Prejudice, social stress and mental health in lesbian, gay and bisexual populations: Conceptual issues and research. *Psychological Bulletin*, *129*: 674–692.

Pickering, J. (2011). Bion and the couple. *Couple and Family Psychoanalysis, 1* (*1*): 49–68.

Renzetti, C.M. (1992). *Violent Betrayal: Partner Abuse in Lesbian Relationships*. Newbury Park, CA: Sage Publications.

Renzetti, C.M. (1998). Violence and abuse in lesbian relationships: theoretical and empirical issues. In L. Berkowitz (Ed.) *Issues in intimate violence, pp.* 117–127. Thousand Oaks: Sage Publications.

Rey, H. (1994). *Universals of Psychoanalysis in the Treatment of Psychotic and Borderline States*. London: Free Association Books.

Ristock, J.L. (2002). *No More Secrets: Violence in Lesbian Relationships*. New York: Routledge.

Rollè L, Giardina G, Caldarera AM, Gerino E and Brustia P (2018) When Intimate Partner Violence Meets Same Sex Couples: A Review of Same Sex Intimate Partner Violence. Front. *Psychol.* 9:1506. doi: 10.3389/fpsyg.2018.01506

Rosso, A. (2001). *Taking Back our Lives: A Call to Activity for the Feminist Movement*. New York: Routledge.

Ruszczynski, D. (2007). The problem of certain psychic realities: Aggression and violence as perverse solutions. In D. Morgan & S. Ruszczynski (Eds.) *Lectures on Violence, Perversion and Delinquency* (pp. 23–42). London: Karnac Books.

Stith, S.M., McCollum, E.E., Rosen, K.H., Locke, L., & Goldberg, P. (2005). Domestic violence focused couples treatment. In J. Lebow (Ed.) *Handbook of Clinical Family Therapy* (pp. 406–430). New York: John Wiley.

Stoller, R.J. (1975). *Perversion: The Erotic Form of Hatred*. London: Quartet.

Stoller, R.J. (1976). *Perversion: The Erotic Form of Hatred*. Sussex: The Harvester Press Ltd.

Turell, C.S. (2000). A descriptive analysis of same-sex relationship violence for a diverse sample. *Journal of Family Violence, 15*: 281–293.

Vall, B., Paivinern, H., & Holma, J. (2018). Results of the Jyvaskyla research project on couple therapy for intimate partner violence: Topics and strategies in successful therapy processes. *Journal of Family Therapy, 40*: 63–82.

Vetere, A., & Cooper, J. (2001). Working systemically with family violence: Risk, responsibility and collaboration. *Journal of Family Therapy, 23*: 378–396.

Wood, H. (2007). Compulsive use of virtual sex and internet pornography: Addiction or perversion. In D. Morgan & S. Ruszczynski (Eds.) *Lectures on Violence, Perversion and Delinquency* (pp. 157–178). London: Karnac Books.

Index

Abse, S. 193–194
abuse: domestic 206–207, 209; gay male partner 207; from homophobia 170; isolation and 123; and neglect 48, 50; psychological 205; sexual 197, 209; verbal 154; violence and 205–212, 215; *see also* violence and abuse
acceptance: body 161; exclusion from parental couple 31; family 47–49; family of origin 63; healing and 115; of Oedipal configurations 12; self-affirmation and 201; of triangular relations 12
adaptive functioning 96
adaptive illusion 93
adaptive skills 13
adolescence 197; challenges 137; impetus in 11; LGBTQ+ 151; overt familial interdictions in 14; sexual identity from 176
adoption 179, 183
adult: children and 9, 26, 38, 90; couple relationships 94; development 26; intimate relationships 75, 198; middle-aged 174; older 177; older LGB 170; patients 11; personality 10; relationships in non-heteronormative couples and families 24; sexuality 8–9, 46; single 114; transgender 47; young 98, 156, 169–170, 174–175, 184
aesthetic conflict 94, 100; *see also* conflict
affective mirroring 10
African women 65
ageing *see* older same-sex couples
aggression 12, 155; defense against 197; dissociated 138; expressions 32; libido and 138, 160; physical 69;
self-preservative 214; sexuality and 194; unexpressed 155
agnosticism 18
Altman, N. 45
American Psychiatric Association (APA) 46, 153
American Psychoanalytic Association (APsaA) 1, 46, 51, 179–180, 193
American Psychological Association 46
anal sex 154–158
Anapol, D. 144
anatomy, gender 14–15, 18–19
anti-homosexual bias 13; *see also* homosexual/homosexuality
Antunes-Alves, S. 210
anxiety(ies) 17, 152, 186; abandonment 216; abjection affects 91; conscious/unconscious 32, 34, 75; depression and 93, 145; female genital 15; managing 17; Oedipal 26, 30, 152; personal 110; primal scene 28, 35–36; shame and 13–14, 153; shared 124, 213; social admonition 13; transitioning 124; *see also* unconscious anxieties
apologies 179–180
Arbery, A. 45
Aron, L. 27
assisted reproductive technologies 179
attachment 124, 132, 136; anxieties and 53; behaviours 158; emotional 33; mirroring and 48; needs 215; open relationship 138–140; perspective 144; as "perversion" 14; relationships 54; secure/insecure 29, 208, 215; separateness and 137; theory 75, 139, 215; traumas 52; violence/abuse and 215

attitudes: implicit bias 182; towards ageing LGB people 166
attraction 172–173
autonomy in couple relationships 76–78
Ayouch, Thamy 61

Baldwin, J.R. 47, 64
Barker, M. 136
Barnes, R. 207
Bartholomew, K. 215
Basson, R. 163
BDSM (bondage/discipline, dominance/submission) 159, 162–163
behaviors 13, 92, 96; body and 9; clinical 20; desires and 13; gender role 18, 61; human 17; masculine 63; non-conforming identities and 17
being of the same mind 76
Belkin, M. 45
Benioff, L. 139
Bernstein, D. 15
Berry, D. 152–153
Bhati, K. 196
bias(es): anti-homosexual 13; explicit 55, 180–181; family 55–56; heterosexist 24, 26, 38; homophobic 70; implicit 48, 55, 141, 179–189; internal 202–203; patriarchal 71; preconceived 38; traditional 20; unconscious 24, 55, 85, 87, 181–182
Bigner, J.J. 184, 187
binarism 66–68
binary gender 12, 15–16, 90, 203; *see also* gender
Bion 79, 87, 110, 131; model of the mind 30
bisexuals/bisexuality 1, 89–102, 210, 214–216; biphobia 96; community 89; container 93; couple relationship and 95–97; fantasies 92–93; gay men and 140–141, 206; identity 89, 96, 102; in individual mind 89–90; object 93; otherness 95; partner 91; self-identified 89; sexual expression 100; sexual politics 91; in society 89–90; subjectivity 112; theorists 91; uncertainty and 90–91
"bi-valent" 89
Black, Indigenous, and People of Color (BIPOC) 45
Black trans women 44
Blair, L. 129

Blechner, M.J. 55
Bonello, K. 141
Bos, H. 185
Boston Psychoanalytic Society and Institute 45
boundary violations 31, 32–35, 37
Bowen, D. 188
Brazil: gender identity in 63; household work 64–65; same-sex couples in 69; sex and gender in 63–65
British Psychoanalytic Council 1
British Psychoanalytic Society 45
Britton, R. 27, 77, 111, 137
Burke, S.E. 180–181
Butler, J. 15–17, 49, 61, 67–69, 107
Butler, M. 83
Buttigieg, P. 56

Callan, S. 208
Call Me by Your Name 173
Canada 66
capacity to think 30
Carlson, T.S. 181
Carol 173
Carone, N. 27
Carrascosa, S. 64
Carvalho, M.A.de. 66
case studies: cisgender woman 49–50; difference and desire 126–132; family 49–53; Korean-American transfeminine 50–52; older same-sex couples 168–169; open relationship 142–147; psychosexual considerations and therapy 154–163; same-sex parents/parenting 186–189; violence and abuse 210–212; white transgender woman 52–53
Castañeda, M. 68
Catherall, D.R. 213
charmed circle 107
Chen, M.Y. 114
Child & Adolescent Consultation Service 2
child/children/childhood 9, 170; abuse and neglect 50; adoptive 185; adult development and 26; affections for a same-sex parent 12; attachment between mother and 10; atypical gender development 183; born through donor insemination 184; detrimental effect 157; development 26, 27; gay fathers 184–185, 187–188; gender

dissonance in 52; gender dysphoria 128; gender non-normativity 52; household and 65; lesbian mothers 183–184, 186; middle 180; neglected 78; psychosexual development of 24; queer 48; same-sex relations 63; school 86, 184; sexual feelings 11; shared 97; starved healthy 101; struggles 12; transference 152; transgender 25; wellbeing of 184; *see also* same-sex parents/parenting
Chused, J.F. 196
cissexism 48–49, 53, 55
civil rights 44, 66, 189
Clarke, Jeremy 83
classism 45
claustrophobic and agoraphobic dilemma 216
client-affirmation and normalizing 153
Clinical Encounters in Sexuality: Psychoanalytic Practice and Queer Theory 2
Clulow, C. 139, 144
coercive controlling violence 209–212; *see also* violence and abuse
collusion 95–97, 102, 201
Colman, W. 95, 137–138, 147
compersion 147
competition 11–12, 36–37
complexity 12, 27, 29, 99, 101–102, 115, 119, 124, 198, 209
conflict 19; about primary femininity 15; aesthetic 94, 100; ambivalence and 90; external 188; internal 1, 54, 82, 124, 131, 170, 186, 188; marital 53; Oedipal 31, 37, 138; stress and 208; universal human needs 89; *see also* violence and abuse
confused power dynamics 206
conjugality and gender 64–65; *see also* gender
Conley, T. 136
conscious anxiety 32; *see also* anxiety(ies)
Constantine, J. 141
Constantine, L. 141
containment 29–30, 34, 76–78, 138, 143, 212, 215–216
contemporary psychoanalytic theory 26–28
Corbett, K. 16, 28, 67
core complex 215–216

core gender identity 15
Costa, J. F. 65
countertransference 19–20, 35–36, 74, 84; dynamics 3; managing 76; transference and 75–76, 124, 148, 152–153, 168, 203
coupledom 169
couple fit 78–79, 122, 124–125, 129, 212–213, 215
couple psychotherapy 35–36, 75–76, 80, 84–86, 135–136, 146–148, 213
couple relationships 81; aesthetic conflict in 94; autonomy in 76–78; and bisexuality 89–90, 95–97; changes 61; dyadic 138, 140, 146–147; gay male 143; heterosexual 64–65, 67; intimacy in 76–78; intimate 205; psychoanalytic theory 136; sexual difficulties 28; 'specialness' 135; transitioning and 122–124; *see also* older same-sex couples; same-sex couples
couple state of mind 28, 74, 81–82, 125, 129, 136–138, 195
couple therapy 33, 70, 82, 87; psychoanalytic theory to 94, 124–126
COVID-19 50
creative couple/creative coupling 28, 31, 74, 80–81, 136–138, 143, 195
Crenshaw, Kimberlé 44
Crespi, L. 186
cultural and intercultural considerations 60–71; culture and psychoanalysis 60–62; same-sex couples 60–63, 65–69; sex and gender in Brazil 63–65
culture 16, 19, 52, 54; American 43–44; heteronormative 202; impact on heterosexual couple 61; and psychoanalysis 60–62; of psychoanalysis 44–49

Dajani, K.G. 45
Davies, J.M. 27
Da Vinci, L. 13
decolonization 61
"Deconstructing Heterosexism: Becoming an LGB Affirmative Heterosexual Couple and Family Therapist" (McGeorge and Carlson) 181
decoupling sex 138
defensive triangulations 37
de-legitimized desires 13–14
depressive position 29–31

D'Ercole, A. 185–186
Deri, J. 141, 144, 146
desire 12, 97–102; adolescent 12; behaviors and 13; for couple intimacy 76; de-legitimized 13–14; erotic 13, 33; homosexual 49; needs and 102; open relationship 138–140; trans 124; *see also* sexual desire
DeSouza, E. 64
De Stefano, J. 210
Diagnostic and Statistical Manual (DSM-II) 46
difference and desire 122–133; case studies 126–132; psychoanalytic theory to couple therapy 124–126; transitioning and couple relationship 122–124; *see also* desire
different-ness 52
Dimen, M. 19
discrimination 166; Black trans women 44; and cultural trauma 53; due to sexual orientation 1; misogyny and patriarchal 175; prejudice and 182; state sanctioned violence 54
dissociative collusion 96
domestic violence and abuse 206–207, 209; *see also* violence and abuse
donor insemination *see* insemination
Donovan, C. 216
Dovidio, J.F. 180–181
Downey, J. 48
Downs, A. 52–53
Drescher, J. 45
Dreyer, Y. 195
DSMV classification system 153
dyadic anxieties 34; *see also* anxiety(ies)
dyadic foundation 29
Dykstra, R. 209

Eagle, M. 139
Eaton, M. 207
economic inequalities 176
Edelman, L. 112
Ehrensaft, D. 28
enigmatic signifiers 10–14
envy 15, 37, 152
Equalities Act 177
Erikson, E. 168
erotics 9, 29; desire 13, 33; otherness 92–95; position(s) 91; and sexuality 26; trajectories 91
Evzonas, N. 11, 19

exclusion 26, 28, 31, 34–37, 35–36, 68–69
experiential conglomerate 154
explicit biases 55, 180–181; *see also* bias(es)
explicit dangers 12–14

family 13, 15, 28, 43–56, 62, 93, 98; acceptance 47–49; biases 55–56; case studies 49–53; contexts 55–56; expansion 63; heterosexuals 141; intersections 53–55; link and intersectionality 44; non-biological 119; nuclear 65, 114, 146, 179; psychoanalysis 44–49; queer/queering 56, 105, 113; relations 25; theory 28–30; *see also* same-sex parents/parenting
Family Acceptance Project, The 48
Farmer, E. 208
Farr, R. 183, 184–185
fatphobia 115
favelas 69
fear of penetration 154–157
female homosexuality 62
femininity 15–17, 49, 61, 65, 77, 93, 96, 107–108
feminist 61, 175, 205–207
Fiorini, L.G. 12
Floyd, G. 45
fluidity 18, 27–28, 96, 109–111, 140
Fonagy, P. 10, 211
Forsell, S.L. 184–185
Fraser, L. 55
Freud, S. 1, 13, 25, 29, 75, 106, 151; *Interpretation of Dreams, The* 61; *Leonardo Da Vinci and a Memory of His Childhood* 13; static gender of anatomic destiny 18; *Three Essays on the Theory of Sexuality* 8–9
Friedman, R.C. 48
From Psychoanalytic Bisexuality to Bisexual Psychoanalysis: Desiring in the Real 2

gay community 98, 155, 167, 206
gay couples 28, 66–67, 69, 81, 83, 86–87; *see also* same-sex couples; same-sex parents/parenting
gay marriage 46, 166, 179
gay rights campaign 3
Gay Rights Movement 43
Gay Straight Alliances 56
Gelso, C.J. 196

gender 180; analyst/therapist 196–198; anatomy 14–15, 18–19; in background 16–18; binary 12, 15–16, 90, 203; and conjugality 64–65; differences 46; in foreground 16–18; identity/identifications 17, 20, 37–38, 63; melancholia 69; minorities 18; non-normativity 52; orientation 27; regulation of 15–16; and sex 63–65; and sexuality 1, 53, 55; social construction of 15–16; "soft assembly" 38; stereotypes 17–18; subjectivity 19; trouble 69
Gender Spectrum 48
Gender Trouble (Butler) 107
genital sexuality 10
gerontophilia 173
Gerontophilia 173
Giffney, A.N. 1
Gilbert and George 173–174
Girl, Woman, Other (Evaristo) 156
Glasser, M. 215
Glazer, D.F. 189
Goldberg, A. 187
Golombok, S. 179, 183, 184, 185
González, F.Z. 18
Green, Andre 10
Green, R.J. 208
Greene, B.A. 45
Greenwell, G. 141
group approach 145
Gulati, R. 13
Gump, J. 45
Guthrie, C. 198, 200

Halberstam, J. 112
Halperin, D. 107
Hansbury, G. 45
Haraway, D. 117
Harris, A. 12, 38, 45, 96
Hart, A. 45
Hertzmann, L. 28, 55, 85, 195, 199, 202
heteronormative: assumptions 181; couples and families 38; thinking 2; *see also* implicit bias
heteronormativity 1, 32, 38, 43, 46, 71, 169–170, 175, 184, 193–195, 194–195, 202
heterosexism 1, 46, 54, 116, 181–182; impact 181; institutional 181
heterosexist language 182
heterosexual 3, 12–13, 46–47, 152; and cisgender 56; cis-gendered 156; community 86; couples 63–64, 67, 171, 186; genital and non-genital sex for 159; lifestyles 91; marriages 60, 62, 70, 170; men 13, 64, 174; parental couple 55; privilege 27, 29, 181; two-parent families 26; women 64, 66, 174; youth 47
heterosexual privilege 181; *see also* implicit bias
Hinshelwood, R. D. 108
HIV/AIDS 174
holding, Winnicottian concept of 154
Holmes, Dorothy 45
Holtzman, D. 11
homo-parental families 62; *see also* family
homophobia 28, 45–46, 48, 54, 68–69, 116, 166, 206; analytic work and 193; heteronormativity and 195; therapist's 199; *see also* internalized homophobia
homosexual/homosexuality 1, 47, 62; as an illness 180; anti-homosexual bias 12; child 12; desire 49; healthy 13; male and female 1; misguided beliefs about 27; orientation 1; public denigration of 86; relationships 68; societal indictment of 81; travestility and 64; *see also* bisexuals/bisexuality; monosexuality
Hopper, E. 45
hormone therapy 160
Horney, K. 14
household work 64–65
hysterectomy 2

implicit bias 48, 55, 141, 179–189; areas of 181; explicit bias *vs.* 180–181; heteronormative assumptions 181; heterosexual privilege 181; impact on research 183–185; institutional heterosexism 181; language and attitudes 182; managing 185–189; mental health professionals and 181; same-sex parenting 182–189; as stereotypes 180; *see also* bias(es)
indeterminacy 99
insemination 179, 183
institutional heterosexism 181; *see also* implicit bias
institutionalized hetero 48

intergenerational relationships 172–173; attraction 172–173; cinematic portrayal 173
internal conflicts 1, 54, 82, 124, 131, 170, 186, 188
internalization 27–31
internalized hetero 55
internalized homophobia 86, 168, 182, 194, 212; *see also* homophobia
International Journal of Psychoanalysis, The 19
International Psychotherapy Institute 45
Interpretation of Dreams, The (Freud) 61
interpretive action 154
intersectionality 44, 207
intersections 12, 44, 53–55, 69
intimacy 34; in couple relationships 76–78; obstacle to 108; sameness with 34; with sex 13, 138; sexual and emotional 31, 50, 83, 135, 141
intimate coupling 75
intimate partner violence *see* violence and abuse
IPA (International Psychoanalytic Association) 180
Isay, R.A. 12, 167, 172
Island, D. 206–207

Jaffe, L. 46, 51, 180
Jamieson, L. 135
jealousy 12, 37
Jenkins, A. 56
Johnson, M.P. 209, 214

Kaplan, L. 16–17
Keats, J. 110
Kelly, J.B. 209, 214
Kennedy, A. 54
Kernberg, O.F. 95, 137–138
Khalaf, R. 156
Khanna, R. 114
Kilborne, K.J. 138
The Killing of Sister George 173
Kilomba, G. 61
Klein, M. 9, 26–27, 29–30, 44, 74, 79, 80
Kleinian Oedipal model 29–30
Kort, J. 153
Koyanagi, J. 144–145
Krafft-Ebing, R.V. 173
Kulish, N. 11

lack of desire 162–163; *see also* sexual desire
Langridge, D. 3
Laplanche, J. 11
Laufer, L. 19
Lemma, A. 20, 52, 124
Leonardo Da Vinci and a Memory of His Childhood (Freud) 13
lesbian, gay, bisexual, transgender, queer (LGBTQ) 2–3, 24, 38, 108, 123; community 48, 114; couples 83; equality 55; rights 43, 46–47; youth 47–48; *see also* bisexuals/bisexuality; homosexual/homosexuality; psychosexual considerations; same-sex couples
lesbian couple 28, 77–78, 79, 84; *see also* same-sex couples; same-sex parents/parenting
Letellier, P. 206–207
Lewes, K. 193
Lezos, A. 152–153
liberal/neoliberal patriarchies 91
Libido theory 9
Lingiardi, V. 27
link and intersectionality 44
linked separateness 28, 30, 36
love in open relationship 138–140
Lowen, L. 140

Macklin, E.D. 141
male same-sex couple 78–79, 80–83, 85–86
Malpas, J. 122
marginalized communities 53
marital triangle 28
masculine woman 64, 66
masculinity 16–17, 61, 65, 109, 117, 187
mastectomy 160, 161
Masters, D. 83
masturbation 154, 157, 161
Matsick, J. 136
mature intimate relationships 30–32
Mayer, E.L. 15
McCann, D. 125
McDade, T. 45
McGeorge, C. 181
melancholy gender 16; *see also* gender
Meletti, A. T. 66
Meltzer, D. 94
mental health professionals 46, 181
mentalization 10, 211–212

mentalization-based techniques 211–212
Merrill, G.S. 208
Messinger, A.M. 206
Meyer, I.H. 208
microaggressions 48, 181–183, 182
microinvalidations 182
minority stress 208
Miskolci, R. 67
misogyny 45, 49, 109, 175
Mitchell, S. 118
Mitchell, V. 208
modern couples and families, model for 25–26
monogamy 174
monosexuality 1; *see also* bisexuals/bisexuality; homosexual/homosexuality
mono-shaming 140
Morgan, M. 81, 125, 136, 143, 195, 197, 198
Morgenroth, T. 194–195
Moss, D. 85
"Moving Counselling Forward on LGB and Transgender Issues: Speaking Queerly on Discourses and Microaggressions" (Smith, Shin and Officer) 181–182
multiple self 95–97
multiplicity 24, 27, 32; of family configurations 25; openness to 118; of relationships 38
mutual touching exercises 162

Nagoski, E. 161
Nathans, S. 193
National Association of Social Workers 46
The Nearest Exit May be Behind You (Bergman) 161
negative capability 110
neglect 217; and abuse 48, 50; childhood 78; microaggressions 181; same-sex couple 167; *see also* abuse
Ness, Patrick 156
The New Male Sexuality (Zilbergeld) 155
Nichols, M. 152, 153, 163, 164
Nico, M. 65
non-binary parental couples 26
non-heteronormative couples and families 24–25, 38, 71
non-normativity 52, 109

non-penetrative sex 156–157
non-traditional family romance 28
Notes on a Scandal 173

Obergefell v. Hodges Supreme Court 46
object relations and the couple 94–95
"the Oedipal" 20
Oedipal anxieties 26, 37, 152
Oedipal complexity/Oedipus complex 8, 10, 20, 27
Oedipal conflicts 31, 138
Oedipal development 111
Oedipal dynamics 32, 37
Oedipal father 90, 93
Oedipal situation 26, 29–31, 77, 137
Oedipal structure 37
Oedipal theory 24–39; capacity to think 30; clinical material 37–38; contemporary psychoanalytic theory 26–28; exclusion 35–36; in family theory 28–30; mature intimate relationships 30–32; model for modern couples and families 25–26; primal scene anxieties 35–36; in psychoanalytic couple 28–30; rivalry 35–36; sexual boundary violations 32–35; transference/countertransference 35–36; triangulation as defense against separation 32–35
Oedipal triangle 29
Oedipus Rex (Sophocles) 24
Officer, L.M. 181–182
Ogden, T. H. 154
older same-sex couples 166–177; case example 168–169; dependency 171; heterosexual marriage and 170; intergenerational relationships 172–173; internal developmental process 170; lived experience 175–176; opaqueness about sexual selves 170, 171; sex and 174; sexual identity and 171; social and support services for 167; specific thinking about 166–167; therapist considerations 176; visible or invisible appearance 173–174
open relationship 135–148; attachment 138–140; case study 142–147; couple state of mind 136; creative couple 136–138; desire 138–140; love 138–140; polyamorous relationships and 144–147; primacy of monogamy 135–136; sex 138–140

opposite sex 14, 16–17, 105, 170
Ortmann, D. 161
otherness 166
oxytocin 163

Pacey, S. 151, 154
patriarchy 67, 91, 206
Patterson, C. 184–185
Paul, R. 56
Pauley D. 13
pedophile 70–71
Peirce, C.S. 90
Pellegrini, A. 203
Pelúcio, L. 64
penetration, fear of *see* fear of
 penetration
Perrell, E. 129
PFLAG (Parents and Friends of
 Lesbians and Gays) 48
philosophical perspectives 90–91
phobia 182; *see also* homophobia
Pichon-Rivière, E. 44
Pickering, J. 212
Pliskin, R. 194–195
polyamory (or poly) 33, 144–147
Powell, Dionne 45
Preciado, P.B. 67
prejudices 1, 19–20, 109; complex
 effects of 109; conscious 180; cultural
 attitudes and 46; discrimination and
 social 53; LGBTQ people 46; societal
 107
pre-Oedipal phenomenon 26
primacy of monogamy 135–136
primal scene 28, 35–36
primary femininity 15
primary partner and others approach
 144–145
projective gridlock 125
projective identification 79, 213
projective processes 74, 79–81
promiscuity 168
Przedworski, J.M. 180–181
psychic toxicity 212
psychoanalysis 44–49, 60–62
Psychoanalytic Center for the
 Carolinas 45
psychoanalytic couple 28–30
psychoanalytic institutes 45
psychoanalytic theory 8, 25, 124–126
psychoanalytic thinking 1, 46, 125, 138,
 179

psychosexual considerations 151–164;
 BDSM 159, 162–163; clinical principles 152–153; fear of penetration
 154–157; lack of desire 162–163;
 shame and humiliation 157–160;
 specific considerations 151–153; trans
 and non-binary clients 160–162
psychosexual development 8–9, 24, 27,
 170
psychosexuality 9–10, 15

Queer Art of Failure, The (Halberstam)
 112
queering: consulting room 114–119; of
 social contexts 56
*Queerly Beloved: A Love Story Across
 Genders* (Anderson-Minshall and
 Anderson-Minshall) 162
queerness 114
queer people of color (QPOC) 53
queerphobia 115
queer relationships 105–119; stake in
 107–111; stepping sideways 111–119

racism 48, 115–116
Raphling, D. 196
Rapoport, E. 112
Rasmussen, P.R. 138
recidivism 209
relational psychoanalytic couple therapy 89–102; aesthetic conflict in the
 couple relationship 94; bisexuality in
 individual mind 89–90; bisexuality
 in society 89–90; couple relationship
 and bisexuality 89–90, 95–97; desire
 97–102; multiple self 95–97; object
 relations and the couple 94–95;
 philosophical perspectives 90–91;
 tolerating erotic otherness 92–95;
 uncertainty and bisexuality 90–91
Release (Ness) 156
Renzetti, C.M. 206, 207
reproductive technology 28
responsive desire model 163
Rey, H. 216
Richards, D. 167
Ristock, J.L. 207, 216
rivalry 35–36
Riviere, J. 17
Rodrigues, E. 65
Rohleder, P. 54
Rosa, F.H. 64

Rose, S.H. 12
Rubin, G. 61, 107
Ruszczynski, D. 212, 214
Ruszczynski, S. 124, 136–137

sadistic act 214
sadomasochistic couple fit 213–214
Sáez, J. 64
Sage 167
Saketopoulou, A. 19, 45, 123, 203
same-sex attractions 17, 43, 171–172
same-sex couples 60–63; in Brazil 69; choice of therapist 192–203; different paradigms 65–68; violence and abuse 205–216; *see also* older same-sex couples; psychosexual considerations; therapists/analysts, choice of
same-sex difference 32
same-sex marriage 46, 61, 175
same-sex parents/parenting: case scenarios 186–189; challenges 183; coming to parenthood 183; implicit bias 179, 182–189; internalized homophobic feelings and attitudes 186; managing implicit bias in 185–189; non-biological parental arrangements 188–189
São Paulo 66, 69
Scarfone, D. 11
Scorsolini-Comin, F. 66
"secure attachment" 29
Sedgwick, E.K. 61, 68, 106
Seidel, E. 28
self-alienation 54
self-disclosure 200–201
self-esteem 54
self focus exercises 154, 157, 159, 160, 161; *see also* psychosexual considerations
self-hatred 168, 194, 196, 201, 202, 208
self-preservative aggression 214
self reflection 152
sensate focus exercises 154, 159, 161; *see also* psychosexual considerations
separateness/separation 26, 28, 30, 32–36, 137, 146, 214
sex and older couple 174
sexism 67, 207
sex life 34
sex reassignment surgery (SRS) 126
sexual abuse 197, 209; *see also* abuse
sexual boundary violations 32–35

sexual desire 92; exercises rebooting 162–163; lack of 162–163; responsive desire model 163
sexual differences 46
sexual identity development 199
sexual intimacy 83, 128, 141, 144
Sexualities: Contemporary Psychoanalytic Perspective 2
sexuality 2–3; in body 10–11; and erotics 26; and gender 1, 53, 55; genital 10; in mind 10–11; in the "Oedipal" mind 11–12; in relationship 10–11
Sexuality and Gender Now: Moving Beyond Heteronormativity 2
sexuality of analyst/therapist 198–202; difference in individuals 199; homophobia 201–202; identity development 199–200; self-disclosure 200–201
sexually transmitted disease 83
sexually transmitted infections (STI) 156
sexual minorities 1, 18, 82, 152, 182, 205
Sexual Offences Act (1967) 169–170, 174
sexual orientation 1, 19, 20, 25, 27, 32, 55, 63, 70, 76, 83, 85, 152, 170, 176–177, 179, 181, 185, 200
sexual preferences 29, 37–38
shame and humiliation 157–160
shaming 48, 140
shared relationship 75
shared superego 95, 102
Shernoff, M. 153, 164
Shin, R.Q. 181–182
Siegel, S. 195, 199, 202
Silva, G. W. S. 63
A Single Man 173
situational couple violence 209, 210, 214; *see also* violence and abuse
skepticism 20
skills *see* adaptive skills
Smith, L.C. 181–182
social attitudes 166
social change 45–46, 55
social construction of gender 15–16, 18
social contagion 19
social isolation 68, 206
social justice 44
social learning theory 207
social psychological model 207
societal ageism 166
societal indictment 82
soft assembly 12, 38, 96

solo approach 145
Somerville, S. 114
Sophocles 24
Spears, B. 140
Spence, H. 135
stage discrepancy 216
Steiner, J. 81
stigma: Black trans women 44; and oppression 54; transgenderism 20; transgender people 52
Stoller, R.J. 213
Stonewall Inn riots 179–180
stop-start technique 157
straight therapist working with gay couples 83
Suchet, M. 110
Sullivan, N. 13
superego 13, 70, 95, 102, 202
supervision 74, 76, 82, 84–86, 152

Tantric sex 159
Target, M. 10–11, 211
Tasker, F. 184
Tatchell, P. 3
Tavistock Clinic 28
Tavistock Relationships 74, 198
Taylor, B. 45
therapeutic relationship 84
therapists/analysts, choice of 192–203; gender 196–198; sexuality 198–202; transference 195
therapist stance 81–82
"the simplicity principle" 90
Thompson, C. 14
Three Essays on the Theory of Sexuality (Freud) 8–9
tolerating erotic otherness 92–95
trans and non-binary clients 160–162
transference 35–36, 84
transgenderism 19–20
transgender/trans: adults 47; couples 25; identity 19, 43, 52
transitioning: and couple relationship 122–124, 132; gender 18
trans patient 19
transphobia 45, 48, 116
transsexuals/transsexuality 1, 18, 72n1; *see also* bisexuals/bisexuality
trans subjectivities 18
travestis 64, 71–72n1
Trevor Project 47
"triadic space" 28

triangular competition 12
triangular relations 12, 20
triangular space 77, 137
triangulations 20, 34–35; as defense against separation 32–35; defensive 37

uncertainty and bisexuality 90–91; *see also* bisexuals/bisexuality
unconscious anxieties 32, 74–87; autonomy in couple relationships 76–78; countertransference 84; couple fit 78–79; couple psychotherapy 75–76; couple state of mind 81–82; intimacy in couple relationships 76–78; projective processes 80–81; sexual intimacy 83; straight therapist working with gay couples 83; supervision 85–86; therapeutic relationship 84; therapist stance 81–82; transference 84; *see also* anxiety(ies)
unconscious bias *see* implicit bias
Uncoupling Convention: Psychoanalytic Approaches to Same-Sex Couples and Families 2
United States Supreme Court 54

Vall, B. 209
van Balen, F. 185
van den Boom, D.C. 185
Van der Toom, J. 194–195
Vaughans, K. 45
verbal abuse 154; *see also* abuse
victimization 206
violence and abuse 205–217; attachment and 215; case example 210–212; coercive controlling violence 209–212; conditions for offering therapy to 211–212; core complex 215–216; dynamics 212–216; factors correlated with 207; feminists 205–206; gender-based analysis 207; mentalization-based techniques for 211–212; nature of 205–208; patriarchy and 206; projective identification 213; sadistic act and 214; sadomasochistic couple fit 213–214; self-preservative aggression and 214; silence on 206; societal contexts 207–208; theories of 207
Vulnerable Child Protection Act 51
Vuong, O. 158

Walker, G. 195, 199, 202
Waseda, D. 63
Washington Baltimore Psychoanalytic Institute 45
Weitzman, G. 141, 144, 146
western societies: growing up in 166; role of women in 175
White, C. 45
white supremacy 45, 48
"the widening scope" 10
Winnicott, D.W. 45, 47, 118, 154
Wittgenstein, L. 90
Wolfe, V.A. 208
Womanliness as Masquerade (Riviere) 17

women: cisgender 49–50; masculine 64, 66; in western societies 175; *see also* bisexuals/bisexuality; homosexual/homosexuality; older same-sex couples; same-sex parents/parenting
Wood, H. 215
World War II 45

Yanof, J. 18
Yay! You're Gay! Now What? (Khalaf) 156
YouGov 140

Zell, M.-G. 144
Zilbergeld, B. 155

solo approach 145
Somerville, S. 114
Sophocles 24
Spears, B. 140
Spence, H. 135
stage discrepancy 216
Steiner, J. 81
stigma: Black trans women 44; and oppression 54; transgenderism 20; transgender people 52
Stoller, R.J. 213
Stonewall Inn riots 179–180
stop-start technique 157
straight therapist working with gay couples 83
Suchet, M. 110
Sullivan, N. 13
superego 13, 70, 95, 102, 202
supervision 74, 76, 82, 84–86, 152

Tantric sex 159
Target, M. 10–11, 211
Tasker, F. 184
Tatchell, P. 3
Tavistock Clinic 28
Tavistock Relationships 74, 198
Taylor, B. 45
therapeutic relationship 84
therapists/analysts, choice of 192–203; gender 196–198; sexuality 198–202; transference 195
therapist stance 81–82
"the simplicity principle" 90
Thompson, C. 14
Three Essays on the Theory of Sexuality (Freud) 8–9
tolerating erotic otherness 92–95
trans and non-binary clients 160–162
transference 35–36, 84
transgenderism 19–20
transgender/trans: adults 47; couples 25; identity 19, 43, 52
transitioning: and couple relationship 122–124, 132; gender 18
trans patient 19
transphobia 45, 48, 116
transsexuals/transsexuality 1, 18, 72n1; *see also* bisexuals/bisexuality
trans subjectivities 18
travestis 64, 71–72n1
Trevor Project 47
"triadic space" 28

triangular competition 12
triangular relations 12, 20
triangular space 77, 137
triangulations 20, 34–35; as defense against separation 32–35; defensive 37

uncertainty and bisexuality 90–91; *see also* bisexuals/bisexuality
unconscious anxieties 32, 74–87; autonomy in couple relationships 76–78; countertransference 84; couple fit 78–79; couple psychotherapy 75–76; couple state of mind 81–82; intimacy in couple relationships 76–78; projective processes 80–81; sexual intimacy 83; straight therapist working with gay couples 83; supervision 85–86; therapeutic relationship 84; therapist stance 81–82; transference 84; *see also* anxiety(ies)
unconscious bias *see* implicit bias
Uncoupling Convention: Psychoanalytic Approaches to Same-Sex Couples and Families 2
United States Supreme Court 54

Vall, B. 209
van Balen, F. 185
van den Boom, D.C. 185
Van der Toorn, J. 194–195
Vaughans, K. 45
verbal abuse 154; *see also* abuse
victimization 206
violence and abuse 205–217; attachment and 215; case example 210–212; coercive controlling violence 209–212; conditions for offering therapy to 211–212; core complex 215–216; dynamics 212–216; factors correlated with 207; feminists 205–206; gender-based analysis 207; mentalization-based techniques for 211–212; nature of 205–208; patriarchy and 206; projective identification 213; sadistic act and 214; sadomasochistic couple fit 213–214; self-preservative aggression and 214; silence on 206; societal contexts 207–208; theories of 207
Vulnerable Child Protection Act 51
Vuong, O. 158

Walker, G. 195, 199, 202
Waseda, D. 63
Washington Baltimore Psychoanalytic Institute 45
Weitzman, G. 141, 144, 146
western societies: growing up in 166; role of women in 175
White, C. 45
white supremacy 45, 48
"the widening scope" 10
Winnicott, D.W. 45, 47, 118, 154
Wittgenstein, L. 90
Wolfe, V.A. 208
Womanliness as Masquerade (Riviere) 17
women: cisgender 49–50; masculine 64, 66; in western societies 175; *see also* bisexuals/bisexuality; homosexual/homosexuality; older same-sex couples; same-sex parents/parenting
Wood, H. 215
World War II 45

Yanof, J. 18
Yay! You're Gay! Now What? (Khalaf) 156
YouGov 140

Zell, M.-G. 144
Zilbergeld, B. 155